Praise for
Jesus Speaks

"Jesus' words can replace stress with peace, sadness with joy, confusion with guidance, and fear with faith. That's why *Jesus Speaks* will not only change your day, but it can also change your life, your relationships, and your eternity!"

—CHRISTINE CAINE, best-selling author of *Unstoppable;*
founder of The A21 Campaign and Propel Women

"There is absolutely nothing more important for the growing child of God than spending time daily in His Word and presence, and Steve Scott's inspiring new devotional book, *Jesus Speaks,* helps us do just that. Mr. Scott's personal application of Scripture and impressive understanding of Jesus' heart for His people are evident on every page. I'm certain readers will be blessed and challenged and will grow in their intimate relationship with the Father as they focus on Jesus' words daily through Mr. Scott's profound and encouraging writing."

—DR. CHARLES STANLEY, senior pastor of First Baptist Church,
Atlanta; founder and president of In Touch Ministries

"Jesus promised that if we abide in Him and His words abide in us, our prayers will be answered, and we will bear much fruit. *Jesus Speaks* provides an amazing springboard for any believer to abide in His words as never before."

—TOMMY BARNETT, senior pastor of Phoenix First Assembly of God

"A treasure-trove of comfort, encouragement, and wisdom. Scott expounds on Jesus' own words in a daily format that is easy to incorporate into a habit. The devotions are short, but the impact will be far reaching. True intimacy with Christ is achievable. *Jesus Speaks* can be your first step every morning into His presence."

—DR. ED YOUNG, senior pastor of Second Baptist Church, Houston

"I absolutely love *Jesus Speaks*! I am coming to love Jesus more and more as I gain a deeper understanding of who He is through what He says in His own words!"

—SANDI PATTY, Grammy Award–winning Christian artist

"*Jesus Speaks* is like reading a daily love letter from our Lord and Savior. Steve Scott has focused on the spoken words of Christ in one of the most powerful, clarifying ways possible. Based entirely on Scripture, this devotional will transform readers' lives as it unites their hearts with God's will day by day."

—CHRIS HODGES, senior pastor of Church of the Highlands,
    Alabama; author of *Fresh Air* and *Four Cups*

"When books surface that open the human heart to the magnitude, magnificence, and depth of God's timeless Word to us, I'm keen to lean in. *Jesus Speaks* will give you an eternal perspective and will bring Christ's stunning teaching, perspective, and heart into your everyday experience."

—BOBBIE HOUSTON, Hillsong Church, Sydney, Australia

"Jesus' words are the key to growing your faith, following Him, becoming His disciple, and knowing the truth. They are the only way to infuse His life, spirit, peace, and joy into our lives. With *Jesus Speaks* you can immerse your mind, heart, and soul in His words every day!"

—JOSH D. MCDOWELL, author and speaker

"We express God's love language when we hear His Son's words and obey them. That's why *Jesus Speaks* can be so transformational for those who want true intimacy with God."

—DR. GARY CHAPMAN, author of *The Five Love Languages*

"With 365 daily teachings centered exclusively on the statements of Christ, *Jesus Speaks* can help every believer experience the heart and mind of our dear Savior."

—RICH WILKERSON, senior pastor of Trinity Church, Miami;
    founder of Peacemakers

JESUS
SPEAKS

FOREWORD BY DR. GARY SMALLEY

JESUS
SPEAKS

365 Days of Daily Guidance and Encouragement,
Straight from the Words of Christ

STEVEN K. SCOTT

WATERBROOK
PRESS

JESUS SPEAKS

All Scripture quotations, unless otherwise indicated, are taken from the Holy Bible, New International Version®, NIV®. Copyright © 1973, 1978, 1984 by Biblica Inc.® Used by permission. All rights reserved worldwide. Scripture quotations marked (ESV) are taken from The Holy Bible, English Standard Version, copyright © 2001 by Crossway Bibles, a division of Good News Publishers. Used by permission. All rights reserved. Scripture quotations marked (KJV) are taken from the King James Version. Scripture quotations marked (NASB) are taken from the New American Standard Bible®. Copyright © 1960, 1962, 1963, 1968, 1971, 1972, 1973, 1975, 1977, 1995 by the Lockman Foundation. Used by permission. (www.Lockman.org). Scripture quotations marked (NKJV) are taken from the New King James Version®. Copyright © 1982 by Thomas Nelson Inc. Used by permission. All rights reserved. Scripture quotations marked (NLT) are taken from the Holy Bible, New Living Translation, copyright © 1996, 2004, 2007, 2013. Used by permission of Tyndale House Publishers Inc., Carol Stream, Illinois 60188. All rights reserved.

Italics in Scripture quotations reflect the author's added emphasis.

Hardcover ISBN 978-1-60142-842-4
eBook ISBN 978-1-60142-843-1

Copyright © 2015 by Steven K. Scott

Cover design by Mark D. Ford; photography by Reto Puppetti/Trevillion Images

Published in the United States by WaterBrook, an imprint of the Crown Publishing Group, a division of Penguin Random House LLC, New York.

WATERBROOK® and its deer colophon are registered trademarks of Penguin Random House LLC.

Library of Congress Cataloging-in-Publication Data
Scott, Steve, 1948-
Jesus speaks : 365 days of daily guidance and encouragement, straight from the words of Christ / Steven K. Scott. — First Edition.
      pages cm
    ISBN 978-1-60142-842-4 — ISBN 978-1-60142-843-1 (electronic) 1. Jesus Christ—
Words—Meditations. 2. Devotional calendars. I. Title.
    BT306.S4325 2016
    232.9'54—dc23

                                            2015029806

Printed in the United States of America
2017

10 9 8 7

SPECIAL SALES
Most WaterBrook books are available at special quantity discounts when purchased in bulk by corporations, organizations, and special-interest groups. Custom imprinting or excerpting can also be done to fit special needs. For information, please e-mail specialmarketscms@penguin randomhouse.com or call 1-800-603-7051.

To the Lord Jesus Christ:
Everything I have that I value, You have given me.
Lord Jesus, I know the Father because of You.
I have forgiveness of my sins because of You.
I have eternal life because of You.
I stand amazed by Your life, Your words,
and Your amazing grace every day.

To my heavenly Father:
How can You love me, a sinner so deserving of Your disdain?
I marvel at Your mercy.
Oh Father, thank You for sending Your dear Son.
Oh, what a Savior! I love You, I love You, I love You!

To my grandchildren:
Maddy, Julia, Melody, Ian, Colin, Harrison, Ettie,
and those yet to be born—
Jesus is alive and loves you more than anyone
on this earth loves you.
He wants you to intimately know Him and your Father in heaven.
Oh, how He loves you!
Grandpa's prayer for you is that you come to know
Him as He really is.
The more you get to know Him, the more you will love Him.
I love each of you so very much!

To my children:
Mark, Carol, Zach, Devin, Ryan, Sean, and Hallie Rose.
I love you so much—more than you will know in this life.
And yet my love is but a minuscule, dull reflection of His.
Oh, may you come to know and love Him more and more
each day for the rest of your lives on this earth.
There is none like Him!

To my precious wife:
My sweet Shannon, you are my daily example
of how God wants me to be.
The love of Christ flows out of your heart so freely
in ways far too numerous to expound.
I am amazed by your kindness, generosity, compassion,
patience, and forgiveness of this unworthy soul.
I love you so much.

To my dear friends who by their example
have taught me to love Christ:
Gary Smalley, Jim Shaughnessy, Herb and Helen Selby,
Wayne and Mary Shuart, Dave and Sandy Heinze
and your amazing family,
Elmer Lappen, Dr. Jim Borror,
and, of course, my mom and her godly family.

✈ Foreword ✦

An Important Word from
Dr. Gary Smalley

I n a week of reading, I had more reality and intimacy with Jesus than I had ever known.

Is it possible to have a relationship with Jesus Christ that is as real as your most treasured earthly relationship? The answer is absolutely yes! In fact, your relationship with Christ can be more fulfilling and more intimate than any relationship you have ever known. But the question is how. How can you experience that level of daily reality and intimacy with Jesus?

Steve Scott, one of my dearest friends, has introduced me to a level of intimacy with Christ that is greater than I have had at any other time in my life. Steve showed me what Jesus Himself revealed to His disciples two thousand years ago as they shared a meal in the upper room the night before Jesus' crucifixion.

On that night Jesus said, "He who has My commandments and keeps them, it is he who loves Me. And he who loves Me will be loved by My Father, and *I will love him and manifest Myself to him*" (John 14:21, NKJV). What an amazing promise.

If you will discover and do what He tells you, He and the Father will love you in a special way. And there is more: He will *manifest,* or *reveal,* Himself to you! *That* is intimacy.

But He didn't stop there. He went on to say, "If anyone loves Me, he will keep My word; and *My Father will love him, and We will come to him and make Our home with him*" (verse 23, NKJV). Can you imagine the Father and Son taking up residence with *you*? The only condition is that you begin to discover and to do what Jesus said.

Years ago Steve Scott did something that no one had done before. He organized by topic all nineteen hundred statements of Jesus that are recorded in the New Testament. His work was published as *The Greatest Words Ever Spoken: Everything Jesus Said About You, Your Life, and Everything Else.* In the two years it took Steve to do this, and in the years that have followed, he has become more transformed and even more passionate about the teachings of Christ. Before I knew it, he had infected me with this same passion.

The result is that Jesus' words have become the lenses through which I see everything in life. I see the Father through Jesus' words about the Father. I see life on earth through His words about life. I see every opportunity and every trial through the lenses of His words. I see Him everywhere I look. And when my mind and heart are thinking about His words, I experience His presence in a way that is greater than I had ever known before.

In this daily devotional you are going to receive 365 personal messages from the teachings of Jesus. The devotional entries are focused 100 percent on *His* words, and every thought expressed flows wholly from the recorded words of Christ. Jesus promised that if you and I would abide, or dwell, in His words, we would become His true disciples. He said if we would *build* our lives on hearing His words and doing them, our lives would be like houses built upon the rock. By dwelling in His words, we can withstand all the storms of life as well as God's judgment. It is foolish not to live this way. Jesus said those who hear His words but choose not to act on them are like a foolish person who built his house on sand. The house was completely destroyed.

The more you come to know Jesus, the more you will fall in love with Him. I am convinced that *Jesus Speaks* will help you come to know Him in a greater way than you have ever imagined possible.

Oh, what a Savior. There is none like Him!

⤜ ACKNOWLEDGMENTS ⤛

L ord Jesus, thank You for the incredible joy of Your words and the spirit and life they bring to my soul. Thank You for Your patience and kindness to me during the writing of this book.

To my wonderful editor, Ron Lee, thank you for your sensitivity to the Spirit as you labored over these words. I'm so grateful!

Thanks to Alex Field, Laura Barker, Carol Bartley, and all the wonderful folks at WaterBrook who made this book possible.

To Jan Miller and Lacy Lynch, thank you for your belief and dedication to see this book become a reality. I love you both and the entire Dupree/Miller family!

✦✕✦

What I whisper in your ear,
shout from the housetops for all to hear!

—Matthew 10:27, NLT

Before You Begin,
Please Read This

This devotional is written to followers of Christ and those who want to follow Him.

Jesus is alive and wants to have an intimate relationship with every one of His followers. He prayed to His Father, "And *this* is eternal life, that they may know You, the only true God, and Jesus Christ whom You have sent" (John 17:3, NKJV). Jesus made nearly two thousand statements that are recorded in the New Testament. He said, "My words are spirit and life" (see John 6:63). His words can infuse *His* Spirit and life into your spirit and your life. When your spirit becomes full of His Spirit, your fears and despair are replaced with faith, hope, and courage—as well as with the love of Christ.

Jesus gave us more than one hundred conditional promises, *life-changing* promises. If we meet the conditions of those promises, He will fulfill them.

He also gave us more than one hundred commands—commands that don't weigh us down but lift us up! They *empower* us to see everything in life from God's point of view. They turn on His light in the dark world that surrounds us. They reveal everything God values and everything He detests. They make His will clear in every situation we encounter and in every choice we face.

Beyond that, Jesus' commands empower us with the grace and faith we need to do God's will in every situation. When we obey His commands, the act of obedience increases our faith. And perhaps best of all, obeying His commands provides the means for us to love God the way *He* wants to be loved.

Listening to the words of Jesus with the desire to obey and love God will change your life. Your faith will be strengthened, you will know God's desires for your life, and your doubts and fears will evaporate. That is why this book is based *entirely* on the words of Jesus.

The red-letter statements on every page are direct quotes of Jesus.

Each daily devotional is a paraphrase of the teachings of Christ. The devotionals do *not* carry the weight of inspiration, which is reserved exclusively for Scripture. However, each entry begins with a red-letter statement of Jesus, followed by text written as if in the voice of Christ. The first-person usage—such as I, Me, My, and Mine—refers to Christ. At the bottom of each page, you will see topics and page numbers listed. These direct you to *The Greatest Words Ever Spoken,* where you can read *everything* Jesus said on the day's topic.

How to Get The Most Out of This Devotional

1. Each day read and think about the red-letter statement at the top *before* you read the entry that follows.
2. After you have read the day's entry, set aside time to read *everything* Jesus said about that day's topic by reading the referenced topics in *The Greatest Words Ever Spoken* (noted at the bottom of each page).

There is no problem you face, no important question you can ask, that Jesus hasn't answered. The more you get to know Him, the more you will love Him. May God bless you in your growing intimacy with our dear Savior.

Come into the Moment

Do you not say, "There are still four months and then comes the harvest"? Behold, I say to you, lift up your eyes and look at the fields, for they are already white for harvest! John 4:35, NKJV

My dear child, why do you keep focusing on the future? Whether your mind drifts five minutes into the future or five months, dwelling in the future prevents you from experiencing My presence. You can know My nearness *only* when your mind is fully in the moment. All stresses and fears enter your mind when you are thinking about the future. And all regrets and bitterness come into your mind when you are focusing on the past. But when you come into the moment, you will not only experience My presence, but you also will become sensitive to the needs of those around you. Only when your mind is in the moment will My love, compassion, and kindness flow through you to those who share the moment with you. They will see Me in you, and you and I will make a difference in their day that can impact their lives for eternity. Today dedicate your time and attention to living with Me in the moment.

Therefore do not worry about tomorrow, for tomorrow will worry about itself. Each day has enough trouble of its own. Matthew 6:34

✦ *The Greatest Words Ever Spoken,* Living in the Present (pp. 277–78)

Don't Let Your Work Keep You from the Work That Matters Most

Do not work for food that spoils, but for food that endures to eternal life, which the Son of Man will give you. John 6:27

When I dined in the home of Martha and her sister, Mary, Martha worked hard preparing our meal while Mary sat at My feet listening intently to every word I spoke. Martha was upset that she was doing all the work and Mary seemed to be doing nothing. Truly, the food Martha was working so hard to prepare would last only a few minutes, but the food Mary was receiving from Me would last a lifetime. My words were preparing Mary for eternal life. Like Martha, *you* often spend so much time working on things that matter so little. I want you to spend more of your time feasting on My words. You will become more intimate with Me, and My words will transform your day and empower you to make an eternal difference in the lives of others. Prayerfully feast on My words today and every day. If you will do that, My Father and I will make Our home with you, and I will continually reveal Myself to you.

But seek first his kingdom and his righteousness, and all these things will be given to you as well. Matthew 6:33

✦ *The Greatest Words Ever Spoken,* Spiritual Priorities (pp. 328–37)

Take Control of Your Heart and Trust My Father and Me

Don't let your hearts be troubled. Trust in God, and trust also in me. John 14:1, NLT

My disciples witnessed every miracle I performed. They saw Me calm a stormy sea, heal the sick, give sight to the blind, and even raise the dead. And yet they still found it hard to take control of their troubled hearts and trust Me and My Father. Their unbelief didn't stop Me from loving them, but it kept them from experiencing the joy, peace, and power of My presence. The same is true with you. Whenever you find yourself stressed or worrying, realize that you are *choosing* to withhold your heart from Me. You are choosing *not* to trust Me or your heavenly Father, who loves you so. You are not hearing My words or obeying them. If you will begin to spend more time listening to My words and thinking about them throughout your day, your faith will grow and even soar. And as you obey My teachings, you will experience a new level of intimacy with Me and with My Father. Your love, faith, and power will grow beyond anything you have ever imagined. I promise.

Don't be afraid; just believe. Mark 5:36

→→ *The Greatest Words Ever Spoken,* Anxiety, Worry, and Fear (pp. 190–93)

Love My Father and Me
the Way *We* Want to Be Loved

Those who accept my commandments and obey them are the ones who love me. And because they love me, my Father will love them. And I will love them and reveal myself to each of them. . . . All who love me will do what I say. My Father will love them, and we will come and make our home with each of them. John 14:21, 23, NLT

Have you ever wondered how My Father and I want to be loved? The love We desire is obedience. I have always expressed My love for the Father through obedience, and it is the way We want you to express your love for Me. When you love Me by obeying My teachings, you will experience true intimacy with Me. The Father and I will come to you and will make Our home with you. I also promise to reveal Myself to you. Although We delight in your worship and praise, it is your obedience that truly expresses your faith in Us and your love for Us. It brings you to a place where We can shower Our love upon you. My commands will not weigh you down but will lift you up. They reveal the Father's will for every situation and empower you with the grace and faith to *do* His will in each situation.

He who does not love me will not obey my teaching. John 14:24

❧ *The Greatest Words Ever Spoken,* Loving Christ (p. 280); Commands of Christ (pp. 206–17)

If You Truly Abide in Me, You Will Bear Much Fruit

I am the vine, you are the branches. He who abides in Me, and I in him, bears much fruit; for without Me you can do nothing. John 15:5, NKJV

The value of a branch is not measured by its height or width but by the amount and quality of the fruit it bears. The same is true of My followers. You were not created simply to exist. You are not here merely to do that which entertains you and gratifies your desires. My Father is glorified when you bear much fruit and show yourself to be My disciple. Fruit that is eternal flows out of a heart that is being continually transformed by the washing and regenerating power of My words. This can happen only as you abide in Me. And you abide in Me when you spend time reading, studying, and prayerfully meditating on My teachings. As you do this, you will discover My promises and commands. As you step out in faith, believing My promises and obeying My commands, you will begin to bear much fruit in your life and the lives of those I bring into your path. Set aside time today to pour My words, My life, and My Spirit into your mind and heart. Let Me show you My heart and My desires for you.

You did not choose me, but I chose you and appointed you to go and bear fruit—fruit that will last. John 15:16

→→ *The Greatest Words Ever Spoken,* Fruitbearing (pp. 257–60); Following Christ (pp. 245–53)

Let Me Pour My Spirit and Life into You

The Spirit gives life; the flesh counts for nothing. The words I have spoken to you are spirit and they are life. John 6:63

There are so many times you feel as if you are running on empty. You're going through the motions, but your heart feels drained. There is a dull ache or subtle sadness that won't go away. Even when you get a lot done, you feel as if you've achieved nothing important. Though you seek guidance from others, nothing satisfies your deepest longing. That's because the words and counsel of others can only convey information, and more information isn't what you need! You need *spirit*. You need real life. Unlike the words of everyone else, My words do not merely provide information. They infuse My Spirit and My life into the minds and hearts of those who will dwell in them. In My words you will find answers to your every question, light when you are in darkness, comfort when you are hurting, and hope when you are in despair. Most important, you'll discover My perfect will for the moment you are in. My words will put My Spirit and My life into your spirit and life. I'm waiting for you right now.

Therefore everyone who hears these words of mine and puts them into practice is like a wise man who built his house on the rock. Matthew 7:24

→→ *The Greatest Words Ever Spoken,* Jesus' Words, Their Role and Power (pp. 62–64)

Don't Let Your Past Come Between Us

No one who puts his hand to the plow and looks back is fit for service in the kingdom of God. Luke 9:62

I have called you into a life of eternal purpose. I have placed you in a field that is ready to be harvested. But when your focus drifts into the past, whether minutes ago or months ago, it breaks our fellowship. It prevents you from following Me and staying close to My side. Your attention turns away from Me and keeps you from accomplishing what My Father set before you for that moment. Looking back is natural but foolish. It can be distracting, even destructive to *your* soul and to *our* intimacy. I know the hurts you have suffered can cause you to dwell in the past. Instead, follow Me by asking your Father in heaven to forgive those who have hurt you, just as I asked Him to forgive you as I was hanging on the cross. Then come back into the moment and let Me love people through you. I am your Shepherd, and you are My precious lamb. Hear My voice and follow Me. Let's reap the harvest in front of us together. I love you.

Even now the reaper draws his wages, even now he harvests the crop for eternal life, so that the sower and the reaper may be glad together. John 4:36

→ *The Greatest Words Ever Spoken,* Living in the Present (pp. 277–78)

Today Show Mercy to Others as We Have Shown Mercy to You

It is not the healthy who need a doctor, but the sick. But go and learn what this means: "I desire mercy, not sacrifice." For I have not come to call the righteous, but sinners. Matthew 9:12–13

My Father sent Me to earth to rescue sinners from the binding power and terrible consequences of their sin. Child, I anguished on the cross to pay the debt of your sins. I experienced the unbearable pain of separation from My Father to pay the price of your failure to love Him with all your heart, mind, soul, and strength. I became every evil thought, word, and deed that has ever entered your mind or flowed out of your heart. You will never know the number of sins My Father could count against you. And yet His tender mercies toward you outnumber your sins millions to one. That's how much My Father and I love you. Knowing the boundless mercy We have shown you, do you understand why We want *you* to show unlimited mercy to everyone who has hurt you? Every one of them! I'm asking you to forgive them and to bless them. Pray for them and be kind to them. Then you, too, will share the joy and glory of being a physician to those ailing souls who so desperately need Me.

Blessed are the merciful, for they will be shown mercy. Matthew 5:7

↠ *The Greatest Words Ever Spoken,* Commands of Christ (pp. 206–17)

My True Followers Must Forgive

For if you forgive men when they sin against you, your heavenly Father will also forgive you. But if you do not forgive men their sins, your Father will not forgive your sins.
Matthew 6:14–15

When I first told My disciples that they must forgive others seven times in the same day, they cried out, "Increase our faith!" They found it hard to forgive someone even once a day. They didn't realize that the Father and I had forgiven each of them thousands of times. How about you? Do you find it hard to forgive someone? My Father demands that you forgive others, not because they deserve it, but because He has forgiven you. Your offenses against Him created a far greater debt than anyone could inflict on you. Forgiveness is not a feeling; it is a choice to release the offender from your condemnation or vengeance. Instead of repaying their evil with judgment, I want you to pray for them and their redemption. When you refuse to quickly forgive someone, you are *choosing* to disobey My command. This dishonors Me and belittles all that I suffered to pay off the debt of your sin. I'm asking you now, repent and choose to obey My command to forgive all who have offended you.

Forgive us our debts, as we also have forgiven our debtors.
Matthew 6:12

↠ *The Greatest Words Ever Spoken,* Forgiveness (pp. 253–57); Commands of Christ (pp. 206–17)

I Want You to Rejoice Every Day— Here's How

However, do not rejoice that the spirits submit to you, but rejoice that your names are written in heaven. Luke 10:20

When I sent out seventy of My followers, giving them the authority to perform miracles, they returned rejoicing over their newfound power and the miracles they had performed. They proclaimed, "Lord, even the demons are subject to us in Your name." As wonderful as that was, it was *nothing* compared to an even greater miracle that they failed to recognize. A miracle so great and eternal that it should inspire daily rejoicing. It is the miracle that My Father performed when He separated them from the unrelenting power and terrible consequences of their sin. They would be spending eternity in the glorious presence of our loving Father! My child, God has done the same for you! When you were born again, your name was written in heaven. It will never be erased. If you truly understand this, you will celebrate it regardless of your circumstances. Your trials are only momentary afflictions, but your life with Me is eternal. Rejoice in this knowledge today and every day!

I have told you this so that my joy may be in you and that your joy may be complete. John 15:11

✦ *The Greatest Words Ever Spoken,* Joy (pp. 273–75)

Come to Me First!

Come to me, all you who are weary and burdened, and I will give you rest. Matthew 11:28

My dear one, whenever you face a difficult question, struggle with a hard issue, or walk through a trial, come to Me *before* you go to anyone else. Hear My words and prayerfully think about them. So often you do just the opposite. You seek answers, solutions, comfort, and guidance from others before you run to Me. No one else can give you the answers, comfort, or guidance that I can. I will bring My light even to your darkest times. I want you to know that My counsel is not Mine alone; it comes to you directly from the Father. I am delighted when you seek counsel from wise counselors, but come to Me and My words *first.* My words are spirit and life. They not only provide the perfect counsel; they pour My Spirit and My life into your spirit and life. When you are confused, discouraged, or in despair, the spirit and life you will receive from My words will provide more of what you need than the advice of a thousand counselors.

For I did not speak of my own accord, but the Father who sent me commanded me what to say and how to say it. John 12:49

→→ *The Greatest Words Ever Spoken,* Anxiety, Worry, and Fear (pp. 190–93); Jesus' Words, Their Role and Power (pp. 62–64)

Harness Yourself to Me
So I Can Carry Your Load!

Take my yoke upon you and learn from me, for I am gentle and humble in heart, and you will find rest for your souls. For my yoke is easy and my burden is light.
Matthew 11:29–30

I not only want you to come to Me first, but I want you to *harness* yourself to Me in an intimate relationship. I want you to learn from Me by listening to My words and looking at My life. There is no other way. In My words you will find answers to all your greatest questions, issues, and problems. My words provide the rock-solid foundation for your faith. In fact, whenever you *act* on My words, your faith will grow like never before. When you harness yourself to Me, I promise that I will *carry* your load and *perform* My words in your life. This will lighten even your heaviest load. You harness yourself to Me when you do what I say. How often do you read My words? Child, you can't follow Me or harness yourself to Me if you don't receive My words into your mind and heart. When you keep My words, you will know a level of intimacy with Me and My Father that will go beyond anything you have experienced before. I promise!

Therefore everyone who hears these words of mine and puts them into practice is like a wise man who built his house on the rock.
Matthew 7:24

↠ *The Greatest Words Ever Spoken,* Coming to Christ (pp. 452–53); Jesus' Words, Their Role and Power (pp. 62–64)

This Is Eternal Life

Now this is eternal life: that they may know you, the only true God, and Jesus Christ, whom you have sent. John 17:3

My Father said, "Let not the wise man glory in his wisdom, let not the mighty man glory in his might, nor let the rich man glory in his riches; but let him who glories glory in this, that he understands and knows Me." Understanding and intimately knowing Him should become your number-one priority. Coming into intimacy with My Father and Me is a greater glory than any other achievement you will ever experience. Until now you have made only a slight effort to get to know Me. You often spend more time tending to other desires than drawing near to Me. Your eternal life must begin in *this* life. Knowing Us the way We want to be known *is* eternal life. I promise that if you will spend time in My Word, hearing My teachings and obeying them, you will come to know Me and the Father as never before. As We become intimate with you, you will find yourself doing the works that I did when I was on earth. The Father and I will perform Our miracles in you and in the lives of those We bring into your path.

If anyone loves Me, he will keep My word; and My Father will love him, and We will come to him and make Our home with him. John 14:23, NKJV

↠ *The Greatest Words Ever Spoken,* Knowing God and Knowing Christ (pp. 275–77)

When You Worry, You Choose to Disobey Me and Not to Believe Me

---

So don't worry about tomorrow, for tomorrow will bring its own worries. Today's trouble is enough for today.
Matthew 6:34, NLT

A re you worried or afraid? Focusing on the future blinds you to the opportunities that My Father brings into the immediate moment. I tell you, stop worrying and start trusting Me. You may ask, "With all the cares and troubles that fill my days, how am I supposed to stop worrying?" Begin your day in My words and think on them throughout the day. As My promises and teachings fill your mind, they will seep into your heart. They will transform you and empower you. They are the solid rock your faith can rely upon. They will reveal My will for each decision you face. As you do My will, your faith will grow, and it will supplant your doubts and fears. Focus on the moment at hand. Set your mind on My words right now, and act on them. Then *My* joy will fill your heart, and *your* joy will overflow.

I have told you these things, so that in me you may have peace. In this world you will have trouble. But take heart! I have overcome the world. John 16:33

✦ *The Greatest Words Ever Spoken*, Anxiety, Worry, and Fear (pp. 190–93); Living in the Present (pp. 277–78)

I *Want* Your Prayers to Be Answered!

If you abide in Me, and My words abide in you, you will ask what you desire, and it shall be done for you. By this My Father is glorified, that you bear much fruit; so you will be My disciples. John 15:7–8, NKJV

I know you have wondered why so many of your prayers seem to go unanswered. Sometimes My Father has answered, but not in the way you expected because His plan is better than yours. But many times your prayers go unanswered because you have *not* abided in Me, and My words have not abided in you. You must dwell in My words and let them seep into your heart. Read them, pray about them, and apply them to your attitudes and behavior. Then, whenever you need a word from Me, the Holy Spirit will bring My words to your mind. And when you obey My words, My desires will become *your* desires, and then your prayed desires will be answered. My love and joy will fill your heart, overflowing to those around you. This will demonstrate My love and power to the world, proving you are My disciple.

But the Helper, the Holy Spirit, whom the Father will send in My name, He will teach you all things, and bring to your remembrance all things that I said to you. John 14:26, NKJV

↠ *The Greatest Words Ever Spoken,* Prayer (pp. 295–98); The Promises of Christ (pp. 298–304)

Be My Witness

Therefore whoever confesses Me before men, him I will also confess before My Father who is in heaven. But whoever denies Me before men, him I will also deny before My Father who is in heaven. Matthew 10:32–33, NKJV

I have called some to be evangelists and some to be teachers. Child, I have called *you* to be My witness, to tell others about Me and the truths I proclaimed. Be open and honest with others about Me and the Father and the relationship We have with you. The closer you get to Me, the more your life will change and become a beacon to others. When people want to know why you are so loving and forgiving, so patient and generous, so peaceful in troubled times, tell them about your relationship with Me. No one can believe in Me unless they first hear the truth about Me. And how will the people in your world hear the truth about Me if *you* don't tell them? Today let the light of your good works shine before your family and all who come into your path. Let them hear of your gratefulness for all the good things the Lord has done for you. And just as you acknowledge Me before others, I will acknowledge you before My Father.

Go home to your family and tell them how much the Lord has done for you, and how he has had mercy on you. Mark 5:19

↠ *The Greatest Words Ever Spoken,* Evangelism (pp. 227–29)

The Life-Giving Blessing of Believing in Me

He who believes in Me, as the Scripture has said, out of his heart will flow rivers of living water. John 7:38, NKJV

W hen you first believed in Me in your heart, you were given the Holy Spirit, who was promised by the Father. He came to dwell in you and produce in you His life-giving fruit, which includes unconditional love, unlimited joy, unexplainable peace, never-ending patience, active kindness, faithfulness, gentleness, self-control, and a hunger for righteousness. But believing *in* Me means *believing* Me. To believe Me, you must hear My words and make daily choices to *act* on them. If you are apathetic to what I have said or choose to disobey My words, you are choosing *not* to believe Me. This unbelief will prevent the Holy Spirit from flowing out of you to bless and influence the lives of others. But when you choose to abide in My words and act on them, the Holy Spirit and His fruit will continually flow out of your heart like rivers of life-giving water. Believe Me today, and let wonderful rivers of living water flow out of you to everyone I bring into your path. You will impact their lives in ways you cannot imagine.

But you will receive power when the Holy Spirit comes upon you. And you will be my witnesses, telling people about me everywhere—in Jerusalem, throughout Judea, in Samaria, and to the ends of the earth. Acts 1:8, NLT

⤜ *The Greatest Words Ever Spoken,* Living Water (p. 278); The Claims Jesus Made About Himself (pp. 14–22); The Promises of Christ (pp. 298–304)

Don't Panic When Others Say Awful Things About You or Do Terrible Things to You

---

God blesses you when people mock you and persecute you and lie about you and say all sorts of evil things against you because you are my followers. Be happy about it! Be very glad! For a great reward awaits you in heaven. And remember, the ancient prophets were persecuted in the same way. Matthew 5:11–12, NLT

I know you have been surprised and hurt by the words and actions of individuals who did terrible things to you. The world is filled with people who care only about themselves. Many people talk about God, even though their hearts may be far from Me. When I was being crucified, only a few were grieving. Most people were cheering. And yet I asked My Father to forgive them. I chose to die for them. The world hated Me then, and those who love the world's values often hate My followers today. When you are persecuted because of your relationship with Me, don't despair. Instead, *rejoice,* because your reward will be great. You are sharing in My suffering. Even though they think they are hurting you, they are enabling you to store up treasures in heaven. These treasures come from truth, righteousness, love, mercy, and following Me. And someday you will hear Me welcome you into My Father's kingdom saying, "Well done, my good servant!"

If you love those who love you, what reward will you get? Are not even the tax collectors doing that? Matthew 5:46

→→ *The Greatest Words Ever Spoken,* Commands of Christ (pp. 206–17)

You Don't Have to Stumble Blindly Through Life

I am the light of the world. Whoever follows me will never walk in darkness, but will have the light of life. John 8:12

Walking in the dark can be dangerous. You can't see what is in front of you. You may follow a path or a person, thinking you are headed to safety, only to discover you are being led into danger and destruction. In darkness a choice may *feel* right yet be terribly wrong. My dear child, it doesn't have to be that way. If you will draw near to Me, you will have My light to guide you through every choice you make and to lead you on every path you take. You won't have to decide in darkness, walk in darkness, or linger in darkness. But you can have My light only when you follow Me. And you can follow Me only by looking at My life and listening to My words. Hear My commands and obey them. See My promises and believe and receive them. This is how you follow Me. You will see life as it really is and discover what is of true value and what is not. Bathe your mind in My words today. If you will, I will lead you safely through this momentary life into My Father's kingdom, where your life will never end.

I have come into the world as a light, so that no one who believes in me should stay in darkness. John 12:46

✦ *The Greatest Words Ever Spoken,* Light Versus Darkness (pp. 384–85); Following Christ (pp. 245–53)

Let My Food Become Your Food

My food is to do the will of Him who sent Me, and to finish His work. John 4:34, NKJV

The food you eat satisfies you only for a few hours. But My food *never* stops satisfying. It doesn't fill your stomach; it fills your heart with peace and joy. It will fill your days with purpose, accomplishment, and eternal worth. As you eat the food I give, your prayers will be answered, and you will see miracles in your life and in the lives of those I bring into your path. *My* food is doing the will of the Father, and I'm offering this same food to you. In order to do His will, you need to know His will. My teachings reveal His will for your every circumstance. If you abide in My words, the Holy Spirit will bring My words to your mind whenever you need them. He then will give you the grace and power to do the Father's will. Step out in faith by acting on My words and doing as I have said. With each step of faith you take, your faith will grow. Store My words in your mind, listen to the whisperings of the Holy Spirit, and act on them. Your faith brings great pleasure to the Father!

Follow Me, and I will make you fishers of men. Matthew 4:19, NKJV

↠ *The Greatest Words Ever Spoken,* Jesus' Missions (pp. 46–51); Faith (pp. 231–37)

The Way to Start Your Day and End Your Night

Believe Me that I am in the Father and the Father in Me, or else believe Me for the sake of the works themselves.

John 14:11, NKJV

Oh, that you could know the Father as I know Him. That you could understand the radiance and magnitude of His love and the perfection of His righteousness. That you could know the infinite wisdom of His judgments and the never-ending flow of His mercies. To know Him intimately, you must believe that I am in Him and that He is in Me. Everything I said on earth He commanded Me to say and how to say it. Everything I did on earth I did *exactly* according to His will. Do you want to see and really know the Father? Then every day look at *Me*. In My actions you will see Him working. Listen to My words, and you will hear Him speaking. The prophets told *about* My Father and recorded His actions and His words. But I AM His Word! I became flesh and dwelt among people so the world could see the Father as He really is. If you will believe Me in this, you will fill your heart with My words, and nothing will be impossible to you.

All things have been committed to me by my Father. No one knows the Son except the Father, and no one knows the Father except the Son and those to whom the Son chooses to reveal him.

Matthew 11:27

✈ *The Greatest Words Ever Spoken,* Jesus' Relationship with God the Father (pp. 55–60); Commands of Christ (pp. 206–17)

I Want You to Live Abundantly Today

The thief does not come except to steal, and to kill, and to destroy. I have come that they may have life, and that they may have it more abundantly. John 10:10, NKJV

A re you discouraged? Do you live in survival mode, just trying to make it through the day? Satan, your adversary, is a thief. He wants to steal your life from you. He wants to render you useless for the kingdom of God. One way he does this is by turning your attention and desires away from Me, toward the things of this world. Satan wants you to focus on what you don't have, what you have lost, or what has been taken from you. But I am your Shepherd, and I came to give you life, *true life,* which is abundant and eternal. When I gave My life on the cross for you, I defeated Satan and broke his power and authority over you. But when you turn your heart to the temporal things of this world (which is Satan's kingdom), you voluntarily submit to his rule. This robs you of the joy that is found only when your mind and heart are turned toward Me. Start each day and end each day in My words, and My abundant life and joy will be yours.

But seek first his kingdom and his righteousness, and all these things will be given to you as well. Matthew 6:33

✦ *The Greatest Words Ever Spoken,* Joy (pp. 273–75)

Do You Want to Get Well?

Do you want to be made well? John 5:6, NKJV

For nearly forty years a man had been very sick. When I asked if he wanted to be made well, he didn't say yes. Instead, he told Me of his seemingly hopeless circumstances. He secretly hoped that I would solve his problem by changing the circumstances—by carrying him to a place where he believed he could be healed. The man didn't know that My Father had granted Me all of His power and authority. The man didn't need to be delivered from his circumstances; he needed a word from Me! He only needed to say, "Yes, Lord," and then hear My words and obey them. Child, how often do you ask Me to solve your problem *your* way or to deliver you from the problem altogether? That is *not* faith. Don't ask Me for help and then specify how the help should be given. Just say, "Yes, Lord, I want to be made well." Then listen to My words and obey them. Then I will make you well *My* way. The infirmities of your soul are much more serious than the infirmities of your body. If I make you well in your soul, your circumstances and infirmities will no longer restrain your soul. You don't need a change of circumstances; you need a change of heart. Hear Me and obey Me, and I *will* make you well.

Don't let your hearts be troubled. Trust in God, and trust also in me. John 14:1, NLT

→→ *The Greatest Words Ever Spoken,* Faith (pp. 231–37); Healing (pp. 263–67)

Don't Let Seeds of Doubt Block Your Faith

Stop doubting and believe. John 20:27

In spite of all My miracles, My disciples still chose to doubt rather than to believe. I finally commanded Thomas to "stop doubting and believe." Faith is not an emotion; it's a choice to do what I say. When you encounter a situation that requires faith, your natural inclination is to doubt. You question My presence, My calling, and even My words. Child, though you can't keep seeds of doubt from entering your mind, you *can* stop them from taking root in your heart. You can respond to any doubt with the choice to express faith by doing what My words tell you. When following Me requires courage, doubts will cause you to fear. Then the Holy Spirit will bring My words to your mind: "Fear not, be of good courage!" When you follow My words, your faith will replace fear with courage and action. The world wants to see before it will believe. I want you to believe, and then you will see. True faith is acting on My words *before* you see. When you act in faith, I will perform all that I have promised.

Because you have seen me, you have believed; blessed are those who have not seen and yet have believed. John 20:29

→→ *The Greatest Words Ever Spoken,* Faith (pp. 231–37); Anxiety, Worry, and Fear (pp. 190–93)

You Can Overcome
Your Greatest Fears

Do not be afraid of those who kill the body but cannot kill
the soul. Matthew 10:28

I t's only natural to be afraid of any harm, especially death. But if
you will follow Me, I will lead you out of your fears into faith.
Throughout your life you will be confronted by fear. But when you
see My Father and Me as We really are, and when you see life and
your circumstances from Our perspective, overcoming fear will
come easily. I gave My life on the cross to give you *eternal* life. When
you believed in Me and were born again, My Father and I adopted
you into Our family. So even your death will not be a tragedy but a
welcomed *new beginning.* A sparrow doesn't fall to the ground apart
from the Father's will and care. He cares for you infinitely more than
many sparrows. Child, when you are afraid, it is because you are focusing on the things of this life that are temporary. Shift your focus
and bind your heart to Me. Fill your heart with My words. I want to
put My perspective into your mind and My courage into your heart.
Don't be afraid.

Take courage! It is I. Don't be afraid. Matthew 14:27

↠ *The Greatest Words Ever Spoken,* Anxiety, Worry, and Fear (pp. 190–93)

Don't Let Your Eyes
Put Your Light Out

Your eye is a lamp that provides light for your body. When your eye is good, your whole body is filled with light. But when it is bad, your body is filled with darkness. Make sure that the light you think you have is not actually darkness. Luke 11:34–35, NLT

Your eyes are the windows to your mind and your heart. That's why it's so important to be careful what you allow your eyes to see. When your eyes focus on that which is good and righteous, they bring life-giving light into your mind and heart. A heart filled with light produces love, patience, kindness, goodness, and compassion. But when you look on that which is dark or evil, darkness enters your mind and heart and produces deeds of darkness: selfishness, greed, envy, pride, and all sorts of evil. I have called you to be a light in the world, a reflection of Me, My truth, My righteousness, and My mercy. When you subject your eyes to darkness, your life will produce deeds of darkness. When I was in the world, I was the Light of the World. Now My followers are My lights on earth, showing My righteousness and love to the world. Child, you must keep your light burning bright. To do that, you must guard your eyes from that which brings darkness into your soul.

You are the light of the world—like a city on a hilltop that cannot be hidden. Matthew 5:14, NLT

→→ *The Greatest Words Ever Spoken,* The Eye and Seeing with Spiritual Eyes (pp. 230–31)

How to Be Great in the Kingdom of Heaven

Whoever therefore breaks one of the least of these commandments, and teaches men so, shall be called least in the kingdom of heaven; but whoever does and teaches them, he shall be called great in the kingdom of heaven.

Matthew 5:19, NKJV

I gave My disciples a number of commands that revealed the ways and will of My Father. I also revealed that My followers' *response* to these commands would determine who would be called great and who would be called least in the kingdom of heaven. Those who minimize even the least of My commands and teach others to do the same will be called the least in the kingdom. Those who *obey* My commands and teach others to obey them will be called great in the kingdom. In heaven, greatness isn't determined by your intelligence, your age, or your earthly achievements. It is determined by the answers to these simple questions: "Did you trust Me enough to follow Me? Did you believe Me enough to do what I said, and did you teach others to do likewise? Did you obey My commands and follow My example?" Regardless of your past, it's not too late to go from least to great. Hear My commands, believe them, and obey them! The Holy Spirit offers you the grace you need to take each step. He won't let you down.

. . . teaching them to obey everything I have commanded you. And surely I am with you always, to the very end of the age.

Matthew 28:20

→→ *The Greatest Words Ever Spoken,* Commands of Christ (pp. 206–17); Heaven (pp. 143–50)

Follow Me in Righteousness Without Hypocrisy

For I tell you that unless your righteousness surpasses that of the Pharisees and the teachers of the law, you will certainly not enter the kingdom of heaven. Matthew 5:20

Be on your guard against the yeast of the Pharisees, which is hypocrisy. Luke 12:1

When I lived on earth, people thought no one could be more righteous than the Pharisees and scribes. They performed religious deeds that could be seen by everyone. But they ignored the issues that are most important to God, namely, the issues of the heart. Their hearts were full of hypocrisy, greed, pride, envy, hatred, jealousy, and immorality. Today it's easier than ever to fill your life with religious activity. But as good as that activity may be, it is meaningless to My Father if your heart is far from Him. He wants you to be more concerned about what goes on inside your heart than how you appear to others. I want to purify your heart, your thoughts, and your motives and intentions with the cleansing power of My Word. As you will dwell in My words, the Holy Spirit will produce His fruit in your heart. Then your life will be an expression of My words instead of a hypocritical contradiction of them.

Woe to you, teachers of the law and Pharisees, you hypocrites! You are like whitewashed tombs, which look beautiful on the outside but on the inside are full of dead men's bones and everything unclean. Matthew 23:27

↣ *The Greatest Words Ever Spoken,* Hypocrites, Hypocrisy, and Self-Righteousness (pp. 378–83); Pharisees (pp. 387–89)

When Your Troubles Overwhelm You

In this world you will have trouble. But take heart! I have overcome the world. John 16:33

When troubles come your way, you often seem surprised. You may think, *How could this happen? Why did it happen to me? What did I do wrong?* And yet, as I told My disciples the night of My arrest, as long as you remain in this world, you *will* have trouble. It's as much a part of your life as the air you breathe and the water you drink. But, child, you have access to comfort, confidence, peace, and joy that the rest of the world does not have. You have Me, and I have overcome the world. Your troubles will never take Me by surprise, and they will never defeat Me or divert My eternal purposes for you. Even through your greatest trials, I will prevail. I will demonstrate My love, mercy, grace, and power to you and through you. Even when Satan is celebrating what seems to be a victory against you, I will turn his seeming victory into a true victory for My Father and His kingdom. Nothing can separate you from My love and purpose. Hear My voice and follow Me.

Peace I leave with you; my peace I give you. I do not give to you as the world gives. Do not let your hearts be troubled and do not be afraid. John 14:27

✦ *The Greatest Words Ever Spoken,* Anxiety, Worry, and Fear (pp. 190–93)

Set Apart for a Higher Use

Sanctify them by Your truth. Your word is truth. . . . And for their sakes I sanctify Myself, that they also may be sanctified by the truth. John 17:17, 19, NKJV

When I was only a few hours away from the agony of the cross, I prayed for *you*. I asked My Father to sanctify you by His truth, to set you apart for a higher use in His kingdom. We have a plan for you. We want your short time on earth to make an eternal difference in your life and in the lives of others. We want your life to bear much fruit for Our kingdom. This happens only as you are set apart for the Father's use each day. He sanctifies you as you meditate on the Word and embrace it. As you allow My truths to guide your attitudes and behavior, My Father will continually sanctify you. He has forgiven your every sin. He has a purpose and a plan for you that is greater than you can imagine. The Holy Spirit will mold you into My image and grant you the authority and power to represent Me and act in My name. You will bear much fruit, and your fruit will last for eternity.

You are already clean because of the word I have spoken to you. John 15:3

↦ *The Greatest Words Ever Spoken,* Sanctification (p. 315)

Follow Me

My sheep listen to my voice; I know them, and they follow me. John 10:27, NLT

The world is full of sheep, but most are not *My* sheep. Though I call out to all people, most choose to go their own way. They simply follow their own desires. My sheep are different because they *hear* My voice and *listen* to Me. They *know* I love them. Most important, My sheep *follow* Me! They obey My words. My child, don't be fooled. The only way to know if people are truly My sheep is if they are following Me. Are their attitudes, words, and deeds a reflection of Me and My teachings? Do they hunger and thirst for My righteousness? Are they peacemakers and forgiving of others? Do they love My sheep in the manner that I love them? Do they rejoice in their relationship with the Father and with Me? Are they slow to judge and quick to show mercy? My child, your growing desire to follow Me, to discover My teachings and do them, shows you are My sheep. Listen to My voice, whether a whisper or a shout. Hide My words in your heart and follow Me. I love you.

I am the good shepherd. The good shepherd lays down his life for the sheep. John 10:11

→→ *The Greatest Words Ever Spoken,* Following Christ (pp. 245–53)

Spiritual Poverty Is the Only Path to Spiritual Wealth

Blessed are the poor in spirit, for theirs is the kingdom of heaven. Matthew 5:3, NKJV

The world is filled with people who think they are spiritually rich. They think they have enough goodness in themselves to cause My Father to welcome them into heaven. They are wrong. Those who think they are spiritually rich live in darkness. Their ears are deaf to My call, and their eyes are blind to My works. On the other hand, you realize that in yourself, you are spiritually destitute. You know that you desperately need My Father's mercy and forgiveness. You see that apart from Me you have no righteousness. And because you recognize your spiritual poverty, you have run to the foot of My cross. You identify with the man who beat his chest, crying out, "God, have mercy on me, a sinner." You have gratefully accepted My payment for your sins. Child, I want you to continue to remain poor in spirit. I will only fill *empty* hands. Every day come to Me with your empty hands and an open heart. I will fill both with treasures from heaven. My Father and I love you so.

I am the vine, you are the branches. He who abides in Me, and I in him, bears much fruit; for without Me you can do nothing. John 15:5, NKJV

✦ *The Greatest Words Ever Spoken,* Attitudes (pp. 196–98); Humility (pp. 271–73); Gratitude (pp. 262–63)

The Holy Spirit Will Remind You

But the Helper, the Holy Spirit, whom the Father will send in My name, He will teach you all things, and bring to your remembrance all things that I said to you. John 14:26, NKJV

The Father has sent the Holy Spirit to perform His ministries in the lives of My followers. One of His most important ministries is to remind you of everything I have said. To follow Me, you need to be continually reminded of My words, My teachings, My commands, and My promises. The Spirit wants to bring My words to your mind every time you need them and at the very moment you need them. My words should be the deciding factor in the choices you make. His ministry in this area provides the foundation for you to walk by faith and to walk in the Spirit. But how can the Helper remind you of My words if you haven't seen or heard them? Your reluctance to spend time consistently meditating on My words can prevent you from receiving this critical ministry of the Holy Spirit. But when you more consistently abide in My words, the Holy Spirit will perform this miraculous ministry in your life. Your faith will grow, and His power, fruit, and gifts will flow through you.

If you love me, you will obey what I command. And I will ask the Father, and he will give you another Counselor to be with you forever. John 14:15–16

→→ *The Greatest Words Ever Spoken,* The Holy Spirit and His Ministry (pp. 116–17)

Choosing Your Master Today and Every Day

No one can serve two masters. Either he will hate the one and love the other, or he will be devoted to the one and despise the other. You cannot serve both God and Money.
Matthew 6:24

When Satan offered Me all the kingdoms of this world if I would only worship him, I refused, saying, "You shall worship the LORD your God, and Him only you shall serve." Child, you know that God wants to be your only Master, but it's easy to let money and other things attract your heart's affection and pursuit. While this is natural, it also is foolish. It's easy to think you can serve God, money, and things all at the same time. But there can be only one master of your life at any moment. Unfortunately, most people choose money, things, people, or even themselves as masters of their lives. How sad, since no other master can love you as My Father does. No other master knows what's truly best for you now and in the future. What masters have ascended to the ruling throne of your life? What things keep you from meditating on My words, praying, and listening to the whispers of the Holy Spirit? If you will simply follow Me, My Father will become the loving Master you desire.

Worship the Lord your God and serve him only. Luke 4:8

✛ *The Greatest Words Ever Spoken,* Wealth and Possessions (pp. 344–47)

The Subtle Seeds of Greed Can Steal Your Life

Watch out! Be on your guard against all kinds of greed; a man's life does not consist in the abundance of his possessions. Luke 12:15

People don't think they are greedy, because they compare themselves to others who are driven or consumed by greed. But greed is as much a part of human nature as one's desire to satisfy an appetite for food. It is a never-ending quest to pursue even more of what you want, regardless of the consequences. Though you may easily spot greed in others, you may be blind to it in your own life. It can be subtle. Greed begins with a lack of gratitude for what you have. That produces the toxic soil of discontentment and unhappiness. In that soil the seeds of envy and greed grow into deadly vines that can choke your soul. My child, don't let this happen. Look to My life and words to discern those things that have eternal worth and pursue *them*. Focus your thoughts on the wondrous blessings your heavenly Father has given you. This will produce a heart of never-ending gratefulness. The seeds of greed and envy cannot grow in the soil of a humble and grateful heart.

Do not store up for yourselves treasures on earth, where moth and rust destroy, and where thieves break in and steal. But store up for yourselves treasures in heaven, where moth and rust do not destroy, and where thieves do not break in and steal. For where your treasure is, there your heart will be also. Matthew 6:19–21

→→ *The Greatest Words Ever Spoken,* Wealth and Possessions (pp. 344–47)

When You Pray

But when you pray, go away by yourself, shut the door behind you, and pray to your Father in private. Then your Father, who sees everything, will reward you. Matthew 6:6, NLT

Today I want you to set aside a time to get away by yourself, free of all distractions, to pray. Praying alone and in secret for more than a few minutes requires faith. You need faith that the Father and I will truly be with you and will listen to your heart. This is a time to hold *nothing* back—a time to start with matters that are at the top of your mind and then slowly work through everything that is in your heart. This includes your cares, your hopes, your concerns for others, your requests, and your grateful praise. Ask, and you'll receive My Father's answers. Seek His will, and you will know it. Knock on the door of His heart, and He will open it to you. And when you are finished, meditate on My words and listen to the whisperings of the Holy Spirit. We will be waiting for you.

If you then, though you are evil, know how to give good gifts to your children, how much more will your Father in heaven give the Holy Spirit to those who ask him! Luke 11:13

→→ *The Greatest Words Ever Spoken*, Prayer (pp. 295–98)

You Don't Have to Pursue Justice Against Those Who Have Hurt You

And will not God bring about justice for his chosen ones, who cry out to him day and night? Luke 18:7

My dear one, I know you have been deeply wounded by the words and deeds of others. I heard the cry of your heart when you questioned, "How can this be?" There have been times when you were devastated by those who abused you and even by some whom you loved. But I want you to know this: you don't have to pursue vengeance or even justice for the wicked. Don't waste a moment fretting about how they seem to get away with it. Realize that *nothing* escapes the eyes of your Father. Nor has He been deaf to your cries. He will bring about His perfect justice in His perfect time. There will be a day when the evil ones will have no place to hide and no advocate to save them from His righteous indignation. Instead of crying out for justice, I want you to pray for their redemption—that they may come to know Me the way you have come to know Me. Be a mirror of your Father's love, mercy, and grace. Remember Me on the cross when I prayed for you, and follow My example.

But I tell you who hear me: Love your enemies, do good to those who hate you, bless those who curse you, pray for those who mistreat you. Luke 6:27–28

✦ *The Greatest Words Ever Spoken*, Chosen (pp. 200–202)

I Chose You for an Eternal Purpose

You did not choose me, but I chose you and appointed you to go and bear fruit—fruit that will last. John 15:16

The call of My Gospel has gone forth throughout the earth. Many have ignored it. Others have responded with religious commitments, but their hearts were never converted. You, on the other hand, are among those whom I have chosen. Since you have been born again, your mind is being renewed, and your heart is being transformed by the washing of My Word. But I chose you with an eternal purpose in mind: to bear much fruit that will continue to glorify your heavenly Father. The fruit I am talking about is a life of faith and obedience—a life that glorifies God with attitudes, words, and deeds that flow naturally out of a transformed heart. I am the vine, and you are a branch. A branch doesn't struggle to bear fruit. It simply remains in the vine and allows the life-giving sap to flow through it to produce fruit. If you will consistently meditate on My words, the Holy Spirit will produce *His* fruit in you. Listen to His promptings today. Let Him bear His fruit in your life moment by moment. Then the world will see Me in you, and that will bring great glory to our Father.

Abide in Me, and I in you. As the branch cannot bear fruit of itself, unless it abides in the vine, neither can you, unless you abide in Me. John 15:4, NKJV

↠ *The Greatest Words Ever Spoken,* Fruitbearing (pp. 257–60); Chosen (pp. 200–202)

Your Life with Me Is More About *Us* Than You

If any of you wants to be my follower, you must turn from your selfish ways, take up your cross daily, and follow me.
Luke 9:23, NLT

While I was on earth, many people followed Me to see My miracles and hear My words. But when they finally understood what it really meant to be My follower, most departed. They counted the cost, and the cost was too high. They preferred a life focused on satisfying their own desires over one that would lead to eternal life. Following Me includes carrying a cross—setting aside your desires and your "rights" in order to do that which is pleasing to your heavenly Father. You have been purchased at a great price—My blood. You have been called to a purpose that glorifies the Father. Realize there are unimaginable blessings when you take up your cross daily. Because you are giving up your rights, you will receive *everything* as a gift from your loving Father. You will be able to thank Him in all circumstances. Your gratefulness will produce a joy that no one can take away. However, if you find yourself sad, discouraged, or angry, know that it's because you laid down your cross and picked up your rights. Repent and re-yield your rights to Me. You will experience My Father's love and My presence like never before.

Whoever serves me must follow me; and where I am, my servant also will be. My Father will honor the one who serves me.
John 12:26

✦ *The Greatest Words Ever Spoken,* Following Christ (pp. 245–53)

Too Much Worrying About Too Many Things

My dear Martha, you are worried and upset over all these details! There is only one thing worth being concerned about. Mary has discovered it, and it will not be taken away from her. Luke 10:41–42, NLT

L ike Martha, you are often worried and bothered about things of little importance. These things upset and distract you, keeping you from spending time on that which is far more important. Truly, only *one* thing is necessary: more time with Me. When you dwell in My presence and listen to My words, the living waters of My Spirit and life flow into your heart and soul. Only then can you discover My heart, My love, and My peace. As you see My Father through My words, your love for Him will also grow. And because of your love for My Father and Me, the rivers of living water will begin to flow out of you to others. Mary realized this as she listened to Me. Martha missed this as she busied herself with tasks that were far less important. Child, open your mind and heart to My words. Share your heart with Me and listen to Me. Let's have more secret time together today.

Therefore I tell you, do not worry about your life, what you will eat; or about your body, what you will wear. Life is more than food, and the body more than clothes. Luke 12:22–23

→→ *The Greatest Words Ever Spoken,* Focus (pp. 244–45); Loving Christ (p. 280)

Become Like a Little Child

I tell you the truth, unless you change and become like little children, you will never enter the kingdom of heaven.
Matthew 18:3

Why must you become like a little child to enter the kingdom of heaven? Little children believe. They believe with their whole hearts. When they talk to My Father, they rightly believe He is listening. When He answers their prayers, they know that He answered them just because He loves them. When I tell them that something is wrong, they believe it and avoid it. When I whisper that they should do something good, they do it without hesitation. Little children are tender-hearted. They give to those in need, even when they have little to give. They are slow to judge and quick to forgive. They love to love and are grateful for anything they are given. When they see someone hurting, they instantly comfort them. Are they perfect? Of course not. Are they sometimes selfish? Yes. But they always want to do better. Most important, they listen to Me, they trust Me, and they love Me from their hearts and with their actions. They follow Me. My child, though you may be fully grown, you are still My precious lamb. Become like a little child and follow Me, without delay, with your whole heart.

For whoever exalts himself will be humbled, and he who humbles himself will be exalted. Luke 14:11, NKJV

✦ *The Greatest Words Ever Spoken,* Humility (pp. 271–73)

Don't Trade Your Greatest Possession for Worthless Gain

And what do you benefit if you gain the whole world but lose your own soul? Is anything worth more than your soul? Matthew 16:26, NLT

M y dear one, are you distracted or seduced by the treasures of this world? Do you spend your time pursuing the things of this life and neglect your own soul? People often value that which has no worth beyond this life. No matter how much they gain, they always hunger for more. They love the things of this world rather than My Father, Me, and that which is of eternal worth. They have truly lost their souls. Child, don't be fooled. This world is not your home. Your soul is your most precious possession. Nourish it with My words—morning, noon, and night. Don't envy those who trade their souls for the things of this life. All their pleasures will come to an abrupt end, and their woes will last for eternity. When you feast on My words, they will provide the food that will keep your soul healthy and strong, and your heart will be yoked to Mine. My Father and I will become your true delight, and you will be like a giant tree planted by the waters. You will store up treasures in heaven that will bless you and others throughout eternity.

A man's life does not consist in the abundance of his possessions. Luke 12:15

⊁⊁ *The Greatest Words Ever Spoken,* Wealth and Possessions (pp. 344–47)

Fulfillment That Never Fades

Everyone who drinks this water will be thirsty again, but whoever drinks the water I give him will never thirst. Indeed, the water I give him will become in him a spring of water welling up to eternal life. John 4:13–14

H as the joy that once filled your life faded? That happens when you fail to rely on Me for your fulfillment. Although you find things that promise to fulfill you, they all fade. Relationships lose their luster as hurtful flaws begin to appear. Even religious activities may quickly become mere routine. Child, there is only one place from which you can draw *living water,* which will satisfy your deepest longings. I am the only Source of living water. Look at My life and listen to My words. The water of My words will cleanse you from all unrighteousness and guilt. It will flush fears from your mind. My promises will flood your heart with peace, even in the midst of your greatest storms. If your soul is not continuously filled with My love and joy, it's simply because you are not drawing from My well. Stop drawing water that does not satisfy, and come to Me.

Come to me, all of you who are weary and carry heavy burdens, and I will give you rest. Take my yoke upon you. Let me teach you, because I am humble and gentle at heart, and you will find rest for your souls. For my yoke is easy to bear, and the burden I give you is light. Matthew 11:28–30, NLT

✦ *The Greatest Words Ever Spoken,* The Promises of Christ (pp. 298–304)

My Joy Overflowing in Your Life

These things I have spoken to you, that My joy may remain in you, and that your joy may be full. John 15:11, NKJV

K nowing that I was about to be arrested, My grieving disciples were shocked to hear Me talk about a new kind of joy they could experience after I was taken away. I told them it would be joy so great that it would cause their joy to overflow. It's a joy that creates peace, contentment, and a type of happiness that the world can't explain. It is *My* joy, and I'm offering it to you. It's a joy that no person, no circumstance, and no power on earth will ever be able to take away from you. To receive it, you must abide in My love in the same way that I abide in My Father's love. I abide in My Father's love by obeying His commands, and *you* abide in *My* love by obeying My commands. If you are not experiencing My joy, it's not because of your circumstances; it's because you are not hearing My commands and obeying them. If you will begin to discover and do what I say, you will receive My joy, and your joy will be full.

I have loved you even as the Father has loved me. Remain in my love. When you obey my commandments, you remain in my love, just as I obey my Father's commandments and remain in his love. John 15:9–10, NLT

✦ *The Greatest Words Ever Spoken,* Joy (pp. 273–75)

Courage to Replace Your Fears

Take courage! It is I. Don't be afraid. Matthew 14:27

I t was the middle of the night, and the sea was rough. When My disciples first saw Me walking on the water, they thought I was a ghost. I told them to be courageous and cheerful. I told them, "It is I" and gave them a simple command: "Don't be afraid." And so it is with you. You never have to be afraid. Whenever you see adversity ahead, it is only natural to feel afraid. But whether the adversity you see is far off or just around the corner, I want you instead to see *Me*. Even in the middle of your greatest trial, you can *know* that I am with you. No storm that comes your way has taken Me by surprise. I knew about it before you were born. It's okay that fear might get the best of you for a moment. But open the eyes of your spirit and see Me. I am here! Run to My promises, and dwell in them for as long as it takes. I will talk to you and reveal My presence. I will show you how to walk close to My side, and we will pass through your storm together.

Are not two sparrows sold for a copper coin? And not one of them falls to the ground apart from your Father's will. But the very hairs of your head are all numbered. Do not fear therefore; you are of more value than many sparrows. Matthew 10:29–31, NKJV

✈ *The Greatest Words Ever Spoken,* Anxiety, Worry, and Fear (pp. 190–93)

Growing Your Faith into Maturity

But you are to be perfect, even as your Father in heaven is perfect. Matthew 5:48, NLT

When you were born again, you were born into a whole new way of life. At first you continued to act in many of the ways you acted before your new birth. When people offended you, you struck back, delivering a wound for a wound. When people said unkind things about you, you said unkind things about them. You loved people who loved you and behaved in a hateful manner toward those who were hateful. But now it's time to grow up. I want you to become more *mature* and *complete* in your faith. Immature faith loves a neighbor but hates an enemy. Mature faith behaves as your Father in heaven would behave, not just loving your neighbor but loving your enemy as well. Mature faith prays for those who hate you or persecute you. In fact, mature faith looks for ways to bless those who hurt you. I'm not asking you to change your emotions or feelings. I'm asking you to have faith in your Father and in Me and to change your behavior. Do as We do. Then you will be complete and mature, just as your Father is.

Greater love has no one than this, than to lay down one's life for his friends. You are My friends if you do whatever I command you. John 15:13–14, NKJV

✦✦ *The Greatest Words Ever Spoken,* Spiritual Maturity (p. 328); Love (pp. 278–80)

I Know Your Desires, and I Understand Your Weaknesses

Watch and pray so that you will not fall into temptation. The spirit is willing, but the body is weak. Matthew 26:41

For more than three years, I poured My life into My disciples. I loved and nurtured them. I met their every need. I gave them the authority and power to perform miracles. They confessed their faith in Me. And yet, when My heart was breaking and I asked them to keep watch with Me while I prayed, they couldn't stay awake. I asked them to keep watch and pray, but they failed. Though I was deeply saddened, I did not condemn them. I knew that in their spirit they *wanted* to serve Me, but they simply did not have the power to do so in their flesh. I know the same is true with you. There are so many times that you want to obey Me. Your spirit is willing, but your flesh is weak, and you fall short. I do not judge you; I understand you. I understand your weaknesses far better than you do. When you fall, know that I am there reaching out to you. I am your Savior. I love you and I forgive you. Pray that you may avoid temptation, and follow Me.

It is not those who are healthy who need a physician, but those who are sick. But go and learn what this means: "I desire compassion, and not sacrifice," for I did not come to call the righteous, but sinners. Matthew 9:12–13, NASB

→ *The Greatest Words Ever Spoken,* Temptation (pp. 341–42); Prayer (pp. 295–98)

Your Sorrows Will Turn into Joy

Blessed are those who mourn, for they will be comforted.
Matthew 5:4

My dear one, I know your sorrows, and I understand your grief. Even though I knew I was only minutes from raising Lazarus from the dead, his death broke My heart. In Gethsemane My sorrow was overwhelming, nearly to the point of death. But for all who know My Father, sorrow is only temporary—it need not control your heart. As you express your heartaches and sorrows to My Father and Me, We will comfort you. Though your grief may be great, know that the Holy Spirit's miraculous comfort will be greater. In this time draw even nearer to Me. Pray continuously. Listen with your heart to My comforting assurances. The eternal things of your life are as present today as they were the day you came into My kingdom. All other things, even people's lives on earth, are only temporary. But your comfort and hope, your joy and your life with Me are eternal. Because I live, you shall live also. Press in to know Me. As you get to know Me more, your love for Me will chase away even your greatest sorrows. I promise.

I tell you the truth, you will weep and mourn while the world rejoices. You will grieve, but your grief will turn to joy. John 16:20

→→ *The Greatest Words Ever Spoken,* Joy (pp. 273–75); A Broken Heart (p. 357)

The Power of My Words

For I did not speak of my own accord, but the Father who sent me commanded me what to say and how to say it. I know that his command leads to eternal life. So whatever I say is just what the Father has told me to say. John 12:49–50

On earth I was not merely a teacher passing along information. I didn't say what I said so people could simply *consider* My words but so they could do them. The truth is, My Father sent Me to earth to accomplish everything He wanted Me to accomplish. I did everything He commanded Me to do and said everything He commanded Me to say. That's why My words are so critical to your daily life and to your eternal life as well. They are not My words only; they are the words of your almighty Father. They will perform their miraculous power in you if you will abide in them. My words will *never* fail. But if you don't know them, you rob yourself of knowing the ultimate truth, the solutions to your problems, and the source of your faith. By not doing them, you deprive yourself of the powerful miracles they would work in your life. Child, hear My words and do them!

Therefore whoever hears these sayings of Mine, and does them, I will liken him to a wise man who built his house on the rock: and the rain descended, the floods came, and the winds blew and beat on that house; and it did not fall, for it was founded on the rock. Matthew 7:24–25, NKJV

→→ *The Greatest Words Ever Spoken,* Jesus' Relationship with God the Father (pp. 55–60); Jesus' Words, Their Role and Power (pp. 62–64)

Waiting to Give You Good Gifts

If you, then, though you are evil, know how to give good gifts to your children, how much more will your Father in heaven give good gifts to those who ask him! Matthew 7:11

E verything your heavenly Father does flows from who He is. Out of His love, He gives you kindness, mercy, and grace. Out of His righteousness, He gives you that which is pure, good, and holy. And out of His justice, He weighs the motives and intentions of your thoughts, words, and deeds. Out of love, righteousness, and justice, He has provided a way that you can stand before Him cleansed from all your sin. Because of His love, all the judgment for your sin was laid on Me. By the shedding of My blood, all My righteousness was transferred to you. When you were born again, you were freed from all judgment and condemnation. How could you think that He who loves you so much would withhold good gifts when you ask Him? However, He will *not* give you gifts that are contrary to His righteousness or detrimental to your eternal benefit. That's why you can trust His decisions regarding what He gives in response to your requests.

So I say to you, ask, and it will be given to you; seek, and you will find; knock, and it will be opened to you. For everyone who asks, receives; and he who seeks, finds; and to him who knocks, it will be opened. Luke 11:9–10, NASB

⇥ *The Greatest Words Ever Spoken,* God's Goodness (pp. 97–99); The Promises of Christ (pp. 298–304)

Speak My Words and Proclaim My Whisperings

What I tell you in the dark, speak in the daylight; what is whispered in your ear, proclaim from the roofs.
Matthew 10:27

At night before you go to sleep, meditate on My words. Think about them and pray about them. Listen to My teachings. Hear My answers to your heart's concerns. Discover My commands, and see them in relation to your day as it ends. Then think about My words in relation to the day you will begin when you wake up. Dwell in My words so you can more intimately know the Father and Me. If you will do this, you will hear My whisperings as you go to sleep and as you move throughout your day tomorrow. When you awake, think about what you heard in the night. Throughout the day the Holy Spirit will bring to mind the things I have said to you. With gentleness and humility, share what you have heard with My followers and others who enter your path. Without fear or reluctance proclaim the good news of what I have revealed to you. Those who desire truth will come to the light and embrace My words.

Take My yoke upon you and learn from Me, for I am gentle and lowly in heart, and you will find rest for your souls.
Matthew 11:29, NKJV

✦ *The Greatest Words Ever Spoken,* Commands of Christ (pp. 206–17)

It's Not *What* You Know, It's *Whom* You Come To

You diligently study the Scriptures because you think that by them you possess eternal life. These are the Scriptures that testify about me, yet you refuse to come to me to have life. John 5:39–40

My child, Scripture is one of the greatest gifts My Father has given to the world. The Scriptures reveal the truth about My Father, about Me, about the Holy Spirit, and about everything We love. The Father gave the Scriptures so people could come to know Us intimately. But instead, many people have searched the Scriptures simply to gain knowledge, and they did *not* come to know the Father or Me. This is tragic. Not only do they miss the purpose of the Scriptures. They also miss the very purpose of their lives on earth. Child, don't follow their foolish example. Every day come to *Me* for life. Prayerfully meditate on My words so you can get to know Me and the Father. Hear what I say and *do* it. If you will, My Father will love you, and I, too, will love you, and I will reveal Myself to you. We will come and make Our home with you. This is the purpose of your life—to intimately know Me and the Father.

If anyone loves Me, he will keep My word; and My Father will love him, and We will come to him and make Our home with him. John 14:23, NKJV

+> *The Greatest Words Ever Spoken,* Eternal Life (pp. 134–42); The Scriptures (pp. 440–41)

You Don't Have to Be Afraid

Why are you so afraid? Do you still have no faith? Mark 4:40

It was late at night, and I was sleeping on the boat. The winds and waves became violent, and the boat was taking on water. My disciples woke Me, crying, "Teacher, don't you care if we drown?" Did they really think that any adversity could overcome them when I was in their presence? The truth is, at that moment they had no faith. And without faith in Me, fear can overtake anyone. Without faith it's easy to believe that your circumstances control your destiny. Child, nothing can overcome you when you are following Me. In My presence you are safely in My hands and My Father's hands. Nothing can remove you from Our eternal protection. Even death cannot snatch you away from Us. What do you fear today? Don't panic. Your fear is simply a mirror that exposes your lack of faith. If you will fill your heart with faith, your fears will quickly be replaced with confidence and peace. But the only way to *fill* your heart with faith is to abide in My words. When you are afraid, it's because you are *not* abiding in My words and acting on them. Take My words into your heart today, and your fears will flee.

Teach these new disciples to obey all the commands I have given you. And be sure of this: I am with you always, even to the end of the age. Matthew 28:20, NLT

❯❯ *The Greatest Words Ever Spoken,* Anxiety, Worry, and Fear (pp. 190–93)

Filled to Overflowing

If anyone is thirsty, let him come to Me and drink. He who believes in Me, as the Scripture has said, "From his innermost being will flow rivers of living water." John 7:37–38, NASB

H ave you wondered why you lack the peace, joy, and contentment you once had in Me? Have you wondered why you sometimes feel empty? Are you frustrated, wounded, fearful, or overwhelmed by your struggles and unmet needs? Do the needs of others strain or drain your life? It doesn't have to be that way! The problem is that the sources you turn to cannot satisfy the thirst of your soul. People and things can give you only a shallow level of contentment, joy, and purpose. Come to Me. I am the only Source of living water, which can continually fill your soul and refresh your spirit. To receive a continuous flow of My living water, you must believe *in* Me, and you must *believe* Me. You believe *in* Me by abiding in My words, and you *believe* Me by doing My words. Then the rivers of My living water will continually flow from your innermost being. Not only will they bring back the peace, joy, and commitment you long for, but they will flow out of you to bless everyone around you. I know you are thirsty. Come to Me.

Come to me, all of you who are weary and carry heavy burdens, and I will give you rest. Matthew 11:28, NLT

➤➤ *The Greatest Words Ever Spoken,* Living Water (p. 278); Following Christ (pp. 245–53)

Why People Do Terrible
Things to You

And these things they will do to you because they have not
known the Father nor Me. John 16:3, NKJV

I know you often are dismayed by the evil things people do to you
and to others. You may have thought, *How could God allow such
terrible things?* From ancient times wicked people have done evil to
those who love My Father and follow Me. They are ruled by their
self-serving nature. They love the things of the world more than they
love God. They love darkness rather than light. Most important,
they do evil because they do not intimately know the Father or Me.
The only way people can break free from their self-centered nature is
to be born again and to enter into an intimate relationship with My
Father and Me. Once people truly know Me, they flee the darkness
to run to the light. I am the Light of the World. Those who know
Me hunger and thirst for righteousness. They become consumed by
God's love, which moves them to bless lives rather than damage lives.
Child, it doesn't matter what people of darkness do to you. What
matters is what you do to them. Forgive them and bless them, the
way My Father has forgiven and blessed you.

Blessed are you when people insult you, persecute you and falsely
say all kinds of evil against you because of me. Rejoice and be glad,
because great is your reward in heaven, for in the same way they
persecuted the prophets who were before you. Matthew 5:11–12

→→ *The Greatest Words Ever Spoken,* Rejection and Persecution of Christians
(pp. 308–12)

Stop Judging, Show Mercy

Do not judge others, and you will not be judged. For you will be treated as you treat others. The standard you use in judging is the standard by which you will be judged. And why worry about a speck in your friend's eye when you have a log in your own? Matthew 7:1–3, NLT

B efore you were born into My kingdom, it was only natural for you to judge, criticize, and condemn others for their faults and wrongdoings. But, dear one, that was then. When you were born again, you became a vessel of mercy. You were spared all of My Father's righteous judgment, condemnation, and punishment for your sins. Your debt to God was fully paid by My death on the cross. Though you were dead in sin, the Holy Spirit brought you to life. In spite of all your sinful thoughts, words, and deeds, My Father has shown His tender mercies toward you in ways you can't imagine. Knowing everything He has done for you, can you understand why I want you to be a reflection of His grace and mercy to others? You are His light in this dark world. If people don't see His mercy in you, they may never see it anywhere else. Stop focusing on the failings and faults of others, and instead look for ways to demonstrate His grace to them. If you must correct them, do so in humility, with love and gentleness. Spend more time removing the beams from your own eye rather than noticing the tiny splinters in the eyes of others.

He who rejects Me and does not receive My sayings, has one who judges him; the word I spoke is what will judge him at the last day. John 12:48, NASB

→→ *The Greatest Words Ever Spoken,* Judging Others (pp. 483–84)

It Is Worth It All

And everyone who has left houses or brothers or sisters or father or mother or children or fields for my sake will receive a hundred times as much and will inherit eternal life.
Matthew 19:29

I know there are many times when you are discouraged and downhearted. I know you often suffer at the hands of those who seem to have no desire for God. I know you see how they are rewarded with the treasures of this world, and yet their lives are centered on themselves. Surely you must wonder, *Why do they receive blessings that seem to be withheld from me?* The truth is, they will someday lose everything they value the most. And when they die, they will experience the agony of being eternally separated from the light and kingdom of God. They will receive eternal condemnation for their sins. Their joy and glory are but for a moment. This is not true for My sheep. Their sacrifices in this life are only momentary. Child, you, too, will leave behind every earthly treasure you value. You, too, will fall asleep in death. But you will wake up in heaven. And you can't begin to imagine My Father's love that will welcome you. It will be yours forever. Wait till you see what He has prepared for you. It *will* be worth it all!

But store up for yourselves treasures in heaven, where neither moth nor rust destroys, and where thieves do not break in or steal.
Matthew 6:20, NASB

→→ *The Greatest Words Ever Spoken,* Rewards (pp. 172–75)

When You Pray . . .

This, then, is how you should pray: "Our Father in heaven, hallowed be your name, your kingdom come, your will be done on earth as it is in heaven." Matthew 6:9–10

While I was on earth, My greatest joys were found in times of prayer. My heart breaks for My followers who spend so little time praying. When I first taught My disciples how to pray, I told them to begin by remembering whom they are talking to—their almighty Father in heaven. He is to be honored and exalted above all others. He is so holy, so loving, so majestic and awesome that no words of praise can do Him justice. Oh, what a God! Oh, what a Father! And He is *your* Father. Oh, that your spirit would catch a glimpse of His majesty. Oh, that you would know the joy of His endless love and mercy. *He* is the Holy One into whose presence you enter when you pray. If you knew Him as I know Him, you, too, would desire His will to be done rather than yours. His will reflects what is best for you and for His kingdom. You need not doubt that. He already has proved His unequaled love for you by sending Me to lead you into His kingdom.

For my Father's will is that everyone who looks to the Son and believes in him shall have eternal life, and I will raise them up at the last day. John 6:40

❧ *The Greatest Words Ever Spoken,* Prayer (pp. 295–98); God's Will (pp. 106–7)

When You Pray . . .

Give us today our daily bread. Matthew 6:11

Child, your Father understands all your daily needs. Yet He also knows that you worry about not having your daily needs supplied. He delights in you when you openly share your heart's desires with Him in prayer. He wants you to be completely honest in sharing what you want, even if you are afraid it might be against His will. For a brief time in Gethsemane, I wanted to be spared the terrible agony that was in front of Me. But soon after I prayed for *My* will, His peace flowed into My Spirit, and My desire changed to wanting *His* will. I could then honestly ask for His will even though I was dreading what lay ahead. I knew I would become the sin I had never known. I knew I would be separated for the first time ever from My Father. Child, your Father does not supply the grace you need until the moment you need it. You need not ask for next week's needs to be met, because you can live only one day at a time. He wants you to know the daily joy that comes only by trusting Him each day. He delights in your daily dependence on Him. Oh, how He loves you!

My grace is sufficient for you, for my power is made perfect in weakness. 2 Corinthians 12:9

↠ *The Greatest Words Ever Spoken,* Prayer (pp. 295–98); Living in the Present (pp. 277–78)

When You Pray . . .

Forgive us our debts, as we also have forgiven our debtors.
Matthew 6:12

Forgiveness is the greatest gift you have been given and the hardest gift to give. It's natural to want to withhold forgiveness. After all, when you are hurt by the words, actions, or neglect of others, the pain continues long after the wound is inflicted. But you won't be truly free of the pain until you forgive. When you don't fully forgive a person, you remain in bondage to him. Not forgiving becomes a root of bitterness that grows into a forest of anger and resentment. It changes who you are and prevents you from experiencing intimacy with Me. But these aren't the reasons the Father demands that you forgive even your enemies. He requires you to forgive because *He* has forgiven you of all your sins against Him. He wants you to be so grateful to Him for His forgiveness that, in faith and obedience, you forgive all offenses against you. Not to forgive is arrogant and belittles Him, His greatest gift to you, and His will for your life. When you truly forgive, you will be freer and happier than you have ever been. I know, because *I* forgave *you*.

For if you forgive men when they sin against you, your heavenly Father will also forgive you. But if you do not forgive men their sins, your Father will not forgive your sins. Matthew 6:14–15

⤜ *The Greatest Words Ever Spoken,* Prayer (pp. 295–98); Forgiving Others (pp. 481–83)

When You Pray . . .

And lead us not into temptation, but deliver us from the evil one. Matthew 6:13

Satan and his demons know how to tempt you. They are smarter and more powerful than you can imagine. You live in their domain. And when you fall to their temptations, the consequences can be devastating to your soul, to the lives of others, and to your intimacy with the Father and Me. My child, if only you knew the amount of temptation you face that could be avoided if you would but ask the Father to lead you into paths away from temptation. Pray that He will deliver you from the path and power of the Evil One. Satan knows what you react to, and once he creates a spark, he knows how to fan the flames. He knows how to appeal to every aspect of your human nature to lead you into greed, arrogance, lust, envy, jealousy, and anger. Pray at the beginning of your day and throughout each day that you will be delivered from those temptations. If you don't, it is because you either underestimate the power of Satan and his temptations, or even worse you overestimate your ability to overcome them. Each day abide in My words, take up your cross, and follow Me!

Keep watching and praying that you may not enter into temptation; the spirit is willing, but the flesh is weak. Matthew 26:41, NASB

→→ *The Greatest Words Ever Spoken,* Prayer (pp. 295–98); Temptation (pp. 341–42)

Unite with All My Followers

May they experience such perfect unity that the world will know that you sent me and that you love them as much as you love me. John 17:23, NLT

On the night of My arrest, I prayed for My disciples and for everyone who would believe in Me through their message. I prayed that you and all My followers would be united. You may wonder, *With all the different doctrines and churches, how could unity ever be possible?* Unity is possible only when people make following Me their greatest priority. It would be impossible to unite if the basis of unity were agreement on doctrinal issues. I never said doctrines were to be *the* focus of My followers. The focus of My followers should be Me—discovering and doing what I say. When I told My apostles to make disciples of all nations, I didn't say to make disciples of people by perfecting their doctrines. I said make them disciples by "teaching them to obey everything I have commanded you." The *only* way to follow Me is to hear My words and do them. When that is the focus of your daily life, you can have perfect unity with all whose hearts are focused on following Me.

A new commandment I give to you, that you love one another; as I have loved you, that you also love one another. By this all will know that you are My disciples, if you have love for one another. John 13:34–35, NKJV

✦ *The Greatest Words Ever Spoken,* Unity Versus Division (p. 342)

When You Truly Believe in Me . . .

Truly, truly, I say to you, he who believes in Me, the works that I do, he will do also; and greater works than these he will do; because I go to the Father. John 14:12, NASB

D id you know that those who believe in Me can do the works I did on earth? If you are not doing those works of faith, it's either because you have not yet realized the power and authority I have given you or because you don't understand what I mean by *believing* in Me. Believing in Me is *not* simply holding the opinion that I am God's Son. Churches are filled with people who say they believe yet live contrary to My teachings. Many even call Me Lord, but they don't do what I say. The person who says he believes in Me but doesn't do what I say is deceiving himself. To believe in Me is to *hunger* for My words and to follow Me by *obeying* My teachings. Child, I know you want to follow Me. You hunger for My teachings, and you strive to obey them. That's why My promise to those who believe in Me is meant for *you*. If you abide in My words, your faith will grow, and you will do the works that I did.

Therefore whoever hears these sayings of Mine, and does them, I will liken him to a wise man who built his house on the rock. Matthew 7:24, NKJV

→ *The Greatest Words Ever Spoken,* Jesus' Teaching on Miracles and Signs (pp. 61–62)

What Kind of Works?

Truly, truly, I say to you, he who believes in Me, the works that I do, he will do also; and greater works than these he will do; because I go to the Father. John 14:12, NASB

Dear one, I have promised that those who believe in Me will do the works I did while I walked on earth. Have you wondered what kind of works these might be? Even though I was known for the miracles I performed, they were only a small portion of My works. As important as they were, My other works were even more important. I was the Light of the World, showing the true worth of everything the Father loves and values. I not only testified to the truth with My words, but I *demonstrated* the truth with My life and My works of righteousness. I performed works of compassion, works of love, works of mercy, and works of forgiveness. I performed works of patience and of perseverance. And, of course, I performed works of serving, suffering, and sacrifice. The greatest works I performed were My works of obedience to My dear Father. Yes, when you believe in Me, you can do the miraculous works I did, when it's the Father's will. But even more important than any miracle you will perform are My *other* works that you will do.

You are my friends if you do what I command. John 15:14

✦ *The Greatest Words Ever Spoken,* Obedience and Good Works (pp. 289–94)

You Are a Light

You are the light of the world—like a city on a hilltop that cannot be hidden. No one lights a lamp and then puts it under a basket. Instead, a lamp is placed on a stand, where it gives light to everyone in the house. In the same way, let your good deeds shine out for all to see, so that everyone will praise your heavenly Father. Matthew 5:14–16, NLT

While I was on earth, I was the Light of the World. My life demonstrated who God is, and My words proclaimed all that He desires. Those who don't know Me are lost in darkness. Child, you and all My followers are now the lights in the world. Since those in darkness can't see Me, *you* are their only hope of finding Me. If you will let your light shine, they can see My love in the way you honor them. They can see My mercy in the way you deal with their faults. They can see My forgiveness in the way you forgive them. In you, they can find a faithful friend who gives them a glimpse of My unconditional love. In you, they can see righteous behavior that rises above the moral depravity of the world. In you, they can see generosity instead of greed, contentment instead of envy, and peace instead of aggression. In you, they can see concern instead of indifference. Be My light so others may see Me in you!

Peace be with you; as the Father has sent Me, I also send you. John 20:21, NASB

→→ *The Greatest Words Ever Spoken,* Light Versus Darkness (pp. 384–85)

Preserving Righteousness in Your World

You are the salt of the earth. But what good is salt if it has lost its flavor? Can you make it salty again? Matthew 5:13, NLT

My Father's ways are as far above the ways of humanity as heaven is above earth. His loving-kindness, righteousness, and judgment are beyond human imagination. He has chosen *you* to be a vessel of His nature. He has given you the Holy Spirit to empower you to overcome the values and influences of the world. You are His salt on the earth. By living in His love and righteousness, you are the preservative of His values in a world that ignores and even despises Him and all that He stands for. If you stop being that preservative, you are setting aside one of your great callings and purposes on earth. People will judge the Father and Me by *your* behavior. This is why it is so important that you stay salty. Your righteousness can make a difference in the values of those you influence. Your loving-kindness can cause others to want to be more loving, like you. And your just treatment of others can influence them to be just in their treatment of others. Child, you are the salt of the earth. Stay close to Me!

Let your light shine before men in such a way that they may see your good works, and glorify your Father who is in heaven. Matthew 5:16, NASB

↠ *The Greatest Words Ever Spoken,* The Mission of a Christian (pp. 281–89); Attitudes (pp. 196–98)

Do You Want to Be Happy? Learn Gratefulness!

Go home to your family and tell them how much the Lord has done for you, and how he has had mercy on you.
Mark 5:19

Child, I understand what you are going through. I know that your circumstances, struggles, and disappointments steal your happiness. Listen to Me. Though adversity can knock you down, it can *keep* you down only if you let it. It knocks you down because it takes you by surprise. Whenever you *remain* in unhappiness, it is because you allow the Adversary to keep your heart focused on your circumstances. You allow him to magnify the adversity, blinding you to everything My Father and I have given you. You allow the momentary raindrops of your circumstances to blind you to the vast ocean of eternal blessings that We have given you. Your salvation and your relationship with Me are eternal! You remain in unhappiness only because you close your eyes to the Father and to Me and to everything We have given you. Get back into My words and let them continually refresh your heart and remind you of all you have been given. Then go and tell others of the great things I have done for you.

However, do not rejoice that the spirits submit to you, but rejoice that your names are written in heaven. Luke 10:20

✦ *The Greatest Words Ever Spoken,* Gratitude (pp. 262–63); God's Mercy (pp. 101–2)

There Is No Other Way, No Other Hope

I am the way, the truth, and the life. No one comes to the Father except through Me. John 14:6, NKJV

On the night of My last supper with My disciples, I gave them truths they would need to believe in order to fulfill their missions. These are just as important for you. When you believe these truths in your *heart,* nothing can destroy your faith. But if you *don't* believe them in your heart, your faith will be easily shaken. First, I am the one and only way that you can come to the Father. He sent Me to earth to perfectly fulfill the Law and to lay down My life for your sins. Although I was tempted in all things, I never sinned. My thoughts and the motives and intentions of My heart were as holy as the Father's. I purchased your salvation with My blood. You were dead in sin, and I have made you alive in Me. That's how much the Father and I love you. Stay close to Me so you won't lose your way.

Because strait is the gate, and narrow is the way, which leadeth unto life, and few there be that find it. Matthew 7:14, KJV

For God so loved the world that He gave His only begotten Son, that whoever believes in Him should not perish but have everlasting life. John 3:16, NKJV

✦ *The Greatest Words Ever Spoken,* Eternal Life (pp. 134–42); The Narrow Way Versus the Broad Way (pp. 170–71)

All Truth Is in Me and Is Revealed in My Life and Words

I am the way, **the truth,** and the life. No one comes to the Father except through Me. John 14:6, NKJV

I am *the* truth. All truth, everything of eternal value, everything of true worth is contained in Me. It is demonstrated in My life and expressed in My words. My words are the truth by which all else will be measured and judged. By hearing My words, you can know the truth about the Father and the Holy Spirit. You will hear what He loves and what He hates. In My words you can know the truth about everything—that which has great worth to the Father, that which has no value. Although His ways are as far above your ways as the heavens are above the earth, through the truth of My words you can learn His ways and know all that you can do to please Him. By the truth of My words, you can avoid that which is destructive to you. Through the truth of My commands, you can love the Father and Me with your faith and obedience. Through the truth of My promises, you can receive all that We have for you. Let My words reveal the answers to every problem you will ever face.

And you shall know the truth, and the truth shall make you free. John 8:32, NKJV

→→ *The Greatest Words Ever Spoken,* Revelation of God's Truth (pp. 312–13)

Your Life Can Only Be Fulfilled by My Life

I am the way, the truth, and **the life.** No one comes to the Father except through Me. John 14:6, NKJV

I n Me is true life that belongs to Me and to those who receive it from Me. It is a life that loves the Father above all. I love you more than you love yourself. I once died for you, but now I *live* for you! I have asked you to deny yourself, take up your cross, and follow Me. This means setting aside your own desires, rights, and expectations and devoting your life to following Me and serving the Father. As you do, I will pour *My* life into you. The life that you lay aside is a dying life of emptiness, sadness, and no eternal worth. The life you receive from Me is eternal and centered on the Father. I want to pour My life into you, and I will do that as you abide in Me and My words.

But whoever drinks of the water that I shall give him will never thirst. But the water that I shall give him will become in him a fountain of water springing up into everlasting life. John 4:14, NKJV

If anyone desires to come after Me, let him deny himself, and take up his cross daily, and follow Me. For whoever desires to save his life will lose it, but whoever loses his life for My sake will save it. Luke 9:23–24, NKJV

→→ *The Greatest Words Ever Spoken,* Eternal Life (pp. 134–42); Following Christ (pp. 245–53)

You Must Be Born Again

That which is born of the flesh is flesh, and that which is born of the Spirit is spirit. Do not be amazed that I said to you, "You must be born again." John 3:6–7, NASB

From the time you first became aware of Me, you have heard the announcement I gave to Nicodemus. *No one* can enter the kingdom of God and intimately know the Father and Me without being born of the Spirit. I know you have wondered if *you* have been born again. A tree can be known only by its fruit. Have you seen your desperate need for forgiveness and cleansing from your sin? Did you repent and run to Me? Do you desire to know Me intimately? Do you hunger for My words and feast on them? Do you want to follow Me, even if it means turning your back on the treasures of this world? Are you willing to take up your cross and follow Me, even though it means daily surrendering the "rights" you used to cling to? Are you seeing the fruit of the Holy Spirit in your life? These cannot be produced by your old nature but only by a spiritual nature, which has been born from above. My call to you is the same every day: Come to Me. I will never turn you away. Abide in My words and follow Me. I love you.

And whoever comes to me I will never drive away. John 6:37

→→ *The Greatest Words Ever Spoken,* Eternal Life (pp. 134–42)

Oh, How God Loves You!

For God so loved the world, that He gave His only begotten Son, that whoever believes in Him shall not perish, but have eternal life. John 3:16, NASB

When Adam and Eve rebelled against God with their arrogant disobedience, He would have been just and righteous to destroy them and start over with a new creation. But instead, because of His unfathomable love, He promised that He would provide a Savior. The Savior would be the enemy of Satan, the One who would destroy him and his evil work and save Adam and Eve and their descendants. Sin is detestable beyond description to the Father, who is perfect in holiness. Every sin of humanity is a hateful display of arrogance and rebellion against God. Would *you* consider sacrificing your precious, beloved child to save people who show their hatred of you every day—people who defy you and belittle all you have given them? Of course you wouldn't! But your heavenly Father, the God of all creation, loves you with a love so great that He *did* sacrifice His one and only Son so you could be saved. His love is so great that no human can imagine it. Oh, how He loves you! I know, because I am one with Him, and I share His love for you.

May they be brought to complete unity to let the world know that you sent me and have loved them even as you have loved me. John 17:23

※ *The Greatest Words Ever Spoken,* God's Love (pp. 99–101); Eternal Life (pp. 134–42)

Those Who Believe in Him

For God so loved the world, that He gave His only begotten Son, **that whoever believes in Him** shall not perish, but have eternal life. John 3:16, NASB

Whoever *believes* in Me will *not* perish but will have eternal life. Believing in Me is not merely agreeing, accepting, or admitting that I am God's Son. Many people will say, "Lord, Lord, have we not prophesied in Your name, cast out demons in Your name, and done many wonders in Your name?" Tragically, I will tell them, "I never knew you; depart from Me, you who practice lawlessness!" People's behavior is the expression of their heart's true beliefs. Many call Me Lord, but their hearts are far from Me. They choose to set aside My words, doing instead what *they* desire. But those who believe in Me in their hearts follow Me by doing what *I* say. When you truly believe in Me, you will endeavor to love the way *I* love, forgive the way *I* forgive, and show mercy to those who don't deserve it. You will gain a growing desire to abide in My words and to do them. Child, believe in Me and delight in My words, and the Holy Spirit will mold your life into a glorious reflection of My life.

He who believes in Me, as the Scripture has said, out of his heart will flow rivers of living water. John 7:38, NKJV

✤ *The Greatest Words Ever Spoken,* Belief and Faith in Christ (pp. 445–51); The Heart (pp. 374–78)

Eternal Life Now

For God so loved the world, that He gave His only begotten Son, that whoever believes in Him **shall not perish, but have eternal life.** John 3:16, NASB

M y precious lamb, do you really understand the *miracle* that the Holy Spirit has wrought in your life? If you are not rejoicing throughout the day, then you have not fully grasped the greatness of your salvation. Before, you were spiritually *dead.* You didn't have even the tiniest spark of life. You had *no* hope. Dead people with no hope can do absolutely nothing to raise themselves from the dead. But God, being rich in mercy because of His infinite love, made you alive in Me. The Holy Spirit brought about the miracle of your second birth. With this birth you repented of your sin. Instead of being driven by your self-centeredness, you did an about-face and began to follow Me. Instead of a future of eternal darkness and separation from My Father and His kingdom, you became a joint heir with Me to all that He has prepared for you. Today do not let any circumstance take your eyes off this miraculous gift. Though it was free to you, it cost Me everything!

Truly, truly, I say to you, he who hears My word, and believes Him who sent Me, has eternal life, and does not come into judgment, but has passed out of death into life. John 5:24, NASB

✢ *The Greatest Words Ever Spoken,* Eternal Life (pp. 134–42); God's Love (pp. 99–101)

I Will Never Throw You Away

All that the Father gives Me will come to Me, and the one who comes to Me I will by no means cast out. John 6:37, NKJV

Child, I know you have been hurt. I know you have been dishonored by others, even those you have loved. Friends throw away friends and end friendships. Husbands and wives dishonor and discard each other in marriage. Even many parents emotionally discard their children. I know this has caused you to wonder if there is any way you can be truly safe and secure. Listen to Me. My Father gave you to Me, and you came to Me. I will *never* throw you away. In Me alone you are safe. I will never turn My back on you, even when you fail. I came to *save* sinners, not to destroy them. Take My yoke upon you and walk with Me. Bathe your heart and mind with My words throughout your day. Nothing is more devastating to Satan than My followers who hold the Word of God in their hearts and are obedient to My Father and Me. Walk with Me, and watch Satan flee.

For my Father's will is that everyone who looks to the Son and believes in him shall have eternal life, and I will raise him up at the last day. John 6:40

→→ *The Greatest Words Ever Spoken,* Security (p. 315); The Promises of Christ (pp. 298–304)

No One Can Take You Away from Me

And I give them eternal life, and they shall never perish; neither shall anyone snatch them out of My hand. My Father, who has given them to Me, is greater than all; and no one is able to snatch them out of My Father's hand. I and My Father are one. John 10:28–30, NKJV

When you were born again, My Father and I lifted you out of the miry clay of sin. Do you think We will ever drop you back into that pit and abandon you? Absolutely not! Do you think anyone could snatch you out of Our hands? Not even Satan himself could do that. Your security does not depend on *your* strength. It depends entirely on Ours! No one can steal you away. Your greatest shelter from Satan's attacks is close by My side. I am with you even in your most severe trials. Even in death you are secure. I have given you eternal life. Child, I am with you now, and nothing can separate you from Me and My love. When you are feeling vulnerable and insecure, it is only because you are not abiding in Me and My words. Feast on My words today and every day. It's the only way to grow ever closer to Me.

If anyone loves Me, he will keep My word; and My Father will love him, and We will come to him and make Our home with him. John 14:23, NKJV

⊱ *The Greatest Words Ever Spoken,* The Promises of Christ (pp. 298–304); Security (p. 315)

You Don't Have to Be Burdened with Doubts or Worries

Why are you troubled, and why do doubts rise in your minds? Luke 24:38

O n the day of My resurrection, My disciples were terrified when they saw Me. They thought they were seeing a ghost. I often told them that they never had to be afraid of anyone or anything, because of their relationship with Me. Yet even at this glorious moment, they were deeply troubled. I had told them the night of My arrest to take control of their hearts and trust in the Father and Me. But even after My resurrection, they had not learned to rely on My words and trust Me. You, too, struggle needlessly with so many worries. When you are afraid, you are forgetting My words or choosing to set them aside. Child, come to Me now. Take My yoke upon you, and let Me carry your burden. Hear My words, believe them, and act upon them. That's how you show your love for Me and express your faith in Me. You never have to be troubled. Your adversary can take away only what is temporal. Your eternal life is safe with Me!

Therefore whoever hears these sayings of Mine, and does them, I will liken him to a wise man who built his house on the rock: and the rain descended, the floods came, and the winds blew and beat on that house; and it did not fall, for it was founded on the rock. Matthew 7:24–25, NKJV

→→ *The Greatest Words Ever Spoken,* Anxiety, Worry, and Fear (pp. 190–93)

My Word Is the Seed, and You Are the Soil

A farmer went out to sow his seed. As he was scattering the seed, some fell along the path, and the birds came and ate it up. Some fell on rocky places, where it did not have much soil. It sprang up quickly, because the soil was shallow. But when the sun came up, the plants were scorched, and they withered because they had no root. Other seed fell among thorns, which grew up and choked the plants. Still other seed fell on good soil, where it produced a crop—a hundred, sixty or thirty times what was sown. Matthew 13:3–8

I n this parable the *seed* is the message of the kingdom. My kingdom is eternal. It is based on eternal truths, but the kingdoms of this world are built on human ideals. The kingdoms of this world defy God, but My kingdom glorifies Him. The riches of earthly kingdoms are temporary, but the treasures of My kingdom are eternal. The kingdoms of this world lead people down roads of darkness, ending in death. My kingdom is full of light, leading My followers into paths of righteousness and eternal life. The seed that is sown are the truths about My Father, the kingdom, and Me. The people who hear this message of truth are the soils. Looking at this parable, ask yourself, *Which soil am I?*

I am the light of the world. Whoever follows me will never walk in darkness, but will have the light of life. John 8:12

→ *The Greatest Words Ever Spoken,* Spiritual Birth (pp. 178–81); Jesus' Words in Parables (pp. 65–84)

Without Understanding, the Risk Is High

When anyone hears the message about the kingdom and does not understand it, the evil one comes and snatches away what was sown in his heart. This is the seed sown along the path. Matthew 13:19

The message of the kingdom is the same today as it was at the start. It's a message about the Father, His love, His righteousness, and His judgment. It's about Me and My redeeming sacrifice. It's about My sheep. They hear My voice, deny themselves, take up their crosses daily, and follow Me. It's a message about dying to your selfish desires and living instead for My Father and His kingdom. The "seed sown along the path" refers to those who hear this message, and even though they initially embrace it, they don't understand it. It is contrary to their self-centeredness and conflicts with their desires. Because they don't understand it, the Evil One steals the message from their hearts, and they go back to their old ways. They trade that which is eternal for that which is temporal. Child, this is not you. As My truth has been revealed, you have embraced it, and you continue to hold tight to it. Continue to bathe your heart in My words every day, and you will be My true disciple. You will continue to know the truth, and the truth will make you free.

I am the way, and the truth, and the life. John 14:6, NASB

→→ *The Greatest Words Ever Spoken,* Spiritual Birth (pp. 178–81); Jesus' Words in Parables (pp. 65–84)

When Trials Come

The one who received the seed that fell on rocky places is the man who hears the word and at once receives it with joy. But since he has no root, he lasts only a short time. When trouble or persecution comes because of the word, he quickly falls away. Matthew 13:20–21

How could people who received My message with great excitement later abandon their faith? The answer is simple. When they received the Gospel, they thought they were trading their unhappy lives for happier ones. They thought their lives were going to get easier, not harder. No one told them that I had said, "In this world you will have trouble." So when trouble came, their shallow roots gave way, and their faith withered. They didn't know that to follow Me is to deny yourself and take up your cross daily. They embraced a form of godliness but never understood the true nature of becoming My follower. Child, you *know* that following Me means laying aside your self-centered rights, dying to yourself daily, and living to glorify God. When you encounter trials, instead of running *away* from Me, you must run *to* Me. Realize that even your greatest trials are but momentary afflictions, and your enduring faith will glorify the Father and produce for you treasures in heaven!

I have told you these things, so that in me you may have peace. In this world you will have trouble. But take heart! I have overcome the world. John 16:33

↠ *The Greatest Words Ever Spoken,* Spiritual Birth (pp. 178–81); Jesus' Words in Parables (pp. 65–84)

Choked by Life's Worries

The one who received the seed that fell among the thorns is the man who hears the word, but the worries of this life and the deceitfulness of wealth choke it, making it unfruitful.
Matthew 13:22

What distractions and obstacles keep you from following Me with your whole heart? What prevents you from bearing much fruit for My Father's kingdom? Is it not all the time you spend worrying about the temporal things of life? Most of the things you worry about are of little importance to the kingdom. My Father's will for you is that you bear much fruit. He wants you to love others with His unconditional love. He wants you to be an example of His righteousness in this world. He wants those who see you to see His mercy in the ways you show mercy. He wants others to see His generosity in the ways you are generous with your time and possessions. He wants people to see His compassion in the ways you show concern and care. He wants you to be a beacon of truth to those who live in darkness. But none of this will happen if you continually focus on the worries of this life. Instead, take your eyes off yourself and set your focus on Me.

In that day you will know that I am in My Father, and you in Me, and I in you. John 14:20, NASB

↠ *The Greatest Words Ever Spoken,* Anxiety, Worry, and Fear (pp. 190–93); Spiritual Birth (pp. 178–81); Jesus' Words in Parables (pp. 65–84)

Fooled by Wealth's Deceit

The one who received the seed that fell among the thorns is the man who hears the word, but the worries of this life and the deceitfulness of wealth choke it, making it unfruitful.
Matthew 13:22

If I had more money, I could do more for God and people who are needy." "I need a bigger house and a better neighborhood." "If I had more, others would have more respect for me, and I could influence more people." These are a few of the lies that so many of My would-be followers have believed. Today visions of greater prosperity—more than most other stumbling blocks—keep people from truly following Me. Remember, I have said, "No servant can serve two masters; for either he will hate the one and love the other, or else he will be devoted to one and despise the other. You cannot serve God and wealth." I meant that for *all* My followers, including you. Don't be deceived by the lies of wealth. I also said, "But seek first the kingdom of God and his righteousness, and all these things will be added to you." This, too, I meant for *you*. Follow Me, and I will supply whatever wealth you truly need.

Beware, and be on your guard against every form of greed; for not even when one has an abundance does his life consist of his possessions. Luke 12:15, NASB

✦ *The Greatest Words Ever Spoken,* Wealth and Possessions (pp. 344–47); Spiritual Birth (pp. 178–81); Jesus' Words in Parables (pp. 65–84)

Hearing, Understanding, and Bearing Fruit

But the one who received the seed that fell on good soil is the man who hears the word and understands it. He produces a crop, yielding a hundred, sixty or thirty times what was sown. Matthew 13:23

Child, you have heard My words. You have understood My message of the Father's boundless love for you. You have understood His righteousness and judgment. You have understood that your sin created an impossible debt and that the Father chose Me to lay down My life as a ransom for *you*. You understand My call to deny yourself, take up your cross daily, and follow Me. Yet I know you struggle in your efforts to deny yourself, take up your cross daily, and follow Me. Don't be discouraged. All My followers struggle against powers and principalities. We are plundering Satan's kingdom, and he does not surrender his subjects without a fight. I have called you to stand against the strength of your old nature and the attractions and influences of the world. None of this happens without a struggle. But you are the good soil. To win your battles, you must *daily* sow My words into your heart. The Holy Spirit will then use My words to guide you and produce His fruit in your life.

You did not choose me, but I chose you and appointed you to go and bear fruit—fruit that will last. John 15:16

→→ *The Greatest Words Ever Spoken,* Spiritual Birth (pp. 178–81); Jesus' Words in Parables (pp. 65–84)

The Secret for Bearing Eternal Fruit

Abide in Me, and I in you. As the branch cannot bear fruit of itself, unless it abides in the vine, neither can you, unless you abide in Me. John 15:4, NKJV

So many of My followers weary themselves trying to bear fruit. But bearing eternal fruit has little to do with how hard you work and everything to do with your *connection* to Me. For a branch to have life and produce fruit, it must have sap. And the life-giving sap flows *from* the vine *into* the branch. I am the Vine, and you are the branch. The only way you can have a spiritual life that produces fruit is by abiding in Me and My words. As you abide in My words, My life will flow from Me to you, and the Holy Spirit will produce His fruit in you. There is no other way you can bear fruit. Your purpose is to bear much fruit for God's kingdom. To fulfill that purpose, you *don't* need to become more active; you need to become more *connected*. My words are your connection to Me, through which My Spirit and life flow. When you do not dwell in My words, the connection is interrupted. But as you remain in My words, that connection is sustained, and I will remain in you, and you will remain in Me. Then you will bear much fruit!

So whatever I say is just what the Father has told me to say. John 12:50

✦ *The Greatest Words Ever Spoken,* Fruitbearing (pp. 257–60)

The Great Commission and You

Therefore go and make disciples of all nations, baptizing them in the name of the Father and of the Son and of the Holy Spirit, and teaching them to obey everything I have commanded you. Matthew 28:19–20

Child, you have been called into the kingdom, not just for your own blessing, but to bear much fruit. And the greatest fruit you can bear is that of becoming My true disciple and leading others into discipleship. You are My true disciple when you abide in My words and follow My commands. My commands will not weigh you down; they will lift you up. They will reveal the will of the Father for every situation you encounter. They also will *empower* you with grace to *do* the Father's will in every situation. They will set you free from the snares of this world. They will give you the power to glorify the Father in everything you do. But being My disciple isn't the end of your calling; it's only the beginning. I have called you to *make* disciples of others. You do this by teaching people to discover and obey My commands. If you will accept this call, I will give you the power to make disciples of everyone who wants to follow Me. This includes your family, your friends, and people you haven't yet met.

If you abide in My word, you are My disciples indeed. And you shall know the truth, and the truth shall make you free. John 8:31–32, NKJV

✦ *The Greatest Words Ever Spoken,* Evangelism (pp. 227–29); Following Christ—Discipleship (pp. 245–53)

No Harvest Without Sowing

And he who reaps receives wages, and gathers fruit for eternal life, that both he who sows and he who reaps may rejoice together. For in this the saying is true: "One sows and another reaps." John 4:36–37, NKJV

The seed of My words must be sown before anyone can come to Me. As you testify of Me, you sow My words into the minds and hearts of those who hear. My words will be rejected by many, listened to by some, and tasted by others. They will take root in the hearts of some, where they will grow and bring forth fruit unto eternal life. Child, although there is great joy in reaping the harvest, sowing requires labor and faith. Often, you can't see the harvest while you are sowing. But never cease from this labor. If you don't sow, there will be no harvest. Believe Me, the harvest will come! Though someone else might reap the harvest, in My Father's kingdom all who sow will rejoice with those who reap. My Father is glorified by your sowing just as He is glorified by your reaping. I have called you to both sow *and* reap. Bring others to Me, and teach them all that you have learned from Me. You are My witness with your life and with your words.

Do not work for food that spoils, but for food that endures to eternal life, which the Son of Man will give you. For on him God the Father has placed his seal of approval. John 6:27

➤➤ *The Greatest Words Ever Spoken,* Evangelism (pp. 227–29); The Mission of a Christian (pp. 281–89)

Guard Your Heart
by Protecting Your Eyes

Your eye is a lamp that provides light for your body. When your eye is good, your whole body is filled with light. But when your eye is bad, your whole body is filled with darkness. Matthew 6:22–23, NLT

As it is written, "Guard your heart above all else, for it determines the course of your life." Now that you have given your heart to Me, it is critical that you diligently protect it. Your eyes are the windows of your mind and heart. What you see enters your mind and then quickly flows into your heart. Because your behavior flows out of your heart, the best way to protect your heart from evil is to carefully control what you allow yourself to see. If you set your gaze on things that reflect the world's dark influences, the dark influences will enter your mind and heart. The longer you allow them to remain in your heart, the more dominant they will become over your thinking, feelings, and actions. The darkness can steal your life and destroy your relationships. It can destroy your impact for the kingdom. Worst of all, it can obstruct your intimacy with Me. Child, flood your heart with the light of My words. They will expel the darkness and cleanse your heart from all unrighteousness.

And if the light you think you have is actually darkness, how deep that darkness is! Matthew 6:23, NLT

✦ *The Greatest Words Ever Spoken,* The Eye and Seeing with Spiritual Eyes (pp. 230–31); The Mind (pp. 385–86); Light Versus Darkness (pp. 384–85)

Lead and Feed My Sheep

Do you love Me? . . . Feed My sheep. John 21:17, NKJV

Have you ever felt like a complete failure—like you were worthless and a disappointment to God? Have you ever been overcome by guilt and shame? That's how Peter felt on the night of My arrest after he denied that he knew Me. Earlier he had told Me, "Even if I have to die with you, I will never deny you!" And yet when the time came, he denied Me three times! After My resurrection he still felt worthless and ashamed. Then I told him how he could express his love for Me in spite of his past failure. I told him to *feed* and to *lead* My sheep. Child, you can express your love for Me in the same way. You can feed My sheep by sowing My words into their hearts. You don't have to be a great teacher; you only need to be a messenger. My teachings are recorded in the Word, and you need only to present them. You can feed My sheep with this food they so desperately need, and you can lead My sheep by the example of your life as you obey My words. Follow Me closely, and My sheep will follow you.

My food is to do the will of Him who sent Me, and to finish His work. John 4:34, NKJV

→ *The Greatest Words Ever Spoken,* Loving Christ (p. 280); Commands of Christ (pp. 206–17)

You Are More Than a Servant— You Are My Family

For whoever does the will of My Father in heaven is My brother and sister and mother. Matthew 12:50, NKJV

One day while I was teaching the multitudes, one of My disciples said My mother and brothers were trying to get closer. Everyone was surprised when I replied with a question: "Who is My mother, or My brothers?" I then answered, "Here are My mother and My brothers!" I had a family that I was born into. But I have an even greater family that isn't defined by a blood relationship but by the *fruit* of their lives. They have been born again by the Holy Spirit, and they do the will of My Father. Everyone (including you) whose heart, mind, and actions are focused on doing the Father's will are members of My eternal family. How can you know the Father's will for anything you face or do? My words reveal His will for every situation you face. The Holy Spirit will empower you with the grace to act in faith on My words. In this you will be doing the Father's will, and you will have the constant assurance that you, too, are a member of My eternal family.

Not everyone who says to Me, "Lord, Lord," will enter the kingdom of heaven, but he who does the will of My Father who is in heaven will enter. Matthew 7:21, NASB

→ *The Greatest Words Ever Spoken,* God's Will (pp. 106–7); Family (pp. 240–42); Children of God (pp. 199–200)

A Disciple's Identifier

A new command I give you: Love one another. As I have loved you, so you must love one another. By this all men will know that you are my disciples, if you love one another. John 13:34–35

How can you know if you are one of My disciples? It's not by how you look or even what you say. My *true* disciples have a number of identifying marks. They are defined by their hunger for My words and their growing obedience to them. They forgive people who most others could never forgive. They are empowered by the Holy Spirit, so they experience the fruit of the Spirit. They show unconditional love for even the most unlovable. But the greatest proof of their discipleship is their patient, supportive, and sacrificial love for one another. Child, don't be discouraged if you struggle to experience and express that kind of love for My followers. The more intimate you become with Me, the more this type of love will grow in your innermost being. You already know that your intimacy with the Father and Me grows as you obey My teachings. As you experience My love for *you,* you will become more and more comfortable expressing it to My other followers. You will find your love growing so much that you won't be able to contain it. It will flow out of you, like streams of water.

Whoever believes in me, as Scripture has said, streams of living water will flow from within him. John 7:38

⤜ *The Greatest Words Ever Spoken,* Commands of Christ (pp. 206–17)

Strengthening the Weak

And you, when once you have turned again, strengthen your brothers. Luke 22:32, NASB

O n the night of My arrest, I told Peter that he would soon deny his relationship with Me. I also knew that in time he would repent and turn back to Me in faith. But coming back to Me wasn't the end; it was the beginning. You see, his coming back wasn't just about him; it was about his ministry with My other followers. Child, the same is true with you. I know there have been times when you, too, have turned your back on Me, choosing to put your desires above Me and My calling on your life. My word to you is the same as My word to Peter: returning to Me isn't the end; it's the beginning. I don't want you to focus only on yourself. I want you to *strengthen* My followers. Let them see how My words apply to their issues and choices. Let them see Me in the way you live your life. In addition to proclaiming My love and mercy, lead and teach them to abide in Me. Love them unconditionally, not with your feelings but with your behavior. As you strengthen your brothers and sisters, you are storing up treasures in heaven.

And if you give even a cup of cold water to one of the least of my followers, you will surely be rewarded. Matthew 10:42, NLT

→→ *The Greatest Words Ever Spoken,* Following Christ (pp. 245–53)

I Want to Reveal the Truth to You, Make You My True Disciple, and Set You Free

---

If you abide in My word, you are My disciples indeed. And you shall know the truth, and the truth shall make you free. John 8:31–32, NKJV

D o you want to know the truth about Me, My Father, and the Holy Spirit? Do you want to know the truth about every situation, problem, and question you encounter? There is one activity that will make you My true disciple, setting you free from the cruel taskmaster of sin. It won't make you sinless, but it will empower you to sin less. That activity is *abiding* in My words. Child, I know you want to follow Me. But you can't follow Me if you don't know what I have said. That's why it is so important to abide in My words. The Holy Spirit will use My words to continually transform your heart and your life. They reveal perfect truth about you, your life and circumstances, and about the Father and Me. They reveal the true worth of everything the Father and I value and the lesser worth of everything else. The Holy Spirit will use My words to guide you into all that My Father has prepared for you.

However, when He, the Spirit of truth, has come, He will guide you into all truth; for He will not speak on His own authority, but whatever He hears He will speak; and He will tell you things to come. John 16:13, NKJV

✦ *The Greatest Words Ever Spoken,* Jesus' Words, Their Role and Power (pp. 62–64)

Remove Anything That Causes You to Stumble

If your right eye makes you stumble, tear it out and throw it from you; for it is better for you to lose one of the parts of your body, than for your whole body to be thrown into hell. If your right hand makes you stumble, cut it off and throw it from you. Matthew 5:29–30, NASB

I know that every time you fall to temptation, you are discouraged and saddened. You have thought, *How could God forgive me this time? How could He still love me?* Child, let Me tell you: He *does* forgive you. And He loves you so much He gave *Me* as a sacrifice to pay the full debt of your sin. But often you face temptation needlessly. Instead of avoiding the source of a temptation, you put yourself near it. You wander into paths that lead to temptation. Often your only hope of avoiding the sin is to avoid the path. Stay away from the sources of temptation. Sin is like a magnet: the closer you get to it, the stronger its attraction. If any activity puts you in proximity to temptation, avoid that activity when possible. Your soul is too precious to subject it to the continuous assault of temptation. As King David discovered, hiding My word in your heart is your best way to avoid the path that leads to temptation.

Keep watching and praying that you may not enter into temptation; the spirit is willing, but the flesh is weak. Matthew 26:41, NASB

+> *The Greatest Words Ever Spoken,* Temptation (pp. 341–42)

Why Focus on the Faults of Others?

And why worry about a speck in your friend's eye when you have a log in your own? . . . Hypocrite! First get rid of the log in your own eye; then you will see well enough to deal with the speck in your friend's eye. Matthew 7:3, 5, NLT

Why do you focus on the faults of others and yet do little to correct your own faults? The answer is *pride.* By focusing on the faults of others, you are able to view yourself as more esteemed than you really are. And by directing attention to the faults of others, you think you are elevating yourself. When you do this, you are seeking the praise of people rather than the praise of God. My apostle Peter reminded My followers, "God is opposed to the proud, but gives grace to the humble." Do you want My Father to oppose you, or do you want His favor beyond measure? Peter went on to say, "Therefore humble yourselves under the mighty hand of God, that He may exalt you at the proper time." When you acknowledge your own shortcomings and repent, you are humbling yourself under My Father's hand. Though you may lose the praise of other people, you will be praised by God and safely lifted up by His almighty hand.

Whoever exalts himself shall be humbled; and whoever humbles himself shall be exalted. Matthew 23:12, NASB

✈ *The Greatest Words Ever Spoken,* Judging Others (pp. 483–84); Commands of Christ (pp. 206–17)

The Tragic Fate of Those I Do Not Know

Many will say to Me in that day, "Lord, Lord, have we not prophesied in Your name, cast out demons in Your name, and done many wonders in Your name?" And then I will declare to them, "I never knew you; depart from Me, you who practice lawlessness!" Matthew 7:22–23, NKJV

Can you imagine anything worse than being at the entrance to heaven and hearing Me declare that you must depart from Me? That will be My announcement to many who did much in My name and yet their hearts were never converted. They never became My followers in righteousness. This being true, many have wondered, *How can I know if I will be invited in or told to depart?* Your eternal destiny will not be determined by church attendance or religious activities. Your destiny will be determined by whether or not you have been born of the Spirit. Those who have been born again have believed on Me and repented of their sins. They hear My voice and follow Me. They live in joyful obedience to My words. Child, listen to My words and follow Me. As you do, you can be confident that when that day comes, you will hear Me say, "Come, you who are blessed of My Father, inherit the kingdom prepared for you from the foundation of the world."

Now this is eternal life: that they may know you, the only true God, and Jesus Christ, whom you have sent. John 17:3

✦ *The Greatest Words Ever Spoken,* The Judgment (pp. 150–60); Eternal Life (pp. 134–42)

The Ultimate Proof
That I Know You

Therefore whoever hears these sayings of Mine, and does them, I will liken him to a wise man who built his house on the rock: and the rain descended, the floods came, and the winds blew and beat on that house; and it did not fall, for it was founded on the rock. Matthew 7:24–25, NKJV

How can you know if *I* know *you*? The answer is, I know My sheep. My sheep hear My voice and follow Me by hearing My words and *doing* them. This creates a foundation of solid rock upon which the lives of My followers securely rest. No matter what they encounter, the house of their lives will stand safe and secure. On the other hand, hearing My words and *not* doing them forms a foundation of sand. And building a house on sand will result in a total collapse when the person experiences the storms of life. Child, be of good cheer. I know you long to hear My words, not to merely consider them but so you can *do* them. Today and every day abide in My words, and let them guide your choices and your behavior. In doing this you will build your life securely on the rock of hearing and obeying My words.

I tell you the truth, if anyone keeps my word, he will never see death. John 8:51

→ *The Greatest Words Ever Spoken,* Eternal Life (pp. 134–42); Jesus' Words, Their Role and Power (pp. 62–64)

Don't Be Deceived by False Teachers

But everyone who hears these sayings of Mine, and does not do them, will be like a foolish man who built his house on the sand: and the rain descended, the floods came, and the winds blew and beat on that house; and it fell. And great was its fall. Matthew 7:26–27, NKJV

Child, I know you have been puzzled, even discouraged, by the words and actions of some who claim to be My followers. How can people who claim to be Christians do what they have done? It is easy to claim to be My follower. But as I told My disciples, "You will know them by their fruits." The only way to rightly discern people's relationship with Me is to look at their lives. My true followers hear My teachings and follow them. Not perfectly, but they hunger for My teachings and strive to obey. Those who hear My words and choose not to do them are building their lives on sand. Although they may know all about Me, they do not know Me intimately. If you see people living contrary to My teachings, realize that their lives reflect the world, not Me. As for you, dear child, set your eyes on Me . . . My life and My words. Do what I say, and you will build your life on the rock instead of sand.

Beware of false prophets, who come to you in sheep's clothing, but inwardly they are ravenous wolves. You will know them by their fruits. Matthew 7:15–16, NKJV

✦ *The Greatest Words Ever Spoken,* Knowing God and Knowing Christ (pp. 275–77); False Prophets (pp. 368–69)

The Time Is Now—
Don't Put It Off!

Follow me now. Let the spiritually dead bury their own dead. Matthew 8:22, NLT

One day a young man told Me that he really wanted to follow Me as a disciple. However, he also wanted to return home and take care of his ailing father's business. He wanted to bury his father when he died and *then* follow Me. What seemed to be a reasonable request was actually shortsighted and foolish. Why? Because it showed that he greatly undervalued Me, My mission, and My calling. He was willing to set aside the eternal impact he could make in the lives of others and instead settle for the temporary gain of caring for the family business. He had been given the opportunity to know Me intimately and be one of My disciples—to be My witness and to feed and lead My sheep. Instead, he wanted to address a temporary need that would quickly pass. Child, My challenge to him was the same as it is to you: Don't let temporary demands on your time keep you from following Me, even for a day! Don't make such a foolish trade. Follow Me today and every day.

But seek first His kingdom and His righteousness, and all these things will be added to you. Matthew 6:33, NASB

✦ *The Greatest Words Ever Spoken,* Following Christ (pp. 245–53)

Your Perfect Teacher

But the Helper, the Holy Spirit, whom the Father will send in My name, He will teach you all things, and bring to your remembrance all things that I said to you. John 14:26, NKJV

When I told My disciples that I would soon leave them, they panicked, thinking they would no longer have Me as their Teacher. That's when I revealed that the Father would send them a new Teacher. The Holy Spirit would teach them everything they would need to know. My followers need to be continually taught and guided into truth. Child, the teaching ministry of the Holy Spirit is *critical* for your life. That's because My Father's ways are contrary to your natural inclinations. As My Father said through the prophet Isaiah, "For as the heavens are higher than the earth, so are My ways higher than your ways, and My thoughts than your thoughts." But your learning must begin with Me. As you study My life and meditate on My words, the Holy Spirit will teach you, writing those teachings on your heart and conforming *your* heart to *My* heart. And because all of your behavior flows out of your heart, your behavior will then be My behavior, bringing glory to our Father.

Heaven and earth will pass away, but My words will not pass away. Mark 13:31, NASB

↦ *The Greatest Words Ever Spoken,* The Holy Spirit and His Ministry (pp. 116–17)

Let the Holy Spirit Minister to You in *This* Way

The Holy Spirit—he will teach you everything and will remind you of everything I have told you. John 14:26, NLT

I n every situation you must decide how to respond. How can you know My Father's will in that moment? In some situations a number of choices will glorify the Father. In others there may be only one choice that truly is *His* way. How can you choose the path that is in keeping with His will? Child, this requires a vital ministry of the Holy Spirit. If you hide My words in your heart, the Holy Spirit will remind you of My words, bringing them to your mind at the moment they are needed. He will then empower you with grace to *obey* My words at that moment. As you act in faith and take that step of obedience, you will find yourself living in the perfect center of My Father's will.

He will guide you into all truth; for He will not speak on His own authority, but whatever He hears He will speak; and He will tell you things to come. He will glorify Me, for He will take of what is Mine and declare it to you. John 16:13–14, NKJV

✦ *The Greatest Words Ever Spoken,* The Holy Spirit and His Ministry (pp. 116–17)

My Followers Love to Fulfill My Father's Desires

But go and learn what this means: "I desire mercy, not sacrifice." Matthew 9:13

Freely you have received, freely give. Matthew 10:8

You have received so much mercy from the Father. Why is it sometimes hard to show mercy to those who have wounded you? Perhaps you think they don't deserve your mercy. The truth is, you did nothing to deserve the mercy of God. Mercy is *never* deserved. The Father owes mercy to no one. Yet He chose to extend His love and mercy to you—not just by forgiving your sin, but also by paying its impossible debt. That payment required Me to suffer the agony of the Cross, and it cost you nothing! Every day the Father and I still forgive your sin and extend Our unlimited mercies to you. Beyond this, We gave you the greatest gift ever given, the gift of eternal life. Oh child, stop grieving the Holy Spirit. Demonstrate your gratefulness to the Father by showing mercy to all who have hurt you—not because *they* deserve it, but because *you* have received God's mercy. You cannot be My follower if you don't extend mercy. But when you do, you will enter a level of My joy that cannot be experienced any other way.

Blessed are the merciful, for they will be shown mercy. Matthew 5:7

→ *The Greatest Words Ever Spoken,* Grace and Mercy (pp. 424–27); Commands of Christ (pp. 206–17)

Hunger and Thirst
for Righteousness

Blessed are those who hunger and thirst for righteousness, for they will be filled. Matthew 5:6

C an you remember the last time you were really hungry? What did you think about? Could you concentrate on anything other than your desire for food? Or can you remember the last time you were really thirsty? The longer you went without water, the more desperate you became to get a drink. As important as food and water are, *righteousness* is even more critical to the life and health of your soul. Do you treat righteousness as if it were of little importance? Or do you actively pursue it? Child, I am your Shepherd, and you are My precious lamb. I want to lead you into paths of righteousness. But when you focus on gratifying your other appetites, your soul is filled with everything but righteousness. The only way to gain a driving hunger and thirst for righteousness is to follow Me. Look at My life and activities and imitate Me. Listen to My words and do them. This will cause you to hunger and thirst for righteousness. Other attractions of the flesh will lose their hold on you, and I will satisfy you to the depths of your soul.

Let your light shine before men in such a way that they may see your good works, and glorify your Father who is in heaven. Matthew 5:16, NASB

→→ *The Greatest Words Ever Spoken,* The Pursuit of Righteousness (pp. 305–7)

Will You Be Called a Son or Daughter of God?

Blessed are the peacemakers, for they shall be called sons of God. Matthew 5:9, NKJV

I n this world *conflict* defines humanity in its fallen state. People engage in active conflict with My Father and His ways because they want to be the god of their lives. Their self-centeredness also keeps them in conflict with other people. When you were born again, your nature changed. You wanted God to rule in your life, and your conflict subsided. If you still have inner conflict, it's because you are not yielding to the promptings of the Holy Spirit. You're not obeying My teachings. If you experience active or subtle conflict with others, it's because you demand your way and judge or condemn their ways. But I am calling you *out* of conflict. I want you to be a peacemaker. Enter into a greater peace with God by following and trusting Me. But My peace must not end in you. It must flow out of you to others. Be an active peacemaker by replacing criticism and gossip with love and encouragement. I made peace between you and God when I took your punishment on the cross. Now I want you to make peace among all those you influence. Become a peacemaker like Me, and you will be called a son or daughter of God.

Peace I leave with you; My peace I give to you; not as the world gives do I give to you. John 14:27, NASB

→→ *The Greatest Words Ever Spoken,* Spiritual Priorities (pp. 328–37); Sons of God (pp. 327–28)

Eliminating All Fear by Fearing God

Do not be afraid of those who kill the body but cannot kill the soul. Rather, be afraid of the One who can destroy both soul and body in hell. Are not two sparrows sold for a penny? Yet not one of them will fall to the ground apart from the will of your Father. Matthew 10:28–29

Why should you continue to live in worry and fear? You are often anxious about so many things, and your life is tormented with stress. Child, it doesn't have to be that way. When you are fearful, it is a sign that you are setting your focus on the temporary things of this life. This world is *not* your permanent home. Even death should not be feared by My followers. It's simply the doorway to your eternal home. To be free from all fear, you need only to revere God above all else and love Him by obeying My teachings. I want you to know that nothing will come your way except through My Father's loving will. He knows everything about you, and yet He loves you so much that He sent Me to save you. Turn your eyes and the focus of your heart away from the temporary things of this world and fix them on Me. Fill your heart with My words, and My peace will replace all your fears.

And even the very hairs of your head are all numbered. So don't be afraid; you are worth more than many sparrows. Matthew 10:30–31

✦ *The Greatest Words Ever Spoken*, Anxiety, Worry, and Fear (pp. 190–93)

I Give My Sheep What No Other Shepherd Can Give

I am the good shepherd. The good shepherd lays down his life for the sheep. John 10:11

And I give them eternal life, and they shall never perish; neither shall anyone snatch them out of My hand. John 10:28, NKJV

Some sheep follow shepherds who care only about their own purposes. Some follow shepherds who care and do the best they can, but they are subject to human weakness. They do not know what dangers lie around the corner. I am the *good* Shepherd. I gave My life for My sheep. I alone can take My sheep where no other shepherd can lead. I alone can give My sheep eternal life. I can protect them through this life and lead them safely into the next. Only My sheep have My promise of living with Me forever in the kingdom My Father has given Me. Child, *you* are My sheep. I gave My life for you. Even today I intercede on your behalf before the Father. Your life today is merely the introduction to the life I have prepared for you. You and I have so much to accomplish during your brief time on earth. Listen to My voice today and follow Me.

My Father, who has given them to me, is greater than all; no one can snatch them out of my Father's hand. John 10:29

✦ *The Greatest Words Ever Spoken,* Knowing God and Knowing Christ (pp. 275–77); The Shepherd and His Sheep (pp. 320–23)

How to Know You Are
One of My Sheep

I am the good shepherd; I know my own sheep and my
sheep know me. . . . My sheep listen to my voice; I know
them, and they follow me. John 10:14, 27

When humanity stands before Me, many will *think* they are
My sheep. They will call Me "Lord" and will tell Me of the
miracles they worked in My name. But I will respond, "I never knew
you; depart from Me, you who practice lawlessness!" Here is what
sets My sheep apart from all others: I know My sheep and they know
Me. They have been born again and have become joined to Me. The
whole *direction* of their lives changed. They used to follow their own
paths, doing whatever they wanted, pursuing their own desires. But
when they were born of the Spirit, they began to hear My words and
do them. They left their paths and began to follow Me. The more
they obeyed My words, the more intimate we became. Child, I want
that same intimacy with you. Today and every day set your focus on
My words. Consume them like your favorite meal. Follow Me by
obeying My words. And as you follow Me, we will become more
intimate, and you will *know* you are one of My sheep.

I have other sheep that are not of this sheep pen. I must bring them
also. They too will listen to my voice, and there shall be one flock
and one shepherd. John 10:16

+» *The Greatest Words Ever Spoken,* Knowing God and Knowing Christ (pp.
275–77); Following Christ (pp. 245–53); The Shepherd and His Sheep
(pp. 320–23)

Your Grief Need Not Remain

So you have sorrow now, but I will see you again; then you will rejoice, and no one can rob you of that joy.
John 16:22, NLT

I understand your grief, and I am sorry you are hurting. There is nothing wrong with grief for a season, but it must not become your master. It must not keep you from accomplishing the purpose I have called you to accomplish. Your life on earth is but a brief moment in eternity. I am your Shepherd, and you are My sheep. My sheep must follow Me. When grief is your master, it can steal your life and keep you from following Me. If you will draw close to Me, you will see the Father as He really is. As you grow in intimacy with Me, your earthly sorrows will fade. As you dwell in My words and do what I say, *My* joy will flow into your heart and *your* joy will be so full it will overflow to others. Let My words pour My Spirit and life into you. If you will, the dark clouds of sorrow will soon be replaced by a bright new day. I promise.

I have told you this so that my joy may be in you and that your joy may be complete. John 15:11

➤➤ *The Greatest Words Ever Spoken,* Joy (pp. 273–75)

I Want You to Know My Father

Nor does anyone know the Father except the Son, and the one to whom the Son wills to reveal Him. Matthew 11:27, NKJV

My Father's ways are as far above your ways as heaven is above earth. Though some know a little about Him, no one really *knows* Him except Me and those to whom I reveal Him. Child, I want *you* to know My Father. You will stand in awe of His majesty and glory. You will shudder in amazement at His love, His righteousness, and His justice. I don't want you merely to know *about* Him; I want you to *know* Him. First, look at Me and My behavior. As you look at Me, you will witness My Father firsthand. As you see the way I dealt with people, you will see His dealings. I did *exactly* what pleased Him. He lived His life on earth in Me. Second, listen to My words. Every word I uttered is one He commanded Me to say. My words were His words—perfectly expressed. Finally, act on My words. As you do, My Father and I will come and make Our home with You. And I will reveal Him and Myself to you. Oh child, knowing the Father is the greatest joy in all of life.

Now this is eternal life: that they may know you, the only true God, and Jesus Christ, whom you have sent. John 17:3

↠ *The Greatest Words Ever Spoken,* Chosen (pp. 200–202); Revelation of God's Truth (pp. 312–13); Knowing God and Knowing Christ (pp. 275–77)

The Power to Forgive

Then the master of that servant was moved with compassion, released him, and forgave him the debt. But that servant went out and found one of his fellow servants who owed him a hundred denarii; and he laid hands on him and took him by the throat, saying, "Pay me what you owe!"
Matthew 18:27–28, NKJV

Why do so many who claim to be My followers find it hard to forgive? The reason is, forgiving is *not* a natural response. The natural responses to being hurt are anger, resentment, and even revenge. Child, I know you still find it hard to forgive some who hurt you. But you can't follow Me if you will not forgive. When you withhold forgiveness, you choose to disobey My commands. You belittle My sacrifice on the cross. I died to pay the full debt of your sins. When you forgive, you are obeying My command, loving the Father and Me, and honoring what We have done for you. You forgive not because your offender deserves it but because God has forgiven *you* a far greater debt. You forgive by praying for the one who offended you and releasing him from his debt of sin against you. Set your focus on the cross. In the miracle of My crucifixion, you will find the power to forgive.

For if you forgive men when they sin against you, your heavenly Father will also forgive you. But if you do not forgive men their sins, your Father will not forgive your sins. Matthew 6:14–15

→→ *The Greatest Words Ever Spoken,* Forgiving Others (pp. 481–83)

You Are Worth So Much More Than You Can Ever Imagine

I am the good shepherd. The good shepherd sacrifices his life for the sheep. John 10:11, NLT

I know there are times when you feel like a failure. You think, *How can God still love me?* And yet I'm telling you that My Father and I love you more than you could ever imagine. We don't love you because you have *earned* Our love. And We don't *stop* loving you because you've earned Our disdain. We love you because it is who We are. When you were dead in sin, having no hope whatsoever, My Father loved you with an indescribable love. He sent Me to live and to die for you. We could not unite with you because of your sin. But now, through your faith in Me, you've exchanged your sin for My righteousness. Because of My atoning sacrifice, you have been cleansed of your sin and clothed with My righteousness. Your worth is not based on what you have achieved or earned. It is established forever by Our love for you and proven by what We have done to give you gifts that are greater than any others—mercy, forgiveness, cleansing, and eternal life. I laid down My life for you. *That* is how much you are worth to Me!

For God so loved the world, that He gave His only begotten Son, that whoever believes in Him shall not perish, but have eternal life. John 3:16, NASB

↠ *The Greatest Words Ever Spoken,* The Shepherd and His Sheep (pp. 320–23)

You Make No Sacrifice
When You Sacrifice for Me

And everyone who has given up houses or brothers or sisters or father or mother or children or property, for my sake, will receive a hundred times as much in return and will inherit eternal life. Matthew 19:29, NLT

Many of My early followers gave up their wealth, their livelihoods, and their security. They were disowned by their families, hated by their neighbors, and even martyred because of their faith. Many gave up everything they had just to make sure other followers had what they needed. And the truth is, everything they gave up was temporal, and everything they gained was eternal. They knew that their momentary sacrifices were storing up treasures in heaven. But that is not why they made such sacrifices. They simply answered My call to deny themselves, take up their crosses daily, and follow Me. They experienced the unsurpassed joy of knowing Me intimately. So although they gave up everything, they sacrificed nothing—for their eternal gain was far greater than their temporal loss. Child, I make the same call to you: "Deny yourself, take up your cross daily, and follow Me"—then *great* will be your reward in this life and in heaven!

If you obey my commands, you will remain in my love, just as I have obeyed my Father's commands and remain in his love. I have told you this so that my joy may be in you and that your joy may be complete. John 15:10–11

✈ *The Greatest Words Ever Spoken,* The Promises of Christ (pp. 298–304)

How to Love Those Who Hate You (and Those You Have Hated)

But I say to you, love your enemies, bless those who curse you, do good to those who hate you, and pray for those who spitefully use you and persecute you, that you may be sons of your Father in heaven; for He makes His sun rise on the evil and on the good, and sends rain on the just and on the unjust. Matthew 5:44–45, NKJV

Child, I have called you to love those you might otherwise hate and those who hate you. You may think, *But I don't hate anyone.* That may be true of your feelings, but hatred is a behavior. When you are angry with someone and experience a judgmental or vengeful heart, *that* is hatred. When you gossip about others, you are damaging their reputation, and that is hatred. My disciples asked Me if they should call fire down from heaven to destroy a group of Samaritans who rejected them. I rebuked them and their spirit and then reminded them that I didn't come to earth to destroy lives but to save them. I want you to follow Me in purpose, spirit, and behavior. My purpose is to save people, not destroy them. My Spirit is love, not hate. And My behavior is to forgive and bless My enemies, not curse them. So *bless* those who curse you, do *good* to those who hate you, and *pray* for those who spitefully use you.

For if you love those who love you, what reward have you? Do not even the tax collectors do the same? Matthew 5:46, NKJV

✈ *The Greatest Words Ever Spoken,* Love (pp. 278–80)

Leading Your Family and Others in My Kingdom

You know that the rulers of the Gentiles lord it over them, and those who are great exercise authority over them. Yet it shall not be so among you; but whoever desires to become great among you, let him be your servant. And whoever desires to be first among you, let him be your slave—just as the Son of Man did not come to be served, but to serve, and to give His life a ransom for many. Matthew 20:25–28, NKJV

Leaders often are domineering and overbearing. They often rule with arrogance and use fear to pressure their followers. This is not the way I want *you* to lead. Instead, I want you to lead with humility and gentleness. I want you to lead in a spirit of serving people, including your family. I want you to guide with love and honor instead of demands and fear. I want you to lead by example. Don't just tell your children to trust Me and run to Me, but let them see you trusting Me and running to Me. Teach others My ways with My words as well as with your life as you imitate My ways. As you lead others in this way, they will learn to lead in the same way by following your example. Watch how you lead your family and others. Take notice: Are you leading by lording or by serving? Become an imitator of Me.

Whoever has my commands and obeys them, he is the one who loves me. John 14:21

↠ *The Greatest Words Ever Spoken,* Humility (pp. 271–73); Serving Others (pp. 319–20)

How to Remain in My Love and My Joy

I have loved you even as the Father has loved me. Remain in my love. When you obey my commandments, you remain in my love, just as I obey my Father's commandments and remain in his love. I have told you these things so that you will be filled with my joy. Yes, your joy will overflow!
John 15:9–11, NLT

For more than three years, My disciples experienced the joy of being in the center of My love. On the night of My arrest, they realized I would be leaving them to return to My Father. They were devastated at the thought that they would no longer be able to experience My love and care. I told them they could remain in My love by doing what *I* did to remain in My Father's love. I remained in the Father's love by keeping His commands. My disciples could remain in *My* love by keeping *My* commands. Child, the same is true for you. If you will learn My commands and keep them, you will remain in My love, My joy will flow into you, and *your* joy will overflow to others. If you are not filled with My joy, it's because you are not remaining in My love. Remain in My love by keeping My commands, and My joy will fill your heart. I promise!

I am coming to you now, but I say these things while I am still in the world, so that they may have the full measure of my joy within them. John 17:13

→→ *The Greatest Words Ever Spoken,* Joy (pp. 273–75); God's Love (pp. 99–101); Obedience and Good Works (pp. 289–94)

Your Ultimate Answers
to Any Temptation

It is written, "Man shall not live by bread alone, but by every word that proceeds from the mouth of God."
Matthew 4:4, NKJV

After fasting for more than a month, I was tired, hungry, and physically weak. That was the perfect time for Satan to tempt Me. Child, whenever you are weakened by *anything,* you become more vulnerable to temptation. The devil whispers, "You're only human. Everyone does it. It's really nothing!" But remember, he will say anything to get you to fall. He will offer you what appears to be immediate relief or gratification. When I was desperately hungry, he tempted Me with an offer of food. He told Me to command stones to become bread. However, I knew that My Father wanted to be My only authority. Taking any order or suggestion from Satan would be giving him a place of authority that belongs to My Father alone. So I answered Satan's temptation with the one weapon he cannot overcome—the Word of God! My precious one, when you are tempted, your *only* effective weapon is the Word. It will expose Satan's lies. Always answer temptation with My words. Stand firm on them. At the same time I want you to know that the Word of God is the *only* food that will sustain your spirit and give you the strength you need to overcome temptation.

Sanctify them by the truth; your word is truth. John 17:17

✦ *The Greatest Words Ever Spoken,* God's Word (pp. 108–9); Abiding in the Words of Christ (pp. 186–88)

Your Ultimate Answers
to Any Temptation

It is written again, "You shall not tempt the LORD your God." Matthew 4:7, NKJV

After I overcame Satan's first temptation, he tempted Me again, this time by quoting God's Word to Me. He tried to tempt Me to act contrary to My Father's will and purposes. Had I given in to temptation, I would have been doing it in response to the will of Satan. I would have been doing *his* will instead of the will of My Father. Here again, I used the single most powerful weapon I had against Satan: the Word of God. My dear one, if God's Word was My most effective weapon, wouldn't it also be the most powerful weapon *you* can use? Of course it is! This is why it is so important that you abide in My words. If you don't *know* the Word, you won't be able to use it to overcome the attacks and temptations of your adversary. There is no greater weapon against Satan and his followers than My words. This is one more way that I want you to follow Me.

Heaven and earth will pass away, but my words will never pass away. Matthew 24:35

→ *The Greatest Words Ever Spoken,* Commands of Christ (pp. 206–17)

Your Ultimate Answers to Any Temptation

For it is written, "You shall worship the LORD your God, and Him only you shall serve." Matthew 4:10, NKJV

When Satan failed to draw Me away from the Father with his first two temptations, he made a third attempt, using his most powerful weapon: an offer of glory, wealth, and power. He offered Me all the kingdoms of the world and all their glory—the very things that reflect his values and desires. He wrongly assumed that those same desires could be aroused in Me. But I am holy, as the Father is holy. The values of this world have no place in Me. Child, he will also tempt *you* by trying to appeal to your base desires. He will offer you more recognition, more wealth, more esteem, and more power over others. Although your nature is vulnerable to these temptations, know that you have one and only one safe harbor that will protect you. Your safe harbor is worshiping and serving the Lord your God. *Nothing* makes you more secure against Satan's attacks than worshiping and serving the Father. Harness yourself to Me, and fill your mind and heart with My words. Your spirit will be nourished and empowered to worship and serve God like never before.

No one can serve two masters; for either he will hate the one and love the other, or he will be devoted to one and despise the other. Matthew 6:24, NASB

➤➤ *The Greatest Words Ever Spoken,* Commands of Christ (pp. 206–17)

Now Is the Time to Turn Around and Follow Me

Repent of your sins and turn to God, for the Kingdom of Heaven is near. Matthew 4:17, NLT

I began My ministry on earth with a message that the world desperately needed to hear. As it is written, "There is a way that seems right to a man, but in the end it leads to death." People follow paths that appear to be right, because serving themselves first only seems natural. But those self-serving paths lead to eternal separation from My Father's kingdom. Could anything be worse than spending your entire life going down a path that you thought was right only to find that it was heartbreaking to the Father who loves you? Today many who bear My name embrace the world's values and walk in ways that are contrary to My Father's ways. Child, what are *your* ways? What do you value, and what do you do? How do you spend your time? How do you spend your money? Which activities and distractions have you allowed to become more important than following Me? For your own sake and the sake of all whom you love, *repent!* Turn around today and follow Me. Learn of Me. Walk in My ways. The kingdom of heaven is at hand. I love you so.

It is not the healthy who need a doctor, but the sick. I have not come to call the righteous, but sinners to repentance. Luke 5:31–32

✢ *The Greatest Words Ever Spoken,* Repentance (pp. 462–66); Following Christ (pp. 245–53)

Reconciling Is More Important to Me Than You Can Imagine

Therefore if you bring your gift to the altar, and there remember that your brother has something against you, leave your gift there before the altar, and go your way. First be reconciled to your brother, and then come and offer your gift. Matthew 5:23–24, NKJV

How great is your Father in heaven? He is above all! He inhabits your praise and joyfully receives your worship and the gifts of your heart. But as much as He loves your praise, worship, and service, He wants you to be at peace with your brothers and sisters. He wants you to do what you can to repair any offense that stands between you and those whom you have offended. Even if you are worshiping Him and realize you have offended someone, *stop* and seek forgiveness and reconciliation. Then come back to worship. You may not be able to move the other person to forgive you, but that is not your responsibility. Your responsibility is to sincerely and humbly seek forgiveness and reconciliation. Seek these things not because the other person desires or deserves it but because your Father desires it. And when it comes to reconciliation, He desires it first and foremost with your spouse, your children, your family, and all who follow Me.

Give us today our daily bread. Forgive us our debts, as we also have forgiven our debtors. Matthew 6:11–12

✣ *The Greatest Words Ever Spoken,* Reconciliation Between People (pp. 307–8)

Your Most Important Priority

But seek first the kingdom of God and His righteousness, and all these things shall be added to you. Matthew 6:33, NKJV

I t is natural for you to attend to most everything else *before* you seek My Father's kingdom and righteousness. The countless demands on your time seem to be never ending. My child, you are missing the greatest opportunity of your life. The blessings and rewards of seeking My Father, His kingdom, and His righteousness ahead of all else cannot be received in any other pursuit or activity. When you seek Him *first,* you will gain a level of purpose, fulfillment, and joy that nothing else can give. More important, your life will count for eternity rather than just the few years you have on earth. Begin your day in My words. Let My teachings determine your choices and actions in everything you do. Replace activities that have little worth or relevance to your relationship with Me with activities that do. Begin and end every day meditating on My words. If you will do that, I promise that My Father will provide everything you need.

For what does it profit a man to gain the whole world, and forfeit his soul? Mark 8:36, NASB

✦ *The Greatest Words Ever Spoken,* Spiritual Priorities (pp. 328–37)

Great News About Heaven

And they can no longer die; for they are like the angels. They are God's children, since they are children of the resurrection. Luke 20:36

Ever since Adam and Eve's sin, humanity has been enslaved by sin and its terrible consequences: separation from God, all manner of evil, and the agony of death. But My sacrifice on the cross has changed everything for those who believe, repent, and follow Me. Born again, they have become children of My glorious resurrection and adopted children of God. Child, as My faithful follower you, too, are a beloved child of the almighty, everlasting God. Oh, that you could fully comprehend what this really means! The only thing standing between you and heaven is the completion of your mission on earth. You can't begin to imagine what it will be like once you pass through death's door. You will experience the full love, righteousness, and mercy of the Father. You will never suffer anything that you suffered on earth. No pain, no infirmities, no sorrows or disappointments, no emptiness or needs. And the best news of all, your life in heaven will never end. You will never die. You will live forever in My Father's glorious light and truth. Oh, what a God!

I tell you the truth, whoever hears my word and believes him who sent me has eternal life and will not be condemned; he has crossed over from death to life. John 5:24

→ *The Greatest Words Ever Spoken,* Heaven (pp. 143–50)

Truth Is Simple—
Only Lies Are Complicated

Simply let your "Yes" be "Yes," and your "No," "No"; anything beyond this comes from the evil one. Matthew 5:37

Satan is the Father of Lies. This world is *his* kingdom. Those who don't know Me have grown up in a dishonest world, where people define truth and lies like shades of color. If something is "mostly" true, they view it as true. If there is a slight exaggeration or a few necessary details are omitted, they act as if they have been honest. But God has no part in Satan's dark world. He is light, and in Him there is no darkness at all. You are a child of God. I have called you to walk in the light as He is in the light. Avoid dishonesty in your ways and your words. Your interactions with everyone must be above reproach. When you enter into a commitment, there are to be no lies, no exaggerations, no necessary details hidden or omitted. Whatever you say you will do, you are fully committed to perform. No partiality, no reservations. To children of the light, there is no *degree* of truth, no *degree* of falsehood. The truth is fully true. The smallest lie is not small; it's a lie. Child, I *am* the Truth. If you want the eternal blessings of following Me, then follow Me!

Walk while you have the light, before darkness overtakes you. The man who walks in the dark does not know where he is going. John 12:35

↠ *The Greatest Words Ever Spoken,* Honesty (p. 378); Commands of Christ (pp. 206–17)

What to Do
When You Are Wounded

But I say, do not resist an evil person! If someone slaps you on the right cheek, offer the other cheek also. Matthew 5:39, NLT

My dear child, you live in the midst of a wicked and perverse generation. People love darkness rather than light because their deeds are evil. They have become gods unto themselves, and they have no part with Me. But you need not be discouraged or dismayed, for you are with Me and you are Mine. I am the Light of the World, and because you follow Me, you need never walk in darkness. As My follower, I want *you* to be a light in the darkness that surrounds you. I want you to represent Me with your words of truth, but even more with your acts of righteousness, to everyone I bring into your path. Those in the world will wound you in many ways. They will speak evil to you and about you. Some will act hatefully toward you, and others will simply neglect or avoid you. But I want you to respond to their evil in the same manner that I responded to those who were hateful toward Me. You must not seek revenge or in any way return evil for evil. Forgive them. Pray for them and bless them. Let them see *Me* in *you*. I am with you even now!

Do good to those who hate you, bless those who curse you, pray for those who mistreat you. Luke 6:27–28

↠ *The Greatest Words Ever Spoken,* Enemies and Adversaries (pp. 480–81); Commands of Christ (pp. 206–17)

Giving When It's Not Deserved

And if someone wants to sue you and take your tunic, let him have your cloak as well. If someone forces you to go one mile, go with him two miles. Matthew 5:40–41

So many people do only what's expected or demanded of them. Some do even less. I do not want you to act that way. You do not belong to this world or its king or its values. You are a child of the Most High. You are My follower, and you represent *Me*. So your behavior doesn't affect just your reputation. It also affects Mine. Your behavior either reflects Me or dishonors Me. It either magnifies Me or diminishes Me. If others can't see Me in your life, how will they see Me at all? If they don't experience My unconditional love in your words and actions, how can they know My love? Child, I am joyfully relying on you to represent Me! The treasures of this world aren't important. If someone demands something from you, don't fight them. Just give them *more* than they demand or expect. It will only be a temporary loss of a temporary treasure. Don't get Me wrong. I want you to be a good steward of all that I have entrusted to you. But the things of this world are just not that important.

I have given them your word and the world has hated them, for they are not of the world any more than I am of the world. John 17:14

✣ *The Greatest Words Ever Spoken,* Conflict (pp. 477–80); Commands of Christ (pp. 206–17)

Secretly Do Good

Watch out! Don't do your good deeds publicly, to be admired by others, for you will lose the reward from your Father in heaven. When you give to someone in need, don't do as the hypocrites do—blowing trumpets in the synagogues and streets to call attention to their acts of charity! I tell you the truth, they have received all the reward they will ever get. Matthew 6:1–2, NLT

I have called you to follow Me. I have called you to be a light in the midst of darkness so others can see your works of righteousness and glorify God. But I have *not* called you to be like the ancient Pharisees, who performed religious works and duties hoping to be seen by others. They performed their deeds with the intention of bringing glory to themselves rather than to God. Their reward was the praise of people. They will receive *no* reward from God. On the other hand, everything *you* do, do for the glory of My Father and Me. Let others experience My love, My kindness, and My mercy through you in the way you treat them. Without drawing attention to yourself, give your help and encouragement. Give it without the expectation or hope of receiving anything in return. In doing so, you will lay up treasures in heaven.

But store up for yourselves treasures in heaven, where neither moth nor rust destroys, and where thieves do not break in or steal.
Matthew 6:20, NASB

➤➤ *The Greatest Words Ever Spoken,* Motives (p. 386); Rewards (pp. 172–75); Commands of Christ (pp. 206–17)

The Right Way to Give

But when you give to the needy, do not let your left hand know what your right hand is doing, so that your giving may be in secret. Then your Father, who sees what is done in secret, will reward you. Matthew 6:3–4

I know you want to be more like Me. And yet the enemy of your soul whispers to you that it's hopeless, that you aren't good enough and you don't have the power to change. He's a liar! Because you have been born of the Spirit and have the Holy Spirit with you and in you, you *do* have the power to be more like Me. As you abide in My words, the Holy Spirit will write them on your heart. Then He will empower you with the grace and faith to obey My words, and He will remind you of My words whenever you face behavioral choices. As you obey My words, your soul will be conformed to My image. You will become more like Me. One way to be like Me is to give to the needy secretly. Unlike hypocrites who give to glorify themselves, you give to glorify the Father. He will reward you in His time and in His ways. You will experience an indescribable joy when you serve and give to others in secret.

Give, and it will be given to you. They will pour into your lap a good measure—pressed down, shaken together, and running over. Luke 6:38, NASB

✢ *The Greatest Words Ever Spoken*, Motives (p. 386); Rewards (pp. 172–75); Commands of Christ (pp. 206–17)

Called to Be Wise

Behold, I send you out as sheep in the midst of wolves.
Therefore be wise as serpents and harmless as doves.
Matthew 10:16, NKJV

As it is written, "How much better it is to get wisdom than gold! And to get understanding is to be chosen above silver." Understanding is knowing the ways of the Father. Wisdom is knowing how to walk in the ways of the Father in every moment. Ignorance is *not* knowing the ways of the Father, and foolishness is choosing to walk in *your* own ways rather than the Father's ways. Living in ignorance and walking in foolishness will bring futility, deception, despair, and harm into your life. My Father and I have a wondrous, eternal purpose for you during your remaining time on earth. Ignorance and foolishness are terrible thieves. They will steal your attention away from that which is most important. They will fill your life with distractions that will prevent you from experiencing and accomplishing all that the Father and I have for you. We have given you everything you need to gain godly understanding and the life-changing wisdom to experience the miraculous power of God. The Holy Spirit is in you. Let Him guide you into all truth through My words and empower you with grace to glorify the Father throughout your day, every day.

Take My yoke upon you and learn from Me, for I am gentle and humble in heart. Matthew 11:29, NASB

✦ *The Greatest Words Ever Spoken,* Wisdom (pp. 347–50); Commands of Christ (pp. 206–17)

Called to Be Harmless

Behold, I send you out as sheep in the midst of wolves. Therefore be wise as serpents and harmless as doves.
Matthew 10:16, NKJV

Child, you are surrounded by many who have no love for My Father or for Me. Some are only ignorant participants in Satan's kingdom, but others are like ravenous wolves that desire to tear down and destroy My followers. But do not despair or even be anxious. Your Father is greater than all. What they mean for evil, He will turn to good. Instead of Satan being victorious in tearing down Our kingdom, *We* will ultimately destroy his kingdom. But We will not destroy it with the weapons of this world. We will gain victory by leading My sheep in Our ways. We will plunder his kingdom with the undefeatable weapons of the Father's wisdom, love, and righteousness. You, along with My other sheep, will defeat Satan's wolves. Not by returning their evil with evil, but by answering each arrow of evil with Our arrows of goodness. Return hatred with love, aggression with gentleness, arrogance with humility, greed with generosity, and persecution with joy. One by one We will rescue Satan's captives and plunder his kingdom. And in this, My dear child, you will glorify our Father greatly. *You* will be the eternal victor!

Blessed are the poor in spirit, for theirs is the kingdom of heaven. . . . Blessed are the gentle, for they shall inherit the earth.
Matthew 5:3, 5, NASB

⤜ *The Greatest Words Ever Spoken,* Gentleness (p. 261); Commands of Christ (pp. 206–17)

Called to Be Diligent to Embrace Truth and Avoid Deception

Don't let anyone mislead you, for many will come in my name, claiming, "I am the Messiah." They will deceive many. Matthew 24:4–5, NLT

It is easy for people to claim to be My followers and even My representatives. Some are, but many are *not*. Remember, on the last day many will tell Me of the miracles they performed in My name. But I will tell them, "I never knew you." They have not only deceived others. They have deceived themselves, thinking that performing miracles is proof that they are My followers. But their hearts are far from Me, and their lives are defined by iniquity and lawlessness. Child, do not fall into their deceit. You must discern who are My disciples, not by their words or their works of power, but by their works of righteousness. Do you see them *obeying* My teachings and commands? My true disciples walk in My commands and teach others to obey all that I have commanded. My true disciples will not be revealed by the doctrines they embrace but by the lives they live. Are they building their lives on the rock of hearing My words and *doing* them or on the sand of hearing My words and then *not* doing them? Be vigilant and diligent to follow those who hear My words and act on them.

Beware of the false prophets, who come to you in sheep's clothing, but inwardly are ravenous wolves. You will know them by their fruits. Matthew 7:15–16, NASB

↠ *The Greatest Words Ever Spoken,* False Prophets (pp. 368–69); Commands of Christ (pp. 206–17)

Growing Your Faith

Have faith in God. Mark 11:22

There is so much deception in the world. People talk about believing in themselves, even loving themselves, as if these are powerful redeeming virtues. They are neither powerful nor redeeming. A drowning man cannot save his life, no matter what he believes about himself. And self-love diminishes one's love for God and others. How foolish to place your faith in yourself or in any human. Even angels, in all their power, cannot save a person from the bondage, judgment, and condemnation of sin. Faith in anyone other than God is blind and impotent. Only My Father and I give life to the dead and rescue those who have no strength to rescue themselves. Child, I know you want to grow your faith in the Father and Me. That's what We want as well. But there is only *one* way you can grow your faith: hear My words and do them. To gain the faith to walk on water, Peter first needed to hear from Me. Once he had My command, he could place his entire weight on the rock of My word. Child, I have given you My words. If you will simply hear them and do them, your faith will grow beyond your imagination.

Did I not tell you that if you believed, you would see the glory of God? John 11:40

↠ *The Greatest Words Ever Spoken,* Belief and Faith in Christ (pp. 445–51)

Adding Faith to Your Prayers

I tell you the truth, if anyone says to this mountain, "Go, throw yourself into the sea," and does not doubt in his heart but believes that what he says will happen, it will be done for him. Therefore I tell you, whatever you ask for in prayer, believe that you have received it, and it will be yours.
Mark 11:23–24

M y disciples often struggled with misunderstandings and inconsistent experiences with faith. They prayed but often without believing they would receive what they asked for. Initially they didn't understand the *nature* of faith—what it is and where it comes from. Today many of My followers have the same problem. They think faith is simply a matter of mental agreement or positive thinking. But mental assertion alone does not produce the kind of faith that transforms lives and moves mountains. That kind of faith must live and grow in your *heart.* When you believe in Me in your heart, you gain a driving hunger to know My words. As you learn My words and obey them, the seed of faith grows, and your life is transformed. Your greatest fears are replaced by faith and the peace and confidence it brings. As you abide in My words and do them, I will reveal Myself to you, and you will know My will for every situation you encounter.

If you abide in Me, and My words abide in you, ask whatever you wish, and it will be done for you. John 15:7, NASB

✦ *The Greatest Words Ever Spoken,* Prayer (pp. 295–98); Belief and Faith in Christ (pp. 445–51)

Where Is Your Heart?

For where your treasure is, there your heart will be also.
Matthew 6:21, NKJV

The greatest commandment begins with "Love the Lord your God with all your heart." This is so important because all behavior flows from your heart. Anything you treasure more than the Father will prevent you from loving Him with all your heart. This is because your heart focuses on that which you treasure and becomes *bonded* to it. That prevents you from becoming bonded to God. You may ask, "How can I treasure God more than anything else?" It happens when you get to know Him as He really is. The more you get to know the Father, the more you will treasure Him. The only way to get to know Him intimately is to look at My life and hear My words and do them. When you listen to Me, you will hear the Father. When you obey My words, you will be loving the Father the way *He* wants to be loved. You will treasure the Father more than ever. And as you treasure Him, you will become bonded to Him.

Anyone who has seen me has seen the Father. How can you say, "Show us the Father"? Don't you believe that I am in the Father, and that the Father is in me? The words I say to you are not just my own. Rather, it is the Father, living in me, who is doing his work. John 14:9–10

⤞ *The Greatest Words Ever Spoken,* The Heart (pp. 374–78); Spiritual Priorities (pp. 328–37); Wealth and Possessions (pp. 344–47)

Where Is Your Treasure?

Do not store up for yourselves treasures on earth, where moth and rust destroy, and where thieves break in and steal. But store up for yourselves treasures in heaven, where moth and rust do not destroy, and where thieves do not break in and steal. For where your treasure is, there your heart will be also. Matthew 6:19–21

Child, I want you to see your life and everything around you the way I see it. I am not blinded by the luster of anything this world offers. Nor am I distracted by temporary attractions that have no eternal worth. Tragically, most people overvalue that which is temporary and undervalue that which is eternal. They waste their lives pursuing earthly treasures they will leave behind while failing to pursue treasures of eternal worth. I don't want that to be true of you. Nothing is more worthwhile than getting to know the Father and Me. As you get to know Us, I want you to love others by helping *them* get to know the Father and Me. So many wander aimlessly through life or drown in defeat and despair. They run blindly toward a tragic end. You are a light in their dark world, and you can lead them safely to Me with your life and your love. Please don't waste your limited time. Store up treasures in heaven by leading others to follow Me.

Beware, and be on your guard against every form of greed; for not even when one has an abundance does his life consist of his possessions. Luke 12:15, NASB

⤜ *The Greatest Words Ever Spoken,* Spiritual Priorities (pp. 328–37); Wealth and Possessions (pp. 344–47)

Be Like Me

Take my yoke upon you and learn from me, for I am gentle
and humble in heart, and you will find rest for your souls.
Matthew 11:29

Because I have called you to store up treasures in heaven, I want
you to understand how to do that. The Father wants you to
become more like Me each day. He sent the Holy Spirit to reproduce
My life in you. He desires that others will come face to face with His
loving-kindness, righteousness, wisdom, and justice through you.
The fastest way to accomplish this is for you to *harness* yourself to
Me. When you and I are harnessed together, you will go My way
instead of yours. Instead of relying on your own strength, you will
rely on Mine. Instead of doing your will, you will do Mine. To do
this, you need to *daily* fill your mind and heart with My words. As
you do, the Holy Spirit will perform His ministry in your mind and
heart. He will bring My words to your memory and apply them to
whatever situation you are in. He will empower you with the grace
you need to apply My words to your life, moment by moment. He
will grant you the faith you need to take each step with Me. And in
all of this, He will reproduce Me in you, and our wonderful Father
will be glorified.

On that day you will realize that I am in my Father, and you are in
me, and I am in you. John 14:20

→→ *The Greatest Words Ever Spoken*, Following Christ (pp. 245–53); Spiritual
Priorities (pp. 328–37)

Freely You Have Received

Freely you have received, freely give. Matthew 10:8, NKJV

My dear child, what have you received from the Father and from Me? You were dead in sin and had no hope of eternal life. But We raised you from the dead and gave you eternal life. We replaced your hopelessness with a confident hope. When you deserved My Father's wrath, He showed you undeserved mercy. We forgave all your sins—all of them! Even now We continue to grant you forgiveness every day. When you have been wounded, We have shown you compassion. We show you never-ending patience. We have listened to every cry of your heart, even when you couldn't express yourself with words. We have met all your needs throughout your life. We have protected you from countless dangers, threats, and consequences. I have shared My life and My heart with you. I agonized on the cross for *you*. I became *your* sins. I endured the terrible pain of separation from the Father so I could separate you from the power, condemnation, and consequences of your sin. I paid your debt in its entirety. The Father and I have loved you unconditionally and beyond degree. That is why I want you to freely extend to others *everything* you have received from the Father and Me.

Peace be unto you: as my Father hath sent me, even so send I you. John 20:21, KJV

↠ *The Greatest Words Ever Spoken,* Stewardship, Generosity (pp. 338–41); Commands of Christ (pp. 206–17)

Freely Give

Freely you have received, freely give. Matthew 10:8, NKJV

Think about the people I have brought into your life. They include members of your immediate and extended family, friends, and people at work or at school. It includes people you have a good relationship with and those with whom you have struggled. Are you showing kindness to them without conditions, as the Father and I have shown kindness to you? Do you extend mercy to those who deserve your scorn? Have you forgiven those who offended you, releasing them from your judgment? Do you work to meet the needs of others? Do you bless your enemies and pray for those who abused you? Have you shown compassion, even to people who have done nothing to deserve it? Do you extend never-ending patience to people the way My Father and I extend it to you? Do you reach out to others the way We reach out to you? Child, regardless of how you may have failed in these matters, I want you to follow Me by doing these things in the future.

I will show you what he is like who comes to me and hears my words and puts them into practice. He is like a man building a house, who dug down deep and laid the foundation on rock. When a flood came, the torrent struck that house but could not shake it, because it was well built. Luke 6:47–48

→→ *The Greatest Words Ever Spoken,* Stewardship, Generosity (pp. 338–41); Commands of Christ (pp. 206–17)

Fear or Faith, a Matter of Life and Death

Do not be afraid; only believe. Mark 5:36, NKJV

Jairus's little girl, his only daughter, was dying. Devastated, he begged Me to come to his home and heal her. Then a group of his friends came from his house and told him that his little girl was dead. They said there was no longer a need for Me to visit his house. Brokenhearted, Jairus's greatest fear was realized: he would never again see his daughter alive. I gave him a word, a gentle command: "Do not be afraid; only believe." He had a choice: to remain in his grief and fear *or* to believe Me and act on My words. Would he choose to believe the eyewitness testimonies of his friends and follow their advice, or would he believe Me and act on My words? How about you? How often do you choose to let your circumstances or the words of others determine your beliefs and choices instead of acting on My words? No obstacle is too great for Me to overcome; no timing is too late for you to trust Me. Choosing not to believe My words in a situation may seem insignificant, but the ultimate consequences can be life changing. Jairus didn't realize it, but the life of his daughter would be determined by his decision. Though it seemed to be too late, he chose to believe Me. Will you?

According to your faith will it be done to you. Matthew 9:29

→→ *The Greatest Words Ever Spoken*, Anxiety, Worry, and Fear (pp. 190–93); Faith (pp. 231–40)

When Do You Choose to Stop Believing?

Do not be afraid; only believe. Mark 5:36, NKJV

Jairus had come to Me when his daughter was terribly sick though still alive. He had seen Me heal others and believed I could do the same for his little girl. He was desperate, but He believed. But before we could even start toward his house, his friends arrived to announce that his daughter had died. All hope of healing her was gone—she was dead. But I told him, "Do not be afraid; only believe." Can you imagine how hard that must have been? He chose to ignore the advice of his friends and to believe My words. When we arrived at his home, his faith was tested again. Friends and family members were weeping and wailing in grief. They offered no hope, no encouragement—only unbelief. I told Jairus to move everyone outside, and once again he acted in faith on My word. I brought his daughter back to life, and the lives of his family members were forever changed. All because Jairus didn't stop believing Me. He acted on every word I gave him. Child, faith can be expressed only one moment and one step at a time. Like Jairus, keep listening to My words. It is *never* time to stop believing. Believe and obey My words, and you, too, will be forever changed.

Stop doubting and believe. John 20:27

✦ *The Greatest Words Ever Spoken,* Anxiety, Worry, and Fear (pp. 190–93); Faith (pp. 231–40)

Stress, Fear, or Faith? Your Choice

Do not be afraid; only believe. Mark 5:36, NKJV

I know you struggle with anxiety, stress, and fears. Even though you try to ignore them, they remain in your mind and heart. They infect your perceptions and affect your responses. They hinder your ability to experience peace and joy. Stress and fear reduce your ability to love people. You are more likely to overreact even to a slight irritation. Minor problems can seem overwhelming. Worst of all, your intimacy with My Father and Me fades or disappears altogether. Child, it doesn't have to be that way. In every situation you have a choice between fear and trust. What keeps you from trusting Me? Sadly, the less you know of My words, the harder it is to trust Me. My words not only *reveal* Me to you. They show you which choices to make in any situation. As you express your faith in Me by doing what I say, your faith will grow. As you do what I say, you will become more intimate with Me and the Father. Trusting Me will become part of who you are. And when you trust Me, your trust will drive stress and fear out of your mind and heart. Faith and fear can't control your heart at the same moment. As you choose to believe My words and act on them, you will continually experience My joy and peace.

If you love me, you will obey what I command. John 14:15

❧ *The Greatest Words Ever Spoken*, Anxiety, Worry, and Fear (pp. 190–93); Faith (pp. 231–40); Obedience and Good Works (pp. 289–94)

Your First Assignment

Go home to your family and tell them how much the Lord
has done for you, and how he has had mercy on you.
Mark 5:19

A young man who was possessed by demonic spirits approached
Me. He lived in a graveyard and was tormented day and night
by his captors. When I cast the spirits out of him, his life was transformed. He pleaded to go with Me, but I told him to go home and
tell his people all that the Lord had done for him. He didn't complain or argue but did exactly what I told him to do. Even though he
couldn't travel with Me, he was as much My follower as those who
did. He followed Me in the most important way—by obeying My
words. Child, My Father has a plan for you as well. It may not be
exactly what you want, but it is eternal and it is perfect! You can be
My true follower if you will believe My words and obey them. Your
first mission field includes your family and friends. Let them hear
your testimony of God's amazing love for you. Let them see *Me* in
the life you lead. Let them experience My love, patience, and kindness through *you*. Let them hear My words through your voice and
see My words actively transforming your life.

I tell you, whoever acknowledges me before men, the Son of Man
will also acknowledge him before the angels of God. Luke 12:8

↠ *The Greatest Words Ever Spoken,* Gratitude (pp. 262–63); God's Mercy
(pp. 101–2); Commands of Christ (pp. 206–17)

When Another Believer Hurts You

Moreover if your brother sins against you, go and tell him his fault between you and him alone. If he hears you, you have gained your brother. Matthew 18:15, NKJV

When a brother or sister hurts you, I know that your natural reaction is to complain to other people about the offense. Even though this is natural, it is *not* what I want you to do. Instead, love your offender in the same ways that I have loved you: with patience, mercy, and grace. Make every effort to be unified in spirit with the offender. When someone hurts you, go privately to the person *before* you go to anyone else. Tell the person how he or she offended you. And, child, *how* you go is as important as going. Do not go in a harsh, confrontational, or condescending manner. Approach the person with a humble, gentle, and loving spirit. Go with the purpose of reconciling rather than merely confronting or correcting the offender. Approach the person with the spirit of a loving servant. I know you don't feel like making such an effort since it is so contrary to your nature. But you are My child, and I have given you the Holy Spirit so you can follow Me and do as *I* would do.

A new command I give you: Love one another. As I have loved you, so you must love one another. John 13:34

→→ *The Greatest Words Ever Spoken,* Conflict (pp. 477–80); Forgiving Others (pp. 481–83)

Don't Be Fooled—My Path Is Dangerously Narrow

Enter through the narrow gate. For wide is the gate and broad is the road that leads to destruction, and many enter through it. But small is the gate and narrow the road that leads to life, and only a few find it. Matthew 7:13–14

M y Gospel has been tragically misrepresented. Some of the critical truths I revealed while on earth are now ignored or unknown by many. In an effort to make My Gospel more acceptable, some have set aside My truths that make people uncomfortable. Many have proclaimed that the kingdom of heaven offers an open door to anyone, regardless of how they live their lives. How tragic! *I* am *the* way, *the* truth, and *the* life. No one comes to the Father except through Me. There are no other paths to God. My sheep follow Me, and I lead them on a very narrow path of love, righteousness, and truth. Mine is the *only* path to heaven. Even though other paths may seem right, they lead to death. Child, do not be afraid to proclaim all My truths, no matter how hard or unpopular they may be. Follow Me along the narrow path, and I will lead you to the home I have prepared for you.

I tell you the truth, I am the gate for the sheep. All who ever came before me were thieves and robbers, but the sheep did not listen to them. I am the gate; whoever enters through me will be saved. John 10:7–9

⤖ *The Greatest Words Ever Spoken,* Eternal Life (pp. 134–42); The Judgment (pp. 150–60)

My First Message Needs to Be Proclaimed Today More Than Ever

The Kingdom of God is near! Repent of your sins and believe the Good News! Mark 1:15, NLT

I n this statement I summarized the three essential parts of the Gospel. But today this message often is altered, minimized, or ignored. Child, I want My first message to be *your* message. It all starts with My Father's kingdom. His kingdom is eternal and glorious beyond description. God and His kingdom should be the central focus of everyone's life while on earth. His kingdom is the perfect expression of the Father and all that He is. It is filled with His unlimited love, His perfect righteousness, and His glorious truth. The joy of being in His presence cannot be expressed in earthly terms. The truth that must be announced is this: the kingdom of God is *near*! You don't have to journey a thousand miles to find it. Its gates have been opened by My death on the cross. It can now be entered and experienced by all who hear My voice and follow Me. I have opened My Father's kingdom to you. That is why it's so important that you abide in Me and My words. By knowing Me intimately, you won't have to die to experience the Father's love, peace, and joy. You can have it right now in your relationship with Me.

Blessed are the poor in spirit, for theirs is the kingdom of heaven. Matthew 5:3

✦ *The Greatest Words Ever Spoken,* The Kingdom of God and the Kingdom of Heaven (pp. 161–70); Repentance (pp. 462–66); Faith (pp. 231–40; 445–51)

My First Message Needs to Be Proclaimed Today More Than Ever

I f people understood the miracle of the Father's opening His glorious kingdom to humanity, they would be filled with awe and would be desperate to enter. But most people are not. Until a person is born again, he is walking *away* from the kingdom of God. To enter the kingdom, one must first *turn around.* He must do an about-face, repenting of his sins and turning his heart toward Me. Today repentance is often misunderstood or ignored. And yet it is just as much a part of the Gospel as the necessity of having faith in Me. If a person doesn't repent, he will die in his sins. He will bear the full weight of judgment resulting in eternal separation from God and His glorious kingdom. Child, even though this part of the Gospel message makes people uncomfortable, it must be proclaimed. Following Me must begin with repentance. When you share the Gospel with others, lovingly include this vital element. Then you will be sharing the *whole* Gospel. I will use you to call others to Me. They, too, will become My followers, and the Father will be glorified.

In the same way, I tell you, there is rejoicing in the presence of the angels of God over one sinner who repents. Luke 15:10

✈ *The Greatest Words Ever Spoken,* The Kingdom of God and the Kingdom of Heaven (pp. 161–70); Repentance (pp. 462–66); Faith (pp. 231–40; 445–51)

My First Message Needs to Be Proclaimed Today More Than Ever

The Kingdom of God is near! Repent of your sins **and believe the Good News!** Mark 1:15, NLT

The Good News is that the Father sent Me to earth to take on your sins and to bear all His wrath against your sins. This makes it possible for you to enter His kingdom and receive eternal life. This is the greatest news anyone will ever hear. And yet it's not enough just to hear it. It must also be *believed*. Believing in Me means believing My words to the point of *obeying* them. The person who says he believes in Me but doesn't obey My words is deceiving himself. Those who truly believe listen to My words and follow Me by doing them. They hunger for My words. They devour them, and they live according to them. Child, this is one more reason why it is so important that you abide in My words. You will truly be a light in your world. And as you proclaim the message of the kingdom, My sheep will hear My voice through you!

If anyone loves me, he will obey my teaching. My Father will love him, and we will come to him and make our home with him. He who does not love me will not obey my teaching. These words you hear are not my own; they belong to the Father who sent me. John 14:23–24

↠ *The Greatest Words Ever Spoken,* The Kingdom of God and the Kingdom of Heaven (pp. 161–70); Repentance (pp. 462–66); Faith (pp. 231–40; 445–51); Obedience and Good Works (pp. 289–94)

If Your Heart Is Not Right, Nothing Else Matters

These people honor me with their lips, but their hearts are far from me. Their worship is a farce, for they teach man-made ideas as commands from God. Matthew 15:8–9, NLT

Ask almost anyone and they will talk as if they know all about the Father and Me. But a very different story is told by the way they lead their lives. They value their own ideas and traditions more than they value God's commands. I want you to be aware that even though people may worship the Father and Me with their lips, their *hearts* may be far from Us. I don't want you to be misled by those who say they know Me but do not. It's their behavior that reveals whether or not they truly know Me. People's behavior expresses the *true* beliefs of their hearts. If they say they believe in Me yet live contrary to My commands and teachings, they *don't* believe in their hearts. People who believe in Me in their hearts follow Me by doing what I say. Such people will not be sinless, but the *direction* of their lives will be the same as Mine. They will have a growing hunger to know the Father and Me more intimately. They will hunger and thirst for My words and My righteousness. That is how you can recognize the beliefs of their hearts.

Why do you call Me, "Lord, Lord," and do not do what I say?
Luke 6:46, NASB

↠ *The Greatest Words Ever Spoken,* Honoring and Exalting Christ (pp. 455–56)

Hearts That Need a Miraculous Cleansing

For from the heart come evil thoughts, murder, adultery, all sexual immorality, theft, lying, and slander. These are what defile you. Matthew 15:19–20, NLT

No unclean person can enter God's kingdom. Since Adam's first sin, all humanity has been plagued by evil. The heart became a house of unrighteousness and sin, ruled by self-centeredness. That made it impossible for you to love God with your whole heart or to love your neighbor the same way you love yourself. Your spirit was dead in sin, having no hope. You were headed down a path to eternal separation from the Father and Me. But My Father provided a way to remove all the evil from your sin-stained heart and replace it with *My* righteousness. At Calvary, He placed all your sin on Me. In your place I received all the punishment that you deserved. And by placing your faith in Me, all My righteousness has been transferred to you. You are clothed in My righteousness. That's why the prophet wrote, "'Come now, and let us reason together,' says the LORD, 'though your sins are as scarlet, they will be as white as snow; though they are red like crimson, they will be like wool.'" Oh, what a God! Child, does anyone deserve your heart more than He does?

Blessed are the pure in heart, for they will see God. Matthew 5:8

→→ *The Greatest Words Ever Spoken,* The Heart (pp. 374–78); Lust (p. 385); Sexual Immorality (p. 488)

Your Heart Made Clean

You are already clean because of the word which I have spoken to you. John 15:3, NKJV

I know you get discouraged over your struggles with sin. The Evil One brings a never-ending string of temptations into your path, casting seeds of doubt, greed, envy, pride, anger, and lust into your mind. When they take root in your heart, you stumble and fall. I want you to know that these sins have been paid for with My blood. You have been forgiven completely. But when you fall, you need to quickly wash your heart and mind with My words. They will not only cleanse your heart and mind, but they will stop the roots of sin from growing stronger. They will also empower you to take different paths in the future and to more carefully avoid temptation. My words will not only make you clean; they will *keep* you clean. They make it harder for the seeds of sin that land in your mind to take root in your heart. My words will change your desires and increase your strength and faith. This is what King David meant when he wrote, "I have hidden your word in my heart, that I might not sin against you."

The good man out of the good treasure of his heart brings forth what is good; and the evil man out of the evil treasure brings forth what is evil; for his mouth speaks from that which fills his heart. Luke 6:45, NASB

⤜ *The Greatest Words Ever Spoken,* Jesus' Words, Their Role and Power (pp. 62–64); Cleansing (p. 206)

In Me You Will Have Peace

These things I have spoken to you, that in Me you may have peace. John 16:33, NKJV

You may wonder, *How can I ever have peace in light of everything I am going through?* The strife in the world, your conflicts with others, and the stresses of life make gaining real peace seem impossible. But, child, I want to give you a peace that the world cannot give or even understand. This peace can be found only in Me, and it passes all human understanding. To receive it, you need to believe Me to the point of daily abiding in My words and doing them. This will bring you into *intimacy* with the Father and Me. This peace is so fulfilling that those who have it can joyfully endure any hardship or trial. When you are stressed, worried, or fearful, let that be an alarm warning you that you have taken your eyes off Me. You have stopped trusting Me, and you are no longer abiding in My words and acting on them. Reset your focus and run to My words. Then *rest* in Me. Heaven and earth will pass away, but My words will never fail. Do not go to sleep tonight until you have poured the soothing balm of My words into your mind and heart.

Peace I leave with you; My peace I give to you; not as the world gives do I give to you. Do not let your heart be troubled, nor let it be fearful. John 14:27, NASB

→→ *The Greatest Words Ever Spoken,* The Promises of Christ (pp. 298–304); Anxiety, Worry, and Fear (pp. 190–93)

Cheer Up!

In the world you will have tribulation; but be of good cheer, I have overcome the world. John 16:33, NKJV

Driven by self-centeredness, people have set aside the Father and His laws, opening themselves to all manner of evil. But the Father's love and patience are so great that He has not turned His back on humanity. Instead, He saves all who believe in Me. Until I establish My kingdom on earth, there will never be a time without tribulation. But, child, *you* don't have to fear like those who don't know Me. Your circumstances—no matter how bad they may become—do not need to affect your joy or peace. Realize that your life on earth is only a moment of the eternity that lies ahead. Rejoice daily that your relationship with Me is eternal and more secure than the world itself. Rejoice that I have overcome the world and death itself. And because you are My sheep, the world and death have no power to separate you from My Father and Our love. Don't focus on the past or the future, but live in the moment with Me. I love you far more than you love yourself.

Blessed are you when people insult you and persecute you, and falsely say all kinds of evil against you because of Me. Rejoice and be glad, for your reward in heaven is great; for in the same way they persecuted the prophets who were before you.
Matthew 5:11–12, NASB

→ *The Greatest Words Ever Spoken,* The Promises of Christ (pp. 298–304); Anxiety, Worry, and Fear (pp. 190–93)

Humble Yourself and Let God Exalt You

For whoever exalts himself will be humbled, and he who humbles himself will be exalted. Luke 14:11, NKJV

Your Father detests pride and loves humility. He has given countless warnings against pride and exhortations toward humility. And yet people pursue the praise of others and do little to seek the praise of the Father. Though this is human nature, it must not be true of you. Realize that everything you have is because of the Father's grace and mercy. Knowing that you are My representative, be diligent in all your labors so your efforts will bring glory to the Father and Me. Let your love and good works attract attention to the Father. When you receive praise, turn it toward the One who has given you all your gifts and talents. And when others say or do things that humiliate you, don't react against them. Realize that even if they meant to hurt you, they are unintentionally *blessing* you by helping you to be more humble before God. Child, if you will humble yourself and follow Me, you will be praised and exalted by the Father in His perfect time. A single word of His praise is more glorious than the praise of a million people. And, child, His exaltation is for *eternity.*

Truly I say to you, unless you are converted and become like children, you will not enter the kingdom of heaven. Whoever then humbles himself as this child, he is the greatest in the kingdom of heaven. Matthew 18:3–4, NASB

→→ *The Greatest Words Ever Spoken,* Humility (pp. 271–73); Pride (pp. 391–93)

My Father Will Honor
All Who Serve Me

If anyone serves Me, let him follow Me; and where I am,
there My servant will be also. If anyone serves Me, him My
Father will honor. John 12:26, NKJV

C an you imagine what it's like to be honored by My Father—the
almighty God, the Creator of all things? Can you imagine
being honored by Him before His heavenly hosts of angels and His
redeemed of all nations? Could there ever be a greater promise given
to humanity? *His* honor is not based on your earthly achievements or
religious activities. It's not based on your age or what you can accomplish for Him. A child can receive just as much honor as an adult. For
the Father has chosen to honor everyone who serves Me. You might
wonder how the Son of God, who needs nothing, can be served by
His followers. Child, you *serve* Me by *following* Me. And you *follow*
Me by *obeying* My teachings and commands. You serve Me when
you tell others of My Father and Me. You serve Me when you follow
the promptings of the Holy Spirit and do My Father's will. You serve
Me when you feed and lead My sheep. You serve Me when you let
Me live My life through you. And because you serve Me, My Father
will honor you. I promise.

The greatest among you will be your servant. Matthew 23:11

↠ *The Greatest Words Ever Spoken,* God's Desires (pp. 90–92); Servants
(pp. 316–19)

True Fulfillment Now and Forever

I am the bread of life. He who comes to Me shall never hunger, and he who believes in Me shall never thirst.
John 6:35, NKJV

Look at the people around you. You will see emptiness, discouragement, and unhappiness. Listen to their words. You'll hear them talk about things that merely entertain or bring temporary gratification. You'll also hear talk of people who upset or anger them. Instead of seeing peace, contentment, and joy, you'll see strife, envy, and unhappiness. And no matter what they get, they are never satisfied. Dear one, this is *not* the life I want for you. As My follower, you can be constantly fulfilled. If any traits of emptiness are true of your life, know that it's because you are *fasting* instead of *feasting* on Me. Come to Me and believe in Me. Believe that I will fulfill My promises in your life. Pour My words into your mind today. But don't just come to Me occasionally. Feast on Me and My words *every* day. When you are not filled with peace and joy, it is because you have stopped feasting on the Bread of Life.

For whoever desires to save his life will lose it, but whoever loses his life for My sake will find it. For what profit is it to a man if he gains the whole world, and loses his own soul? Or what will a man give in exchange for his soul? Matthew 16:25–26, NKJV

✦ *The Greatest Words Ever Spoken,* The Claims Jesus Made About Himself (pp. 14–22); The Promises of Christ (pp. 298–304)

From Death to Life

I tell you the truth, whoever hears my word and believes him who sent me has eternal life and will not be condemned; he has crossed over from death to life. John 5:24

Have you heard My word? Have you believed in the Father who sent Me? Do you believe what the Father has said about Me, that I am His Anointed One, His only begotten Son? Do you believe that He will give eternal life to all who look to Me and believe in Me? Are these beliefs in your heart and expressed by your behavior? Then, child, three incomparable gifts are yours! First, you have been given eternal life. It is given by My Father and Me to all who have *truly* believed in Me. Second, you have avoided judgment. All of the Father's wrath that should have been directed at you was instead delivered to Me on the cross. I paid the full penalty for your sin. Finally, you have passed from death to life. Your eternal life has already begun! While most of humanity passes from life to death, you have done the opposite! Though your body will experience physical death, you will simply pass from the *earthly* stage of life to the *heavenly* stage. Oh, how the Father loves you!

For my Father's will is that everyone who looks to the Son and believes in him shall have eternal life, and I will raise them up at the last day. John 6:40

⇝ *The Greatest Words Ever Spoken,* Abiding in the Words of Christ (pp. 186–88); Belief and Faith in Christ (pp. 445–51); Eternal Life (pp. 134–42)

A Reason to Rejoice
All Day, Every Day

Stop grumbling among yourselves. . . . No one can come to me unless the Father who sent me draws him, and I will raise him up at the last day. John 6:43–44

D o you understand what I have done for you and what I'm *going* to do? If you really understand, you will be overflowing with joy. When I healed a man who was born blind, he was so excited he couldn't stop talking about Me. But that miracle can't compare to what the Father and I have done for *you.* You were dead in sin, and yet the Father drew you to Me and gave you a new birth. Had He not drawn you to Me, you would have remained separated from Him and His kingdom forever. On top of all this, I am going to raise you from the dead. Realize that all your troubles are temporary. Child, I want you to live in a moment-by-moment awareness that what We have done for you is *eternal.* When you complain, you are choosing to belittle the Father and Me and Our priceless gifts to you. So stop complaining. Continually set your focus on the Father and Me and the greatness of your salvation. Choose to rejoice throughout today and every day.

Nevertheless do not rejoice in this, that the spirits are subject to you, but rejoice that your names are recorded in heaven. Luke 10:20, NASB

✦ *The Greatest Words Ever Spoken,* God's Sovereignty (pp. 103–5); God the Father (pp. 92–97); Jesus' Missions (pp. 46–51); Eternal Life (pp. 134–42)

I Want You to Be a Child of God, and I Want Your Reward to Be Great

---

But love your enemies, do good to them, and lend to them without expecting to get anything back. Then your reward will be great, and you will be sons of the Most High, because he is kind to the ungrateful and wicked. Be merciful, just as your Father is merciful. Luke 6:35–36

My Father loves you to a degree that is unimaginable. Even when you are at your worst, He is kind to you. Even when you show little gratitude for His love and mercy, He blesses you and demonstrates His patience, mercy, and grace. Doing the will of My Father is My purpose, My joy, My food, and My work. I want *you* to follow Me by following My example and doing what I say. I want you to love your enemies by showing kindness in your actions toward them. Pray for them, forgive them, and bless them. Stop judging them in your mind and in your words. Do for them the same things My Father and I continually do for you. Remember, mercy is never deserved. It is a gift from your Father to you. He wants you to give that same gift to all who have hurt you. When you do this, you will truly be a child of the Most High, and your reward will be great.

My sheep listen to my voice; I know them, and they follow me. John 10:27

↠ *The Greatest Words Ever Spoken,* Commands of Christ (pp. 206–17)

You Can't Follow Me and Remain in Darkness

I have come as a light into the world, that whoever believes in Me should not abide in darkness. John 12:46, NKJV

In darkness it's easy to believe a lie. It's easy to embrace values that seem to be right but aren't. It's easy to believe that something that feels good *is* good. In darkness it's easy to lose your way and stumble. You might even take a life-ending fall. But I am your bright and shining Light! You don't have to remain in darkness. You can see Me and follow Me down the paths you should take. You can see the true worth of everything around you. You can see the tantalizing attractions of this world for what they are—worthless and vile in God's sight. My word is a lamp that lights the way. As you abide in Me and My words, you will dwell in My light. The Holy Spirit will use the light of My words to reveal all truth to you. My Father's ways will become your ways. And you will become a glowing light to those who want to flee darkness and come to Me.

But when He, the Spirit of truth, comes, He will guide you into all the truth; for He will not speak on His own initiative, but whatever He hears, He will speak; and He will disclose to you what is to come. He will glorify Me, for He will take of Mine and will disclose it to you. John 16:13–14, NASB

↠ *The Greatest Words Ever Spoken,* Following Christ (pp. 245–53); Light Versus Darkness (pp. 384–85)

What Do You Value?

You are the ones who justify yourselves in the eyes of men, but God knows your hearts. What is highly valued among men is detestable in God's sight. Luke 16:15

The Pharisees loved to buy things they believed would make them look more important. They even believed their wealth was proof that God considered them more worthy than people with less wealth. They craved the honor of other people and had no desire to truly know God. Though their wealth purchased things that spawned envy in others who shared their values, those same things were detestable to God. Child, what do *you* value? If you envy the wealth or possessions of others, you have been blinded by this world and the Father of Lies. Of course, I want to provide what you need. I want to enable you to bless your family and others. But don't let your wealth distract your heart or draw your affections. Satan's values are a trap, intended to ensnare your heart and keep you away from Me. The Father's values all relate to your heart and what flows out of it. They do *not* relate to what you possess. He wants you to be a vessel of His love, mercy, compassion, gentleness, forgiveness, patience, and truth. He wants you to value Him above all and to be like Me.

Beware of the leaven of the Pharisees, which is hypocrisy.
Luke 12:1, NASB

✦ *The Greatest Words Ever Spoken,* Spiritual Priorities (pp. 328–37)

My Followers Cannot Outgive My Father

Do not judge, and you will not be judged. Do not condemn, and you will not be condemned. Forgive, and you will be forgiven. Give, and it will be given to you. A good measure, pressed down, shaken together and running over, will be poured into your lap. Luke 6:37–38

Child, I want you to give to others as I have given to you. With My sacrifice on the cross, I have spared you all the judgment and condemnation you were due. So I want *you* to stop judging and condemning those who have hurt you. I want you to let your hurt turn your focus away from your offenders and toward Me. I want you to forgive them, just as I have forgiven you. The greater you're hurt, the more you can forgive, bringing glory to the Father and to Me. The more you forgive, the more you will be like Me. I want you to be a faithful and wise manager of all the talents and resources I have given you. Use them to bless the lives of others. The Father didn't entrust you with resources so you could hoard them. He gave them so you could use them to help meet the needs of others and to glorify Him. Don't be afraid that giving sacrificially will drain your resources. What you wisely give will be restored to you at a *greater* level than what you have given, both on earth and in heaven.

Treat others the same way you want them to treat you.
Luke 6:31, NASB

➤➤ *The Greatest Words Ever Spoken,* Stewardship, Generosity (pp. 338–41); Commands of Christ (pp. 206–17)

The Most Important Person Serves the Least Important

Who is more important, the one who sits at the table or the one who serves? The one who sits at the table, of course. But not here! For I am among you as one who serves.
Luke 22:27, NLT

I n the world a wealthy person sitting at a restaurant table is viewed as more important than the server. This is not true in My Father's kingdom. When I was sent to earth, My mission was so important because I was *doing* the will of the Father. In My kingdom your heart to serve the Father is what makes you important. Washing My disciples' feet on the night of My arrest was just as important to the Father as raising Lazarus from the dead. In both situations I was doing exactly what He wanted Me to do. Your importance in the Father's kingdom is determined by your willingness to serve Him by *doing* His will. I was the leader, teacher, protector, and life-giving Messiah among My disciples. And yet, from the time I called them, I never stopped serving them. Doing the Father's will *always* involves serving. In serving the disciples I was serving Him. If you want to be great in the kingdom, serve the Father by lovingly serving others.

If I then, the Lord and the Teacher, washed your feet, you also ought to wash one another's feet. For I gave you an example that you also should do as I did to you. John 13:14–15, NASB

↠ *The Greatest Words Ever Spoken,* Serving Others (pp. 319–20); Commands of Christ (pp. 206–17)

Even the Smallest Faith Can Work Miracles

If you have faith as a mustard seed, you can say to this mulberry tree, "Be pulled up by the roots and be planted in the sea," and it would obey you. Luke 17:6, NKJV

When I told My disciples they were to forgive a brother seven times in the same day, they were shocked. They had a hard time forgiving even once a day. My command seemed impossible, so they pleaded with the Lord, "Increase our faith!" But obeying any of My commands does not require *more* faith; it requires *some* faith. I told the disciples that with even the *tiniest* amount of faith, they could perform miracles. Their inability to obey My command revealed that when it came to forgiveness, they had *no* faith. Their faith could be increased only by obeying My words. Faith grows by hearing My words and obeying them. My disciples didn't need more faith to forgive one another; they needed more *obedience*. You please and glorify the Father with your faith. And growing your faith is as important as anything you will ever do. But the only way to grow your faith is to hear My promises and commands and act on them. The more you do that, the more your faith will grow.

Whoever has my commands and obeys them, he is the one who loves me. He who loves me will be loved by my Father, and I too will love him and show myself to him. John 14:21

→ *The Greatest Words Ever Spoken,* Belief and Faith in Christ (pp. 445–51); Obedience and Good Works (pp. 289–94); Commands of Christ (pp. 206–17)

Don't Be Discouraged
When Others Won't Listen

Anyone who belongs to God listens gladly to the words of God. But you don't listen because you don't belong to God.
John 8:47, NLT

Have you ever wondered why so many people refuse to listen to God's Word? Why do most people live on the broad path that leads to destruction instead of the narrow path that leads to eternal life? It's because they do *not* belong to God. Those who belong to God listen to His words, and they don't just listen with their ears. They listen and embrace God's words in their *hearts,* and their lives show it. Child, *you* belong to My Father and to Me. You are receiving My words and following them. I know that you get discouraged when others reject your witness. Some people may have made you feel alone or caused you to wonder if you are wrong. Child, they are in darkness. And in darkness people believe anything they want to believe. Those who reject you or your witness are really rejecting Me. They reject Me because they do not belong to God . . . *yet.* Pray for them and bless them.

This is the judgment, that the Light has come into the world, and men loved the darkness rather than the Light, for their deeds were evil. For everyone who does evil hates the Light, and does not come to the Light for fear that his deeds will be exposed.
John 3:19–20, NASB

✦ *The Greatest Words Ever Spoken,* Unbelief and Motives of Unbelievers (pp. 466–69)

Don't Prevent the Children from Coming to Me

Let the little children come to me, and do not hinder them, for the kingdom of heaven belongs to such as these.
Matthew 19:14

I was ministering to a group of adults when a number of children were brought to Me. My disciples scolded those who brought them, thinking the children were too young and unimportant to deserve My attention. They had no idea how seriously My Father cares about children. Keeping them away from Me was offensive to the Father and to Me. Dear one, do not view children as less important than adults. They are worthy of your time. They need to hear about Me, My life, and My words. They are able to receive the Gospel in its purest form, in innocent wonder and faith. Teach them about My love. Show them that they need to turn from selfishness and become My follower. Let them see My love for them expressed on Calvary. Let them know they are just as important to Me as you are. Do not hinder them in *any* way from coming to Me. Let them see your love for Me by the way you live. Love them in the same ways that I love you.

And whoever receives one such child in My name receives Me; but whoever causes one of these little ones who believe in Me to stumble, it would be better for him to have a heavy millstone hung around his neck, and to be drowned in the depth of the sea.
Matthew 18:5–6, NASB

→→ *The Greatest Words Ever Spoken*, Children (pp. 357–59)

Forgiving Without Limits

I do not say to you, up to seven times, but up to seventy times seven. Matthew 18:22, NKJV

After I told My disciples to forgive their brothers seven times in the same day, Peter asked once more if he should forgive a brother up to seven times. I told him, "Up to seventy times seven!" The truth is, for My followers there must be *no* limits to how often or how much they forgive. Child, there is no offense so great or so frequent that you shouldn't forgive. Like Peter, you may wonder how you can *possibly* forgive such frequent or such great offenses. You need only to look at how much My Father has forgiven *you*. When you really understand the price that I paid for your sins, you will realize how wrong it would be for you to withhold forgiveness from anyone for anything. You forgive people, not because they deserve it or because their offense is small, but because My Father forgave you. Forgiveness is releasing the other person from his obligation to *you*. It doesn't relieve the other person of his *responsibility* to bear the consequences of his offense before God. It doesn't free him to continue injuring you or others. Forgiveness is not a feeling; it's a choice—a choice to obey Me and please the Father.

And when you stand praying, if you hold anything against anyone, forgive him, so that your Father in heaven may forgive you your sins. Mark 11:25

→ *The Greatest Words Ever Spoken,* Forgiving Others (pp. 481–83)

Who Can See God?

Blessed are the pure in heart, for they will see God.
Matthew 5:8

Do you want to see God in all His unimaginable glory? Seeing God is My promise to all who are pure in heart. Your heart is the *core* of who you are. Nearly everything you do, you do because of the *beliefs* in your *heart.* That's why Solomon wrote, "Above all else, guard your heart, for it is the wellspring of life." What you hear, what you see, and all your thoughts enter your mind first and then become a part of you as they seep into your heart. You can't fully avoid the dark influences of this world. But if you will abide in My words, you *can* establish a shield between your mind and your heart. This shield can prevent evil from taking up permanent residence in your heart. Child, do all you can to protect your mind from encountering evil. But when evil thoughts get past your defenses, *immediately* counter them with My words. My words will protect, cleanse, and purify your heart. Your soul has been cleansed by My atonement. Your heart will be continually cleansed by My words. And with a pure heart, you will have the indescribable, unsurpassable blessing of seeing God in ways that those without a pure heart can't.

You are already clean because of the word which I have spoken to you. John 15:3, NASB

→ *The Greatest Words Ever Spoken,* Purity (p. 305); The Heart (pp. 374–78)

I Am Preparing a Place for You

In My Father's house are many dwelling places; if it were not so, I would have told you; for I go to prepare a place for you. If I go and prepare a place for you, I will come again and receive you to Myself, that where I am, there you may be also. John 14:2–3, NASB

The kingdom of heaven is real! It is more permanent than the world you live in. Though the earth and heavens will pass away, the kingdom of heaven is established for eternity. And I have prepared a place for *you* in that kingdom. You have been born of the Spirit, and your place is with Me. I want you to remember that this world is not your home. It is only a *temporary* dwelling place. I will come again and receive you unto Myself. Whenever you get discouraged, I want you to think about these things. In comparison to eternity, your remaining time on earth is only a moment. All your fears, disappointments, loneliness, and discouragement will become things of the past. In My presence you will never want to look back. All your tears will be gone. Your joy will be indescribable. So persevere in righteousness until I come for you. I love you.

You are in error because you do not know the Scriptures or the power of God. At the resurrection people will neither marry nor be given in marriage; they will be like the angels in heaven.
Matthew 22:29–30

↠ *The Greatest Words Ever Spoken,* Heaven (pp. 143–50); Eternal Life (pp. 134–42)

A Serious Matter for Prayer

The harvest truly is plentiful, but the laborers are few. Therefore pray the Lord of the harvest to send out laborers into His harvest. Matthew 9:37–38, NKJV

While on earth I could be in only one place at a time. My true followers were few, and those who needed to be ministered to were too many to number. As I looked at the multitudes, I was filled with compassion. They were like sheep wandering aimlessly without a shepherd. Today My true followers are few, much as they were during My earthly ministry. Those who need to hear My voice and follow Me are greater than ever. Many more laborers are needed to proclaim the Gospel with their voices and their lives. But the laborers We need can't be persuaded by the words or schemes of men. Laborers are called by the Father, through the power of His Spirit, to proclaim the Gospel to every creature. I know that you request much of Me. Here is *My* request of you. Every day pray that the Lord will send laborers into His harvest. As you pray, listen for His voice. Will He call you? Pray and listen.

Even now the reaper draws his wages, even now he harvests the crop for eternal life, so that the sower and the reaper may be glad together. John 4:36

✦ *The Greatest Words Ever Spoken,* Diligence, Sowing, and Reaping (pp. 219–21); Prayer (pp. 295–98)

Don't Be Misled

Don't let anyone mislead you, for many will come in my name, claiming, "I am the Messiah," and saying, "The time has come!" But don't believe them. Luke 21:8, NLT

Today many people go forth in My name calling out, "Follow me." Some of them shepherd My sheep along the narrow path I ordained. But, tragically, many others are leading people along paths that point them away from Me. They created their own paths that are broad rather than narrow. Many claim a special revelation or calling. Many try to blend the world's ways with My ways. Many glorify themselves rather than My Father and Me. They elevate man-made doctrines above *My* teachings and commands. Child, be careful. You must not allow yourself to be misled. This is one more reason to abide in My words. Let My teachings become the lens through which you look at the teachings of others. The Holy Spirit will never lead you into a teaching that is contrary to My words. If you meditate on My words, you will be My true disciple, and you will know the truth. My words are your only *sure* defense against being misled. They will not let you down.

For false messiahs and false prophets will rise up and perform great signs and wonders so as to deceive, if possible, even God's chosen ones. See, I have warned you about this ahead of time.
Matthew 24:24–25, NLT

✦ *The Greatest Words Ever Spoken,* False Prophets (pp. 368–69)

You Don't Have to Die

I tell you the truth, anyone who obeys my teaching will never die! John 8:51, NLT

For most people death is a tragic passage from life on earth to eternal separation from the almighty God who created them. They've rejected My Father and His laws, so following death they face His judgment and condemnation. But, child, this is not true for you. Anyone who *obeys My teaching* will never die. Yes, their bodies will die, but *they* will not. For those who obey My teaching, death is merely a momentary passage from life in this world to life in My kingdom. I reminded Martha of this when I told her, "He who believes in Me will live even if he dies." Remember that when I talk about believing, I'm talking about believing in your heart. Those who believe in Me in their hearts are the ones who hunger for My teachings and follow them. Those who don't obey My teachings don't believe in Me in their hearts. Your hunger and thirst to know Me and follow My teachings is the expression of your heart's belief in Me.

I am the resurrection and the life; he who believes in Me will live even if he dies, and everyone who lives and believes in Me will never die. Do you believe this? John 11:25–26, NASB

⤜ *The Greatest Words Ever Spoken,* Death (pp. 123–25); Eternal Life (pp. 134–42); Obedience and Good Works (pp. 289–94); Jesus' Words, Their Role and Power (pp. 62–64)

The Real Victory
Belongs to the Gentle

Blessed are the gentle, for they shall inherit the earth.
Matthew 5:5, NASB

Wars have been fought over lands and their treasures by those who rule the earth by force. In My kingdom it is not that way. My kingdom's treasures will not be won through force but will be *inherited*. That inheritance will be given to those of My followers whose lives are expressed through *gentleness*. Though the gentle may be abused and taken advantage of in this world, they will be honored in My kingdom. Even though you live in a world that is ruled by force, I have called *you* into a life of gentleness. My Father sent you the Holy Spirit to bear His fruit in your life—fruit that is expressed through love, kindness, and patience. Child, I want you to be known for your gentle spirit and your gentle ways. I want your children, your family, and your neighbors to be constant recipients of your gentleness. When you are easily provoked to anger, you are quenching the Holy Spirit and expressing your self-centeredness. That is not Me, and I don't want it to be you. Let others see Me in *your* gentle ways.

Behold, I send you out as sheep in the midst of wolves. Therefore be wise as serpents and harmless as doves. Matthew 10:16, NKJV

✈ *The Greatest Words Ever Spoken,* Gentleness (p. 261)

You Have a Friend in the Highest Place

You are My friends if you do whatever I command you.
John 15:14, NKJV

How would you feel if you were given a way to become a close friend to your favorite celebrity or the leader of your nation? How would you feel about gaining open access to this famous person anytime, day or night? I'm sure you would feel privileged and excited beyond description. But, child, no matter how great that would be, it can't compare to being friends with Me. I am God's *only* begotten Son. I am the great I AM of Israel; the Alpha and Omega, the beginning and the end. I am the King of kings and Lord of lords. I healed the sick, gave sight to the blind, cleansed lepers, and raised the dead. I can calm any storm. I can change the course of human events with a single word. I will reign with My Father for eternity. And knowing all of this, I'm saying that *you* can be My friend just as My disciples were. My promise to them is the same promise I make to you. If you will hear My commands and do them, you will be My friend. My commands won't weigh you down; they will lift you up. They are the gateway to intimacy with My Father and Me.

Now a slave has no permanent place in the family, but a son belongs to it forever. John 8:35

✢ *The Greatest Words Ever Spoken,* Commands of Christ (pp. 206–17); Obedience and Good Works (pp. 289–94)

Why the World Hates Me Now More Than Ever

It hates Me because I testify of it that its works are evil.
John 7:7, NKJV

When I walked the earth, I was hated by many because I revealed that the world's values and works were evil in God's sight. Those whose deeds violated God's laws loved darkness and hated the light. They didn't want their hearts or deeds to be exposed. They not only hated the light, but they hated those who carried the light. Today's evil is as great as the evil of the time of Noah. My Father still promises His judgment "to those who call evil good, and good evil; who substitute darkness for light and light for darkness." If you embrace the values of this world, you will be loved by those who remain in darkness. But when you follow Me and let the light of your life shine, realize that those who love darkness will avoid and ridicule you. Some will hate you, just as they hated Me. I have called you out of darkness, so let your light shine. The light of your life will draw others to Me. As you bear the light, those who desire truth will see Me. You are My light in your world.

If you belonged to the world, it would love you as its own. As it is, you do not belong to the world, but I have chosen you out of the world. That is why the world hates you. John 15:19

→ *The Greatest Words Ever Spoken,* Evil (pp. 363–65); The World (pp. 408–9); Hatred for God (p. 455)

The Only Way to Take Charge of Your Heart

Don't let your hearts be troubled. Trust in God, and trust also in me. John 14:1, NLT

You have fallen into a cycle of letting your heart be controlled by your circumstances and the stresses they create. Not only do you carry unresolved worries into your day from the day before, but you encounter new situations that bring additional anxiety. This is *not* the way of life I have called you to. You cannot experience My peace and joy when you carry burdens I never intended for you to carry. When you are drowning in worries, your heart is focused on them instead of Me. Child, I want you to establish a *new* pattern for today, and I want you to repeat this pattern every day. Instead of letting circumstances control your heart, I want *you* to take control of your heart. Do not let it be troubled. Every time a circumstance creates stress or worry, prayerfully hand it over to Me and trust Me with it. I want you to have My attitude. Do as I would do by applying My words. Allow the circumstance to be a springboard into trusting Me. Let Me carry your burden and safely lead you through your circumstances. When your heart becomes troubled, realize that you face an immediate choice to disobey and remain troubled or to trust Me. You can't do both, so choose trust.

Do not be afraid any longer, only believe. Mark 5:36, NASB

→ *The Greatest Words Ever Spoken,* The Heart (pp. 374–78); Anxiety, Worry, and Fear (pp. 190–93)

How to Trust Me Today

But even more blessed are all who hear the word of God and put it into practice. Luke 11:28, NLT

While I was teaching, a listener said that the woman who gave birth to Me was greatly blessed. As true as that was, My earthly mother wasn't nearly as blessed as those who hear the Word of God and put it into practice. The *only* way to trust Me and love Me is to hear My words and obey them. When you hear My words and act on them, you will be loving the Father and Me the way *We* want to be loved. Obeying My words is also the true expression and demonstration of faith in Me. This will bring the blessing of being loved by My Father and Me in a special way. We will demonstrate Our love by continually abiding with you, and I will reveal Myself to you. There is no greater blessing than this kind of intimacy with the Father and Me. I have promised it to *everyone* who obeys My teachings. Throughout your day put them into practice. If you do this, you will be even more blessed than was My earthly mother.

If anyone loves Me, he will keep My word; and My Father will love him, and We will come to him and make Our home with him. John 14:23, NKJV

✦ *The Greatest Words Ever Spoken,* God's Word (pp. 108–9); Obedience and Good Works (pp. 289–94); The Promises of Christ (pp. 298–304)

A Peace That Can't Be Given
by Anyone Else

Peace I leave with you, My peace I give to you; not as the world gives do I give to you. Let not your heart be troubled, neither let it be afraid. John 14:27, NKJV

The world is filled with unrest and conflict. Everyone clamors for peace, but almost no one has it. People may find momentary serenity, but a single circumstance can quickly fill their hearts with fear. There is *no* security in this world, its people, or anything the world offers. In fact, the more you bond with the world and its values, the more conflict and anxiety you will experience. Child, I want to give you a peace that the world cannot provide. I want to give you *My* peace. No circumstance ever takes Me by surprise. Nothing can undo My plan for you. You are safe in My hands. Take charge of your heart today. Fill it with My words. Only as you bond with Me will you experience My peace.

My sheep listen to my voice; I know them, and they follow me. I give them eternal life, and they shall never perish; no one can snatch them out of my hand. My Father, who has given them to me, is greater than all; no one can snatch them out of my Father's hand. I and the Father are one. John 10:27–30

✤ *The Greatest Words Ever Spoken,* Anxiety, Worry, and Fear (pp. 190–93); The Promises of Christ (pp. 298–304)

The Peace That Can
Only Be Found in Me

These things I have spoken to you, that in Me you may have peace. In the world you will have tribulation; but be of good cheer, I have overcome the world. John 16:33, NKJV

In spite of everything I have told you, do you *still* struggle with anxiety and stress? Why is your peace so quickly replaced by worries and fears? Child, the answer is simple: *My* peace is in *Me.* The peace I offer does not reside in knowledge, even knowledge about Me. My peace can only be experienced as you abide in an intimate relationship with Me. And that kind of intimacy is only experienced as you abide in My words and obey them. My words are spirit and life, and as you dwell in them and obey them, My Spirit and life will dwell in your heart and mind. As you bond with Me, you will have My peace. In this world you *will* face trials and sorrows. But take heart and cheer up, because I have already overcome the world. Nothing in this world can take you away from Me. Child, as you dwell in Me and My words dwell in your heart, My peace will calm your greatest fears.

It is the Spirit who gives life; the flesh profits nothing; the words that I have spoken to you are spirit and are life. John 6:63, NASB

→→ *The Greatest Words Ever Spoken,* Anxiety, Worry, and Fear (pp. 190–93); The Promises of Christ (pp. 298–304)

Your Eternal Purpose Will Be Accomplished with My Peace

Peace be with you! As the Father has sent me, I am sending you. John 20:21

Dear one, there is another reason that I want My peace to reign in your heart. I have not called you into My kingdom for your sake alone. I have called you *in* so you may *go forth.* I came into the world to carry out a host of missions that the Father sent Me to accomplish. I came to do His will and to finish His work. As the Father sent Me, so I am sending you to unite with My other followers to finish My work on earth. To accomplish this, My peace must rule your heart. Only then can you persevere through any adversity or trial. Only with My peace can you accomplish what I have planned for you. With My peace your love for Me and My other followers will amaze and confound the world. Child, there are so many that We must reach with the Gospel. They will be reached only by My followers who have My peace and express My love, which knows no limits. As you trust and obey My words, you *will* have My peace, and you *will* accomplish all that I have set forth for you.

Go into all the world and preach the Good News to everyone. Mark 16:15, NLT

→→ *The Greatest Words Ever Spoken,* The Mission of a Christian (pp. 281–89); Anxiety, Worry, and Fear (pp. 190–93)

I Have Not Left You Alone

No, I will not abandon you as orphans—I will come to you.
John 14:18, NLT

Often you act as if you are alone and I am not there. You rely on *your* strength instead of Mine. You react to adversity as if you have no resource other than your own understanding. You exhaust your strength by trying to carry your burdens alone. But I have not abandoned you. I have commanded you to yoke yourself to Me, to let *Me* carry your burdens. I have sent the Holy Spirit to guide you into all truth, so you never have to rely on your own reasoning. I have given you My words to empower you with grace and provide the sure foundation on which your faith can stand and grow. And yet your attitudes, actions, and reactions sometimes ignore My presence and My teachings. Child, I love you. I sacrificed My life so you could intimately know the Father and Me. But when you act contrary to My words, you are choosing unbelief in place of faith. Throughout today continually acknowledge that I have *not* abandoned you and that I am with you. Let's go through this day together.

Come to Me, all who are weary and heavy-laden, and I will give you rest. Take My yoke upon you and learn from Me, for I am gentle and humble in heart, and you will find rest for your souls. For My yoke is easy and My burden is light. Matthew 11:28–30, NASB

✈ *The Greatest Words Ever Spoken,* The Promises of Christ (pp. 298–304)

One Flock United,
Following One Shepherd

I have other sheep that are not of this sheep pen. I must bring them also. They too will listen to my voice, and there shall be one flock. John 10:16

During My ministry on earth, I called My sheep from the house of Israel. But I also have called sheep from all generations and all nations. I called them into one flock—My flock! I prayed they would be one, even as My Father and I are one. But today, instead of becoming one, My followers have been divided. Many are more concerned about being students and scholars than they are about obeying My commands and teachings. I have *not* called you or My other sheep to become masters of doctrines. I have called you to become *followers*. I have called you to deny yourself, take up your cross daily, and follow Me. Instead of letting doctrinal disagreements divide you, let your desire to follow Me unify you with those who share that same desire. Fix your eyes on Me. Learn from Me. Hear My words and *do* them. Then you can become one with another, even as My Father and I are one.

My prayer is not for them alone. I pray also for those who will believe in me through their message, that all of them may be one, Father, just as you are in me and I am in you. May they also be in us so that the world may believe that you have sent me.
John 17:20–21

→→ *The Greatest Words Ever Spoken,* Unity Versus Division (p. 342); Following Christ (pp. 245–53)

Why the Father Sent Me to Earth

For God did not send His Son into the world to condemn the world, but that the world through Him might be saved. John 3:17, NKJV

I f God is a God of love, how could He allow so many terrible things to happen?" How many times have I heard these words uttered by the sons of men? How foolish of anyone to question the love of My Father. Instead of destroying humanity as He could have done, He sent Me to earth to lay down My life as an atonement for sin. Has anyone else sacrificed his only child for the terrible deeds of the very people who hated him? Would you stand by and offer *your* child to be tortured and crucified? No one has ever loved anyone as much as My Father does. He did not send Me to earth to condemn a world that deserved heaven but to *save* a world that deserved hell. Because men and women continue to reject Him, evil continues to reign. But not so with you. Child, you are one of His vessels of mercy. Though evil may reign around you, My righteousness will remain in you as a light in your world. By following Me, your works of righteousness will glorify My Father and light the way for others to come to Me.

For the Son of Man did not come to destroy men's lives, but to save them. Luke 9:56, NASB

✈ *The Greatest Words Ever Spoken,* God's Goodness (pp. 97–99); God's Love (pp. 99–101)

Liberation or Condemnation?

He who believes in Him is not condemned; but he who does not believe is condemned already, because he has not believed in the name of the only begotten Son of God.
John 3:18, NKJV

Death is the great equalizer. The rich and the poor, the master and the servant, the wise and the foolish all die. But *eternity* is the great divider. Some will be separated from the Father's kingdom of light and will dwell forever in darkness. Others will be forever delivered from darkness and remain in the glorious kingdom of My Father. My very name heralds God's love and proclaims His salvation. My name means "Jehovah saves." As the angel told Joseph, "You shall call His name Jesus, for He will save His people from their sins." Those who believe in Me and follow Me have already been delivered from judgment and condemnation. Their inheritance of eternal life is secure. On the other hand, those who have rejected Me and My words are condemned because they have not believed in My name. In arrogance they continue to exalt themselves as the gods of their own lives and reject God and His ways. Child, today I want you to rejoice in the greatness of your salvation and the knowledge of how much the Father and I love you.

I am the way, and the truth, and the life; no one comes to the Father but through Me. John 14:6, NASB

✦ *The Greatest Words Ever Spoken,* Belief and Faith in Christ (pp. 445–51); Eternal Life (pp. 134–42)

Light or Darkness?

And this is the condemnation, that the light has come into the world, and men loved darkness rather than light, because their deeds were evil. John 3:19, NKJV

I came into the dark world as a great light, revealing the truth about My Father and His kingdom. And yet the truth I revealed was rejected. Even today most people reject Me and My words. How can people be so foolish to reject the truth of My Father's glorious kingdom and His offer of salvation? The answer is that people love darkness rather than light because their deeds are evil. They do not want to change from a life of self-gratification to a life of loving and serving God. Child, *you* have chosen light over darkness. You are following Me. I know there are times when you take your eyes off Me and yield to self-centeredness. I want you to know that I am your Advocate and that My blood continually cleanses you from your sin. You may stumble, but you always repent and return to follow Me along the narrow way. Keep holding to My words. They will light the path and empower you with the grace you need to *continue* on that path. I love you.

But he who does the truth comes to the light, that his deeds may be clearly seen, that they have been done in God. John 3:21, NKJV

➤➤ *The Greatest Words Ever Spoken,* Rejecting Christ (pp. 459–61); Light Versus Darkness (pp. 384–85)

Whom Do You Look to?
Whom Do You Trust?

For my Father's will is that everyone who looks to the Son and believes in him shall have eternal life, and I will raise him up at the last day. John 6:40

Before I came to earth, no one had ever seen the Father or Me. While on earth, I said exactly what the Father wanted Me to say. And I did *exactly* what He wanted Me to do. That's why I told My disciples that when they saw Me, they had seen the Father. Whoever heard Me heard the Father. But before anyone could truly *believe* in Me, they had to *look* to Me. From the Samaritan woman to the thief on the cross, their faith was born when they looked to Me. Child, you look to so many others for answers, for joy, for peace, for hope, for fulfillment. Then you wonder why your faith is weak. I want you to know that the only way your faith can grow is to look to Me! Look at My life, and listen to My words every day. I am the Bread of Life, and I want you to feast on Me daily. I am the way, the truth, and the life. In Me *alone* you will find joy, peace, hope, and life that doesn't disappoint. Look to Me today.

He who has seen Me has seen the Father. John 14:9, NKJV

→→ *The Greatest Words Ever Spoken,* Belief and Faith in Christ (pp. 445–51); Eternal Life (pp. 134–42)

Whom Do You Look to?
Whom Do You Trust?

For my Father's will is that everyone who looks to the Son and believes in him shall have eternal life, and I will raise him up at the last day. John 6:40

Before you can truly believe in Me, you must first see Me—My life, My works, and My words. When you looked to Me to be your Savior, the Holy Spirit gave birth to your spirit, and you were born again. Child, I am your Savior, but I am also much more. To see all that I am, you must believe in Me. You believe in Me by obeying My words. I promised My disciples that I would reveal Myself to *everyone* who would obey My commands. Child, the more I reveal Myself to you, the greater your faith will grow. The greater your faith grows, the more you will express that faith by listening to and obeying My words. Your obedience also expresses and increases your love for the Father and Me. We will then love you in a special way and make our home with you, and I will continually reveal Myself to you.

Those who accept my commandments and obey them are the ones who love me. And because they love me, my Father will love them. And I will love them and reveal myself to each of them. John 14:21, NLT

➤➤ *The Greatest Words Ever Spoken,* Belief and Faith in Christ (pp. 445–51); Eternal Life (pp. 134–42)

Only God Can Do the Impossible

Which is easier, to say, "Your sins are forgiven you," or to say, "Rise up and walk"? But that you may know that the Son of Man has power on earth to forgive sins . . .
Luke 5:23–24, NKJV

Friends lowered a paralyzed man through a ceiling. In the room below, he lay before Me with the hope of being healed. Seeing his faith, I told him his sins were forgiven. The religious leaders were shocked and angered that I would claim I could forgive sins. Knowing their objections, I asked, "Which is easier, to say, 'Your sins are forgiven you,' or to say, 'Rise up and walk'?" Both are impossible for a human but possible for God. To show that I had the power to forgive sins, I did something they thought was equally impossible. I healed the man. Healing a person's body is infinitely easier than forgiving his or her sins. To have the authority to forgive sins, I had to live a life totally free of sin so I could become the perfect atonement. Child, I had to take on *your* sin to give you My righteousness. On the cross I had to subject Myself to all of God's holy wrath and judgment of sin. Like My announcement to the paralyzed man, My greatest announcement to *you* is this: your sins are forgiven! If this doesn't cause you to rejoice, you are closing your eyes to the greatest miracle of all time. Open your eyes and rejoice!

With man this is impossible, but with God all things are possible.
Matthew 19:26

✣ *The Greatest Words Ever Spoken,* Forgiveness (pp. 253–57)

Others Want to Weigh You Down, but I Want to Carry Your Load

And you experts in the [religious] law, woe to you, because you load people down with burdens they can hardly carry, and you yourselves will not lift one finger to help them.
Luke 11:46

It is human nature to abuse power, and the more power a person has, the more likely he is to use it to control, manipulate, and minimize others. During My time on earth, many religious leaders used man-made laws to overwhelm people with feelings of inadequacy, guilt, and hopelessness. Even worse, after they would lay heavy burdens on others, they would do *nothing* to help lighten the load. If the Father had lacked compassion—as the ancient leaders did—He would not have sent His Son to die for the sins of others. And yet that's what He did! He not only sent Me to take on your sin; He sent Me to lovingly care for you. Instead of weighing you down, I want to carry your load and lift you up. I don't want you to let others weigh you down. So when you are weary or heavily burdened, come to Me. Even now, cast the weight of your cares, all your anxiety, and all your burdens on Me. I will carry your load and will see you through.

I came that they may have life, and have it abundantly. I am the good shepherd; the good shepherd lays down His life for the sheep.
John 10:10–11, NASB

✤ *The Greatest Words Ever Spoken,* Hypocrites, Hypocrisy, and Self-Righteousness (pp. 378–83)

Even the Smallest Kindnesses Will Be Rewarded

And if you give even a cup of cold water to one of the least of my followers, you will surely be rewarded. Matthew 10:42, NLT

My whole life on earth was one of giving. But no matter how much I gave, people always wanted more. There were times when I felt totally spent—moments when I felt as if I had nothing more to give. And yet I never stopped giving—not to children, not to beggars, not to My followers, not even to the multitudes. It is My Father's nature to give, and I did *exactly* what pleased Him. My giving never depended upon a person's worthiness or response. It depended wholly on My Father's purpose and grace. Child, I have called you to be more like Me. You don't have to wait for big opportunities to give or to serve. Even the smallest kindnesses you do for the least of My followers will not go unnoticed or unrewarded. Whether you give money, time, talents, an encouraging word, or a listening ear, it will all be rewarded. Today look for little things you can do to show My love and give to those who come into your path.

But when you give to the needy, do not let your left hand know what your right hand is doing, so that your giving may be in secret. Then your Father, who sees what is done in secret, will reward you. Matthew 6:3–4

++ *The Greatest Words Ever Spoken,* The Promises of Christ (pp. 298–304); Rewards (pp. 172–75)

If You Knew the Gift of God

If you knew the gift of God, and who it is who says to you, "Give Me a drink," you would have asked Him, and He would have given you living water. John 4:10, NASB

When I met the Samaritan woman, she had no idea who I was. She didn't realize *I* was the Gift of God. In Me, she could have answers to her every question. In My words, she could hear the Father's heart perfectly expressed. And in Me, she could receive the ultimate possession—eternal life. But she did not know Me. Child, do you *really* know Me, or am I a mere acquaintance? Do you know My heart? Do you know what I love and what I detest? Do you know My words? Have they taken root in your heart and produced works of righteousness, grace, and faith? Are *My* priorities *your* priorities? The Father has given you a lifetime of blessings, but His greatest gift to you is Me. I am God's gift to *you.* To go through life without intimacy with Me is to miss the very purpose of your life. I want you to come to know Me more intimately than ever. But that can happen only as you abide in My words and obey them. That is the *only* way you can truly know the Gift of God.

Now this is eternal life: that they may know you, the only true God, and Jesus Christ, whom you have sent. John 17:3

✦ *The Greatest Words Ever Spoken,* The Claims Jesus Made About Himself (pp. 14–22); Knowing God and Knowing Christ (pp. 275–77)

I Will Come and Receive You

And if I go and prepare a place for you, I will come again and receive you to Myself; that where I am, there you may be also. John 14:3, NKJV

As the hour of My arrest drew near, My disciples were deeply troubled. They couldn't imagine their life without Me. At our last supper together, I wanted them to know My departure would *not* be the end of our relationship. I assured them I would come again and receive them to Myself and they would be with Me forever. My promise to them is My promise to you. Even though they had the advantage of being with Me physically, *you* have the greater blessing of *believing without seeing.* Following Me requires more faith on your part than it did for the first disciples. Child, such faith greatly pleases the Father. I also want you to know that the Father has set His perfect time for My return. But we must first reap the full harvest of all who are to be born again. And, dear one, I want *you* to reap the harvest with Me. Keep sowing the seeds of God's Word to those whom I bring into your path. I will come again and receive you unto Myself.

Because you have seen me, you have believed; blessed are those who have not seen and yet have believed. John 20:29

→→ *The Greatest Words Ever Spoken,* The Promises of Christ (pp. 298–304); Jesus' Death, Resurrection, and Second Coming (pp. 23–33)

A Kingdom Prepared for You

Then the King will say to those on his right, "Come, you who are blessed by my Father; take your inheritance, the kingdom prepared for you since the creation of the world." Matthew 25:34

A time is coming when everyone will come face to face with Me. Many will hear those terrible words, "I never knew you; depart from Me, you who practice lawlessness." But those who have believed in Me and followed Me will be invited into the kingdom that was prepared for them even before the world was created. As the Holy Spirit revealed to Paul, "No eye has seen, no ear has heard, and no mind has imagined what God has prepared for those who love him." You have been blessed by My Father beyond your greatest hopes and dreams. The kingdom that has been prepared for you is not yours because you have earned it. No one could do enough to earn a place in the kingdom. It is yours by inheritance—a gift from the Father when you were born again. You looked to Me for your salvation and believed on Me for redemption. You repented, and now you are building your life on the rock of hearing My words and doing them. Oh, what a Father we serve!

Therefore whoever hears these sayings of Mine, and does them, I will liken him to a wise man who built his house on the rock. Matthew 7:24, NKJV

✦ *The Greatest Words Ever Spoken,* Heaven (pp. 143–50)

A Blessing or a Curse

And anyone who welcomes a little child like this on my behalf is welcoming me. But if you cause one of these little ones who trusts in me to fall into sin, it would be better for you to have a large millstone tied around your neck and be drowned in the depths of the sea. Matthew 18:5–6, NLT

Tragically, children often are ignored, neglected, and even abused. I want you to know that children are more important to the Father than I could ever express. When little children are told the truth about the Father and Me, most come running to Us. They want to follow Me. So be an example to them of what it means to follow Me with a joyful heart. Teach them all about the Father and Me. As they see My life unfold in the Gospels, they will see the glorious works of the Father. As they hear you echo My words, they will hear the voice of the Father. When you do this, you will be blessing Me. It's also important to know that those who tear down the faith of little ones or lead them into paths of darkness will suffer consequences they can't imagine. Choose to be blessed of the Father—build and strengthen the faith of children and be their protector from the lies and temptations of the Evil One.

Beware that you don't look down on any of these little ones. For I tell you that in heaven their angels are always in the presence of my heavenly Father. Matthew 18:10, NLT

✦ *The Greatest Words Ever Spoken,* Stumbling Blocks (pp. 488–89); Children (pp. 357–59)

Loved by God,
Hated by the World

I have given them Your word; and the world has hated them because they are not of the world, just as I am not of the world. . . . Sanctify them by Your truth. Your word is truth. John 17:14, 17, NKJV

Why are some people so mean to you? The truth for most people is that until they are redeemed, they don't want to hear the truth. They don't want to know that many of the things they value most are detestable to God. People of the world are more concerned about the things that gratify their flesh than they are about things that glorify God. Child, *you* are seeing the Father and His truth. But you live in a world driven by values that are abhorrent to the Father. Is it any wonder that people whose hearts are driven by pride, greed, anger, jealousy, envy, and self-centeredness act hatefully toward My followers? And yet I want you to love your enemies and pray for those who curse and abuse you. I want your light to shine brightly in the darkness of this world. I want to live *My* life in *you*. You, My child, are one of My lights on earth.

Let your light shine before men in such a way that they may see your good works, and glorify your Father who is in heaven. Matthew 5:16, NASB

→→ *The Greatest Words Ever Spoken,* Rejection and Persecution of Christians (pp. 308–12)

Protection from the Evil One

I'm not asking you to take them out of the world, but to keep them safe from the evil one. John 17:15, NLT

The night I prayed for My disciples, I also prayed for *you*. I asked the Father to give you special protection from Satan. Satan hates the Father and Me, and he hates you because of your love for Me. He wants to prevent you from leading people out of his kingdom of darkness into My Father's kingdom of light. He wants to extinguish your light. But the Father answered My prayer. Child, I have *overcome* the devil and his kingdom. Satan does not have the power to remove you from My Father's loving hand. When I taught My first disciples to pray, I told them to ask the Father to keep them away from paths of temptation and deliver them from the Evil One. So pray as I taught My disciples to pray, not merely mouthing the words, but sincerely and thoughtfully praying each thought. My Father will answer the prayer of your heart and will lead you into paths of righteousness. He will deliver you daily from the Evil One.

Our Father in heaven, hallowed be Your name. Your kingdom come. Your will be done on earth as it is in heaven. Give us this day our daily bread. And forgive us our debts, as we forgive our debtors. And do not lead us into temptation, but deliver us from the evil one. Matthew 6:9–13, NKJV

↠ *The Greatest Words Ever Spoken*, Prayer (pp. 295–98); Satan (pp. 175–78); The World (pp. 408–9)

The Greater Love

If you love your father or mother more than you love me, you are not worthy of being mine; or if you love your son or daughter more than me, you are not worthy of being mine.
Matthew 10:37, NLT

I f you don't love Me more than you love everyone else, you are not worthy of Me. But, child, understand that when I talk about loving Me, I'm *not* talking about your feelings. You love Me in a very different way than you love others. You love *Me* by *obeying* My commands and teachings. The amazing feelings you have for your family aren't offensive to the Father or Me. We created you with a heart that could experience and express such wonderful feelings. The love I desire from you is a much greater love—one that honors the Father's words and My words by acting on them. My Father has exalted His Word even above His Name. On earth I was His Word in human form. I perfectly expressed His Word with My life. Everything I said, He commanded Me to say. When you treasure My words by obeying them, you are not only loving the Father and Me the way We desire to be loved; you are loving Us *more* than you love everyone else.

If anyone loves me, he will obey my teaching. My Father will love him, and we will come to him and make our home with him.
John 14:23

→→ *The Greatest Words Ever Spoken,* Loving Christ (p. 280)

In Me, You Have
What Others Yearned For

For I tell you the truth, many prophets and righteous men longed to see what you see but did not see it, and to hear what you hear but did not hear it. Matthew 13:17

Since the first prophecies of My coming, the prophets and the chosen of Israel yearned for My appearance on earth. They knew My coming would reveal the Father as never before. They knew My life and words would perfectly reveal the glory and truth of the Father. My dear one, what was denied to them has been provided to *you* in the record of the Gospels. In Me you can see the Father's love, mercy, grace, and righteousness. You can see His holiness, patience, truth, and justice in My dealings. You can hear His will perfectly spoken for every choice you face. Sadly, what the prophets would have given their lives to see and hear is all but ignored by most people. Child, don't be like those who give only a passing glance at My life. Fix your gaze on *Me.* Be still and listen to the Spirit whisper My words into your heart. And let this become your blessed daily routine. In Me and My words you have *real* life. You now have what the holy prophets of old longed for.

Your father Abraham rejoiced to see My day, and he saw it and was glad. . . . Most assuredly, I say to you, before Abraham was, I AM. John 8:56, 58, NKJV

→→ *The Greatest Words Ever Spoken,* The Claims Jesus Made About Himself (pp. 14–22)

Losing Your Life for Me Is the Only Way to Find It

He who finds his life will lose it, and he who loses his life for My sake will find it. Matthew 10:39, NKJV

S adly, people look for life in all the wrong places. They believe fulfillment will be found in nearly everything they pursue—relationships, wealth and possessions, and success. But after they finally get what they wanted, they discover they're still not fulfilled. Some are so dedicated to success that their work becomes their life. And though it may occupy all their time and attention, they find it doesn't satisfy their longings. People pour their hearts, minds, souls, and strength into whatever they think will provide fulfillment. At the end of their lives, they leave behind everything they spent their lives acquiring. And to the very end, they lack contentment, fulfillment, security, peace, and joy. They never gained what they craved. Child, that isn't you. *Your* life is found in *Me.* Don't be deceived into seeking life in anything that is temporary. In Me, your life is eternal. You will *never* lose the riches you find in Me. Lose yourself in Me and My words, and your life will count for eternity.

For what profit is it to a man if he gains the whole world, and loses his own soul? Or what will a man give in exchange for his soul? Matthew 16:26, NKJV

→ *The Greatest Words Ever Spoken,* Following Christ (pp. 245–53); Spiritual Priorities (pp. 328–37)

Losing Your Life for Me Is the Only Way to Find It

He who finds his life will lose it, **and he who loses his life for My sake will find it.** Matthew 10:39, NKJV

My dear one, you don't have to be like those who try to find their life in the temporary things of the world! You don't have to reach the end of your life with a soul that is empty. You have decided to follow Me. You know that I am the way, the truth, and the life. To lose your life for My sake is to make *knowing Me intimately* your priority in life. You already know that intimacy with Me comes as you abide in My words and obey them. That's how I reveal Myself to you and how the Father and I inhabit your life. As our intimacy grows, the life that will flow out of our relationship will become your source of joy. Your love of the Father will grow. The fruit you bear for the kingdom will increase—in your own life and in the lives of those around you. As you set aside your self-interest, the life you will find in its place is one that glorifies God now and for eternity. This is the only *real* life, and it is yours in Me. Not just for now, but for eternity.

In that day you will know that I am in My Father, and you in Me, and I in you. John 14:20, NASB

→ *The Greatest Words Ever Spoken,* Following Christ (pp. 245–53)

What Do You Call Me?

So why do you keep calling me "Lord, Lord!" when you don't do what I say? Luke 6:46, NLT

Among Satan's most devastating lies are those that convince people they are My followers when, in fact, they are not. They bear My name and even call Me "Lord," but they do not *do* what I have told them to do. Many don't even know what I have said. They think that because they belong to a church or call themselves Christians, they are My followers. What people think about themselves does *not* determine what they are. Many made a decision to follow Me but then went their own way. They thought the decision itself made them My followers. But what makes people My followers is that they *follow* Me—not with one decision, but with daily decisions to live according to what I have said to do. Child, I know you want to follow Me. All you need to do is *abide* in My words and act on them. As you do what I say, you will know that you are My follower. When you do what I say, you are truly making Me your Lord!

Not everyone who says to Me, "Lord, Lord," will enter the kingdom of heaven, but he who does the will of My Father who is in heaven will enter. Matthew 7:21, NASB

→→ *The Greatest Words Ever Spoken,* Following Christ (pp. 245–53); Spiritual Priorities (pp. 328–37)

The Deception of Wealth

You say, "I am rich, have become wealthy, and have need of nothing"—and do not know that you are wretched, miserable, poor, blind, and naked. Revelation 3:17, NKJV

Wealth is deceitful and can choke the life out of nearly anyone. Those who are wealthy in earthly riches are vulnerable to pride, greed, and independence from Me. In pride they can hold a false, elevated view of themselves and can view others as being less important. Instead of seeing themselves as spiritually destitute, in desperate need of My saving grace, they can view themselves as wholly self-sufficient. Child, do not be distracted or deceived by the allure of riches. Don't let them make you lukewarm in your pursuit of intimacy with Me. My Father will bestow His riches on *all* who follow Me. His riches are purity of heart, unconditional love, mercy, forgiveness, wisdom, and justice. He will give these to you without measure. He will give the riches of this world to those who use them to further His work. But the ruler of this world gives riches to the people he wants to *ensnare.* Resist Satan and his allurements and follow Me.

I counsel you to buy from Me gold refined in the fire, that you may be rich; and white garments, that you may be clothed, that the shame of your nakedness may not be revealed; and anoint your eyes with eye salve, that you may see. As many as I love, I rebuke and chasten. Therefore be zealous and repent. Revelation 3:18–19, NKJV

⤖ *The Greatest Words Ever Spoken,* Wealth and Possessions (pp. 344–47); Stewardship, Generosity (pp. 338–41)

True Riches

I know your works, tribulation, and poverty (but you are rich). Revelation 2:9, NKJV

How can people be rich when they suffer trials and tribulation and live in poverty? The answer is simple. The riches of this world are *not* the riches of My Father. His riches are peace in the midst of conflict, joy in the midst of sorrow, contentment in the midst of poverty, righteousness in the midst of evil, love in the midst of hatred, and forgiveness when a person is subjected to offense and pain. An abundance of money or possessions does *not* elevate you in God's sight. In fact, it only increases your obligation to be a generous steward of that wealth. To whom much is given, much is required. My followers in ancient Smyrna faced more adversity and suffering and lived in greater poverty than any other first-century church. And yet their love for Me and their works of righteousness were a shining example to My followers throughout Asia. Dear one, I want you to focus on spreading the Father's riches. Let His peace, joy, righteousness, love, and forgiveness reign in your heart and flow out to others. Then you will be rich in His kingdom.

You are the salt of the earth; but if the salt has become tasteless, how can it be made salty again? Matthew 5:13, NASB

➤ *The Greatest Words Ever Spoken,* Wealth and Possessions (pp. 344–47); The Mission of a Christian (pp. 281–89)

God Wants to Be Worshiped for Who He Really Is

You Samaritans worship what you do not know; we worship what we do know, for salvation is from the Jews.
John 4:22

I magine if a person thought you were someone else. When they talked about you, they would be describing a different person. Now, imagine that everyone they talked to believed their false notions about you. This happened to My Father. He has been so misrepresented through the ages that most people believe things about Him that are not true. They worship a god of their own imagining rather than God as He truly is. The Father is not an exalted being with the same attributes as a human. The only way to know who He really is and what He is really like is to know Me. Only in Me can you see the Father and His heart in a way you can understand. Only in My ways can you see His ways. Watch Me with My disciples. Watch Me with the woman at the well, the rich young ruler, even the thief on the cross. In the records of the Gospels, you will see the Father in Me. Your Father wants you to worship Him for who He really is, not for someone He is not.

God is spirit, and those who worship Him must worship in spirit and truth. John 4:24, NASB

✈ *The Greatest Words Ever Spoken*, Worship (p. 469)

Worship God the Way *He* Wants to Be Worshiped

Yet a time is coming and has now come when the true worshipers will worship the Father in spirit and truth, for they are the kind of worshipers the Father seeks. John 4:23

S ome people praise God with their lips even though their hearts are far from Him. Worshiping the Father with words while living in a way that is contrary to His desires is a hypocritical act that deeply offends Him. For instance, the woman at the well lived in sin with no desire to change, and yet she foolishly thought her worship of God was acceptable. Many worship the Father with a sincere heart in ways they think are best and yet may not be the ways He wants to be worshiped. The Father wants you to worship Him in spirit and in truth. He wants you to worship Him with your life, including your attitudes and behavior. Child, when you choose to follow Me each day, your heart is worshiping Him with works of righteousness. Then your lips will express your heart rather than contradict it. Following Me is your *spiritual* form of worship. Our dear Father also wants to be worshiped in *truth.* He wants you to know Him intimately and worship Him for who He *really* is. He is the Lord, the one who exercises loving-kindness, judgment, and righteousness on earth and delights in these.

These people honor me with their lips, but their hearts are far from me. They worship me in vain; their teachings are but rules taught by men. Matthew 15:8–9

→ *The Greatest Words Ever Spoken,* Worship (p. 469)

No Matter What They See, They Always Want More

Unless you people see signs and wonders, you will by no means believe. John 4:48, NKJV

What do *you* have to see to believe? From the beginning of My earthly ministry, people came with the hope of being healed. And for every person who wanted to be healed, many more came hoping to *witness* miracles. When they saw Me perform these miracles, some believed, but most did not. They always wanted to see even *more.* Sadly, they hungered more for miracles than they did for Me. They didn't hear the truths My Father had sent Me to proclaim. Truths that could set them free from the power and condemnation of their sins. Truths that could empower them to see the Father as He really is and show them how to love Him the way He wants to be loved. They hungered for signs and wonders but not for the One who could give them eternal life. Child, do you hunger more for signs and wonders than you do for Me? They will not satisfy the longings of your soul nor reveal the glories of your Father. They will not empower you with faith to follow Me step by step on the narrow way. My *words* are spirit and life. Only My words will satisfy your soul and empower you to abide in Me.

This evil generation keeps asking me to show them a miraculous sign. But the only sign I will give them is the sign of Jonah. Luke 11:29, NLT

↠ *The Greatest Words Ever Spoken,* Jesus' Teaching on Miracles and Signs (pp. 61–62); Signs and Miracles (pp. 323–27)

Whenever You Are Stressed, Discouraged, or Overwhelmed

And the very words I have spoken to you are spirit and life.
John 6:63, NLT

Whenever you are overwhelmed, stressed, discouraged, or in despair, your problems aren't caused by your circumstances. The problem is you are running your life without an adequate supply of food for your spirit. What you need is an infusion of "spirit and life" into your mind, heart, and soul. Child, how much time have you spent meditating on My words this week? If your answer is "little to none," then your spirit is starving. You don't need empty advice from people; you need spiritual food. I am the *only* One who can fill up your spirit. The *only* spirit-and-life food I offer are My words. You can fill your mind with knowledge and information; you can fill your heart with feelings and images; you can surround yourself with people. But the *only* way you can fill your soul with the spirit and life you need is by delighting in My words. As you feast on My words, your spirit will be nourished, and you will soar above your problems. I promise!

I am the bread of life; he who comes to Me will not hunger, and he who believes in Me will never thirst. John 6:35, NASB

✦ *The Greatest Words Ever Spoken,* Jesus' Words, Their Role and Power (pp. 62–64)

Hear My Words and Obey Them

Stand up, pick up your mat, and walk! John 5:8, NLT

Can you imagine being flat on your back in sickness and pain for thirty-eight years? That was the condition of the man at the pool of Bethesda. Knowing he had no power to get up and walk in his own strength, I commanded him to do the impossible: to stand up and walk. He faced a choice. He could ignore Me, debate Me, or obey Me. At that moment he chose to believe My words, and he made his move to obey. Strength miraculously flowed into his body, and he received all the power he needed to do the impossible. Child, you linger in your troubles so much longer than you need to. You often are overwhelmed by adversity. Your spirit is tormented by worry and fear. All because you do not dwell in My words. Without hearing My words, you have no foundation for your faith. Your faith can take a stand only when you have a word from Me to stand on. And when you have a word from Me, like this man, you have a choice. You can ignore it, debate it, or obey it. Only when you choose to obey My words can you receive the miracles I offer.

Take My yoke upon you and learn from Me. Matthew 11:29, NASB

→ *The Greatest Words Ever Spoken,* Obedience and Good Works (pp. 289–94); Signs and Miracles (pp. 323–27)

Avoid a Worse Future

Now you are well; so stop sinning, or something even worse may happen to you. John 5:14, NLT

When the man at Bethesda obeyed My words, he was miraculously healed. In a single moment he was given a brand-new life with many new paths to walk and many new temptations to face. I let him know that choosing paths of sin could result in something much worse than his former illness. Sin will *always* bring about an infection of the soul, and a soul that is sick is in much greater peril than a body that is sick. It can make you a vessel of darkness driven by self-centeredness. My dear one, *please* do not underestimate the destructiveness of sin. Your anger can destroy the spirit of another person. Your greed can infect everyone around you. Sin is like a pet snake that appears harmless but can end your life with a single strike. Like the man at Bethesda, I have given you a new life with many new paths and choices. The enemy of your soul makes sin look sweet and harmless. But every bite injects a deadly poison that can paralyze you in your walk with Me. Let My words be lights that reveal the peril of sin. Turn your feet away from sin and follow Me.

I have come into the world as a light, so that no one who believes in me should stay in darkness. John 12:46

→→ *The Greatest Words Ever Spoken*, Sin (pp. 396–99); Light Versus Darkness (pp. 384–85)

Why Some People
Don't Appreciate You

My Father is always at his work to this very day, and I, too, am working. John 5:17

I know there are times when you try so hard to make things good for others, and it seems they don't care. I know how you feel. After I healed the man at Bethesda, instead of rejoicing and glorifying God, the religious leaders wanted to kill Me. They were blinded by religious traditions. When I told them My Father and I were always working, they hated Me even more for calling God "My Father." You live in a world where people embrace the false values of the Evil One. They are blind to the Father's ways and attack those who represent Me. Don't be discouraged. You and I don't labor for the praise of others but because of our love of the Father. Know that He loves you more than you can imagine. He and I *never* cease our labors of doing good, and neither should you. Let's sow the seeds of God's Word together and reap the harvest. You have the privilege of making your remaining time on earth count for eternity.

Do you not say, "There are yet four months, and then comes the harvest"? Behold, I say to you, lift up your eyes and look on the fields, that they are white for harvest. Already he who reaps is receiving wages and is gathering fruit for life eternal; so that he who sows and he who reaps may rejoice together. John 4:35–36, NASB

⤜ *The Greatest Words Ever Spoken,* Jesus' Missions (pp. 46–51); Jesus' Relationship with God the Father (pp. 55–60)

I Did Nothing of Myself, and Neither Should You

Most assuredly, I say to you, the Son can do nothing of Himself, but what He sees the Father do; for whatever He does, the Son also does in like manner. John 5:19, NKJV

I didn't come to earth to do as I pleased. I was sent by the Father to finish His work. He was with Me every moment of My time on earth. I did *nothing* by Myself. Everything I did, I had seen the Father do. Everything I said, He commanded Me to say and how to say it. The power, confidence, and joy of doing *everything* with Him was greater than words can express. Child, if I relied on the Father moment by moment to accomplish His perfect will, why would you think *you* have to walk through your day on your own? You can do with Me what I did with the Father. You can do what you have seen Me do. Every day look at My life. Look at My interactions with others, how I cared, how I listened, what I did and said. And then let the Holy Spirit lead you in My steps. Imitate Me! Every day listen to My words. You don't have to go through a single moment alone. You don't have to overcome a single challenge on your own. I am with you! Lean on Me.

I am the vine, you are the branches; he who abides in Me and I in him, he bears much fruit, for apart from Me you can do nothing. John 15:5, NASB

⇥ *The Greatest Words Ever Spoken,* Jesus' Relationship with God the Father (pp. 55–60); Fruitbearing (pp. 257–60)

I Do Not Seek My Own Will— I Seek the Father's Will

I can do nothing on My own initiative. As I hear, I judge; and My judgment is just, because I do not seek My own will, but the will of Him who sent Me. John 5:30, NASB

In the history of humanity, I am the only son of man who has the ability to judge others with *perfect* judgment. First, I always listen to My Father before I judge. Second, I am the only One who *never* seeks My own will but *always* My Father's will. So My judgment is free of human influence. Child, before you were born again, your nature was to seek your will and reject the Father's will. But now that you have been born of the Spirit, you have the power to set aside your will and seek the Father's will. You can listen to the Spirit in every decision you make. Even though your old nature pushes you to do your will, the Spirit tells you to seek the will of the Father. As you seek the Father's will, you will begin to delight in Him. Then He will plant His desires in your heart and bring those desires to pass. But it all starts with your seeking His will. In My words you will *find* His will *every* time you seek it.

My Father is glorified by this, that you bear much fruit, and so prove to be My disciples. John 15:8, NASB

✈ *The Greatest Words Ever Spoken,* Jesus' Relationship with God the Father (pp. 55–60); God's Will (pp. 106–7); Jesus' Missions (pp. 46–51)

That You May Marvel

For the Father loves the Son, and shows Him all things that He Himself does; and He will show Him greater works than these, that you may marvel. John 5:20, NKJV

The work of creation is not God's greatest glory. He glories in Me and His work that I have finished. He delights in the lives of those whose glory is found in intimately knowing Him. The miracles I performed during My walk on earth glorified the Father. Child, I performed His works so you would marvel and understand the greatness of His power. His greatest delight was not in the miracles I performed but in My obedience. He delighted in the transformed lives of those who believed in Me, repented, and followed Me. Today He delights in you as you walk by faith and follow Me. He has given you the Holy Spirit so that you might bear all the fruit of the Spirit. My great and eternal joy is My Father's love. The more you get to know Him, the more you will experience that same love. Marvel at His miraculous work of your salvation. He is to be praised above all.

Love the Lord your God with all your heart and with all your soul and with all your mind and with all your strength. Mark 12:30

✦ *The Greatest Words Ever Spoken,* God's Works (pp. 109–10); The Claims Jesus Made About Himself (pp. 14–22)

The Life I Gave You
Won't End with Your Death

For as the Father raises the dead and gives life to them, even so the Son gives life to whom He will. John 5:21, NKJV

When I revealed that God was My Father and that He sent Me to provide His gift of eternal life, some believed and rejoiced. Others remained in their unbelief. Most of the religious leaders fumed in anger to the point of wanting Me dead. I announced the greatest news humanity will ever hear, and most people rejected it. But not *you*. Child, you have been birthed by the Holy Spirit, and I have given you eternal life. When you die, I will raise you from the dead. Rejoice in this wonderful truth. Live in the reality that your life on earth is only the beginning of your life. Realize that although the ruler of this world and his followers may take away everything in your life that is temporary, they have no power whatsoever to take away that which is most important. They cannot remove anything from you that is eternal. They can't remove you from My presence, My love, or the eternal life that I have already given you. No matter what circumstances you face today, let this truth cause you to rejoice without ceasing.

My sheep hear My voice, and I know them, and they follow Me; and I give eternal life to them, and they will never perish; and no one will snatch them out of My hand. John 10:27–28, NASB

→→ *The Greatest Words Ever Spoken,* Eternal Life (pp. 134–42); The Claims Jesus Made About Himself (pp. 14–22)

Honoring the Father
by Honoring the Son

Moreover, the Father judges no one, but has entrusted all judgment to the Son, that all may honor the Son just as they honor the Father. He who does not honor the Son does not honor the Father, who sent him. John 5:22–23

People have always held differing views of who I am. Many who claimed to be the chosen of My Father refused to listen to My testimony or accept the testimony of My works. They claimed to love the Father, yet they rejected *Me.* Nothing could be more dishonoring to the One who sent Me. Can you imagine the love of Someone who would sacrifice His only Son to atone for the sins of others? Child, there are so many who say they believe in God and yet refuse to come to Me. This is so offensive to the Father. And yet He is quick to forgive when a person later truly repents and believes in Me. Child, you honor Me when you follow Me. And when you are honoring *Me,* you are honoring the Father. You honor Me when you listen to My words, treasure them in your heart, and obey them. By doing this you are loving and honoring the Father the way He wants to be loved and honored. He deserves to be honored at all times.

Greater love has no one than this, that one lay down his life for his friends. You are My friends if you do what I command you. John 15:13–14, NASB

→ *The Greatest Words Ever Spoken,* Honoring and Exalting Christ (pp. 455–56); God's Desires (pp. 90–92); Reverence for God (pp. 110–11)

Are You Still Throwing Stones?

Let the one who has never sinned throw the first stone!
John 8:7, NLT

The Pharisees brought a woman to Me who had been caught in the act of adultery. She was humiliated and terrified. They reminded the crowd that the Law commanded that she be stoned to death, and then they asked what *I* would tell them to do. I wrote a message on the ground, which let them know that I *knew* about *their* sins. Then I announced that the one who had never sinned could throw the first stone. Realizing that I could expose each one of them, they dropped their stones and walked away. Child, I am the only One who has never sinned, the only One who has the authority to judge. You *have* sinned and have no right to judge *anyone.* I have forgiven all your sin and spared you all judgment. That is another reason you should judge no one—not in your mind, not with your behavior, and not with your words. That means *no* gossiping and *no* throwing stones. When you judge anyone, you grieve the Holy Spirit and demean My work on the cross. Take My yoke upon you and stop judging others.

Do not judge, or you too will be judged. For in the same way you judge others, you will be judged, and with the measure you use, it will be measured to you. Matthew 7:1–2

↠ *The Greatest Words Ever Spoken,* Judging Others (pp. 483–84)

Why Do You Seek Me?

Most assuredly, I say to you, you seek Me, not because you saw the signs, but because you ate of the loaves and were filled. John 6:26, NKJV

After I fed five thousand people, many followed Me to the other side of the sea. But they were seeking Me for the wrong reasons. They didn't want Me; they only wanted more food! In Me, they could have had eternal life. They could have enjoyed permanent peace that would take them through any trial, even death. Child, what do *you* want from Me? Do you merely want temporal gifts that meet your physical needs and gratify your earthly desires? Or do you want *Me*? My dear one, meeting temporal needs or desires will do nothing to fill your soul. You would still feel emptiness. I am the Bread of Life. I want an *intimate* relationship with you. I want to pour My Spirit and life into your spirit and life. You and I can have this kind of daily intimacy if you will continually live in My words. There's no other way, no shortcut. When you neglect My Word, you undermine our relationship. I'm waiting for you—right now. Abide in My Word and get to know Me!

For the bread of God is he who comes down from heaven and gives life to the world. John 6:33

→→ *The Greatest Words Ever Spoken,* Jesus' Identity (pp. 34–42); The Claims Jesus Made About Himself (pp. 14–22); Unbelief and Motives of Unbelievers (pp. 466–69)

The Work God Wants from You

This is the work of God, that you believe in Him whom He sent. John 6:29, NKJV

After I fed the five thousand and they followed Me across the sea, they still didn't get My message. Instead of wanting Me, they wanted the power to do miracles. They asked what they could do to perform the works of God. Rather than telling them how to work miracles, I gave them a much greater revelation. The greatest work of God they could ever do was to believe in Me. The power to feed thousands, heal the sick, or even raise the dead would end at death. But those who believe in Me would do the work of God that is eternal. Child, the Holy Spirit *can* perform miracles through you. But no miracle you will ever experience can compare to the work of God that you do when you truly believe in Me in your heart. For out of your heart comes all your behavior. When you believe in Me, the fruit of the Spirit will flow out of you like rivers of living water. Belief in Me is expressed by obeying My words as you walk through your day. Believing in Me every day is the greatest work of God you will do in your life!

When a man believes in me, he does not believe in me only, but in the one who sent me. When he looks at me, he sees the one who sent me. John 12:44–45

→ *The Greatest Words Ever Spoken,* Belief and Faith in Christ (pp. 445–51); God's Works (pp. 109–10)

My Message Is Not Mine

My teaching is not my own. It comes from him who sent me. If anyone chooses to do God's will, he will find out whether my teaching comes from God or whether I speak on my own. John 7:16–17

O ne of My missions on earth was to perfectly reveal the Father's message. Many people liked some parts of the message and rejected other parts. Most of the religious leaders rejected it altogether, believing that it was *My* message and not the Father's. However, anyone who wanted to do the will of God discovered that My teachings were from the Father. Most people today will decide they do *not* want the truth but instead want to be the god of their own lives. However, those who want to know and *do* the will of God recognize My message as true. Child, that is you! Rather than run away from My message, you have believed it and acted on it. As the Holy Spirit reveals how to apply My words to your daily situations, continue to follow His promptings. I know it's not easy, but you can do it by faith, sustained by My Father's grace and empowered by the Holy Spirit.

Truly, truly, I say to you, he who believes in Me, the works that I do, he will do also; and greater works than these he will do; because I go to the Father. John 14:12, NASB

→ *The Greatest Words Ever Spoken,* Jesus' Missions (pp. 46–51); Jesus' Relationship with God the Father (pp. 55–60); Belief and Faith in Christ (pp. 445–51)

Don't Worry, Even About Your Daily Needs

And who of you by being worried can add a single hour to his life? Matthew 6:27, NASB

Child, your natural response to a potential problem is to worry. And when the problem becomes reality, you worry even more. However, because you are a child of God, you don't have to let your natural reactions rule your heart, mind, or behavior. Worrying can't add even an hour to your life, but it can take years away from it. Worry can steal your joy and distract your attention away from Me. Worry focuses your attention on yourself. After I told My disciples that no one can serve two masters, I commanded them to stop worrying. I said, "Therefore I tell you, do not worry about your life, what you will eat or drink; or about your body, what you will wear." When you worry about anything, you are disobeying that command. You are also making *fear* your master rather than God. Child, as soon as you realize you are worrying, I want you to replace your worry with faith in My promises. I have promised to meet your every need if you will obey My command to seek first My Father's kingdom and His righteousness. I will not let you down.

So do not worry about tomorrow; for tomorrow will care for itself. Each day has enough trouble of its own. Matthew 6:34, NASB

✦ *The Greatest Words Ever Spoken,* Anxiety, Worry, and Fear (pp. 190–93)

How to Know If His Word Abides in You

You do not have His word abiding in you, for you do not believe Him whom He sent. John 5:38, NASB

T he religious leaders of My day thought they lived according to God's Word. But His Word was not dwelling in their hearts. If the Father's Word had been ruling their hearts, they would have believed Me. Child, I know you have wondered if *you* are abiding in My words. Answer these questions: Are you discovering new truths in My words each day? Is your faith growing to the point that you act on My words as you discover them? Are you becoming My true disciple by discovering and obeying more of My commands? Are My truths setting you free from the taskmaster of sin? (I'm not asking "Are you sinless?" but "Are you sinning less?") If you answered "yes," then you *are* abiding in My words. If you answered "somewhat" or "no," then you should make abiding in My words your new priority. My words are your source of spiritual nourishment. Abide in them and obey them, and you and your faith will grow faster than you can imagine.

If you abide in My word, you are My disciples indeed. And you shall know the truth, and the truth shall make you free.
John 8:31–32, NKJV

✈ *The Greatest Words Ever Spoken,* Abiding in the Words of Christ (pp. 186–88); Unbelief and Motives of Unbelievers (pp. 466–69)

Don't Ask "Why?" Ask "What?"

It was neither that this man sinned, nor his parents; but it was so that the works of God might be displayed in him.
John 9:3, NASB

When we came across a man who had been blind since birth, My disciples asked, "Who sinned, this man or his parents, that he was born blind?" They wrongly assumed that when bad things happen, it is always the result of someone's sin. They were surprised when I told them this man's blindness was not caused by *anyone's* sin but was part of God's plan to reveal His glorious works. Child, it is foolish to speculate about God's reasons for anything. If you are dealing with a trial, do *not* try to guess its purpose. Instead of asking *why,* ask *what*—"What do You want me to do?" Ask the Holy Spirit to show you how you should respond. Seek guidance from God's Word. Remind yourself that not even a sparrow falls to the ground without the Father's loving care and that *you* are worth much more than sparrows. The same applies when something good happens. Don't ask why He has blessed you, but ask Him what He wants you to do with that blessing.

Are not two sparrows sold for a penny? Yet not one of them will fall to the ground apart from the will of your Father. And even the very hairs of your head are all numbered. So don't be afraid; you are worth more than many sparrows. Matthew 10:29–31

↠ *The Greatest Words Ever Spoken,* God's Works (pp. 109–10); Sickness (pp. 395–96)

Breaking the Chains of Sin

Most assuredly, I say to you, whoever commits sin is a slave of sin. And a slave does not abide in the house forever, but a son abides forever. Therefore if the Son makes you free, you shall be free indeed. John 8:34–36, NKJV

All sin disguises itself as a friend, but in reality it's an enemy that will lead you into slavery and destruction. When you sin, sin becomes your cruel taskmaster. You can't simply walk away from such slavery. But, child, I came to set the captive free! *I* am the One who can break your chains, and My words are the cutting tools I use. You move yourself into position to be set free when you abide in My words. That's why I said, "If you abide in My word, you are My disciples indeed. And you shall know the truth, and the truth shall make you free." Child, if you are struggling with a continuing enslavement to sin, then you are *not* abiding in My words. You must change the residence of your heart and mind. You must begin to reside in My words and do them. My words reveal the truth about sin and the truth of the Father's will in any situation. The Holy Spirit will use My words to set you free so you can serve the one Master who loves you so.

He has sent Me to heal the brokenhearted, to proclaim liberty to the captives and recovery of sight to the blind, to set at liberty those who are oppressed. Luke 4:18, NKJV

✦ *The Greatest Words Ever Spoken,* Sin (pp. 396–99); Freedom (pp. 423–24)

Whom Do You Believe In?

Do you believe in the Son of Man? John 9:35

After I healed a man who was born blind, the Pharisees asked him what he thought about Me. He told them I was a prophet. They ridiculed and condemned him and threw him out of the synagogue. Later I asked him, "Do you believe in the Son of Man?" He asked, "Who is He, Lord, that I may believe in Him?" When I told him it was I, he confessed Me as Lord. Then he fell on his face and worshiped Me—a crime punishable by death. For the first time in his life, he had his sight. Yet he was willing to lose his life to worship Me. When he saw Me as I AM, everything else, including his sight and even his life, became insignificant by comparison. Child, I want you to know the Father and Me in this same way. I want you to see Me as this young man did. When you see Me clearly, you will see the Father. The better you come to know Me, the better you will know the Father. The Holy Spirit wants to use My life and words to make this kind of intimacy your reality and most valued treasure.

If you really knew me, you would know my Father as well. John 14:7

✈ *The Greatest Words Ever Spoken,* Belief and Faith in Christ (pp. 445–51); Healing (pp. 263–67)

I Know You by Name

The watchman opens the gate for him, and the sheep listen to his voice. He calls his own sheep by name and leads them out. John 10:3

I n the kingdom of this world, people are prisoners of self-centeredness. They are slaves bound to sin. To the Evil One, prisoners have no names. Not so in My kingdom. My dear one, you are not merely an anonymous face among the multitudes of My followers. I not only know your name, but My Father gave you your name before you were born, before He created the world! The greatest sound your ears will ever hear will be the sound of My voice calling you by name when we come face to face. But like My other sheep, during your time on earth you will know My voice by My words. As you listen to My words, you will hear My voice and recognize My heart. Child, I want to lead you steadily along the narrow way. I want to provide the light you need to follow Me safely through this dark world. Harness yourself to Me. Learn from Me. Oh, how wonderful that day will be when you hear Me call your name.

My sheep hear My voice, and I know them, and they follow Me. John 10:27, NASB

✈ *The Greatest Words Ever Spoken,* The Shepherd and His Sheep (pp. 320–23)

You Know Someone
They Don't Know

And I will pray the Father, and He will give you another Helper, that He may abide with you forever—the Spirit of truth, whom the world cannot receive, because it neither sees Him nor knows Him; but you know Him, for He dwells with you and will be in you. John 14:16–17, NKJV

When people say or do terrible things, do you wonder, *Why are they so mean? How could they be so blind? Why don't they care?* Those who are of the world can't see what you see. They can't believe what you believe. They can't feel what you feel. You, dear one, are a stranger in their world. This world does *not* have the promise of the Father. Those who are of this world do *not* know the Holy Spirit, and they don't have His fruit. They can't receive the truth He offers. They can't know, experience, or produce His fruit of selfless love, overpowering joy, storm-calming peace, unlimited patience, unconditional kindness, unrelenting goodness, persevering faithfulness, intentional gentleness, and godly self-control. But you have the Holy Spirit with you and in you. His fruit is available to you every moment. It can flow out of you whenever you yield yourself to His promptings. You have the ultimate Helper! Listen to His every whisper, His every prompting.

He will glorify Me, for He will take of Mine and will disclose it to you. John 16:14, NASB

→→ *The Greatest Words Ever Spoken,* The Holy Spirit and His Ministry (pp. 116–17)

I Loved You at Calvary

When you have lifted up the Son of Man on the cross, then you will understand that I AM he. I do nothing on my own but say only what the Father taught me. John 8:28, NLT

When was the last time your heart was with Me at Calvary? It was the hardest day of My life on earth. Thirty-nine times I felt the excruciating pain of a whip ripping the skin off My back. Later I suffered the pain of spikes being driven into My hands and feet. But that was not My greatest agony. When I saw the faces of the men, women, and children who delighted in My suffering, My heart was filled with sorrow and compassion. That's when I cried out, "Father, forgive them, for they do not know what they are doing." Child, I was praying for you too. I had never known sin, but suddenly I was *all* of *your* sin. And then came My moment of greatest anguish: for the first time in eternity, the Father separated Himself from Me. Oh, how I grieved. Then in a moment My grief turned to an inexpressible peace. It was finished. Your debt had cost Me everything, but now it was paid in full! Child, I loved you then, and I love you now!

For even the Son of Man came not to be served but to serve others and to give his life as a ransom for many. Matthew 20:28, NLT

⤙ *The Greatest Words Ever Spoken,* Jesus' Love (pp. 44–46); Jesus' Missions (pp. 46–51)

I Do Nothing on My Own

But so that the world may know that I love the Father, I do exactly as the Father commanded. John 14:31, NASB

On the cross when I cried out, "My God, My God, why have You forsaken Me?" people thought I was calling on Elijah to save Me. I was not. I had never known the horrible anguish of being separated from My Father. But when I became your sin, He could have no part of Me. As I suffered this, My greatest agony, the Holy Spirit was opening the eyes of some people at the scene. They realized that I was truly the Son of God. A thief on the cross next to Me hungered for My forgiveness and was born again. He saw Me as a King about to pass through death to enter My kingdom. Knowing that he had been born of the Spirit, I told him that he would be with Me in paradise that very day. Child, everything I did on earth, even My journey on that terrible and glorious day, I did with the Father. I did *nothing* on My own. He was always with Me. And now *I* am with *you*. I will never leave you or forsake you. I love you so!

Believe Me that I am in the Father and the Father is in Me; otherwise believe because of the works themselves. John 14:11, NASB

⇸ *The Greatest Words Ever Spoken,* Jesus' Relationship with God the Father (pp. 55–60)

The Only Way to Love and Follow Me

If you love me, obey my commandments. John 14:15, NLT

Loving Me is much less complicated than loving other people. People measure their love for others by their feelings. That type of love is erratic and can easily change with circumstances. The love I desire isn't expressed with feelings but with obedience. Sadly, many who profess to believe in Me know very little of My commands and teachings, and they do little to obey them. Child, hear My words and discover My commands. They won't weigh you down but will lift you up! Obedience isn't your enemy; it's your ally. It provides the *best* way to please the Father and express your love for Me, because it expresses your faith. Obedience to My commands keeps you securely on the narrow way and gives you the confidence of building your life on the *rock* of hearing and doing what I say. There is no other way to follow Me. My commands give you the guidance and power you need to joyfully overcome even your greatest trials. They are the yoke that allows Me to carry your burdens.

When you obey my commandments, you remain in my love, just as I obey my Father's commandments and remain in his love. I have told you these things so that you will be filled with my joy. Yes, your joy will overflow! John 15:10–11, NLT

→ *The Greatest Words Ever Spoken,* Loving Christ (p. 280); Joy (pp. 273–75); Obedience and Good Works (pp. 289–94)

Pleasing the Father

And He who sent Me is with Me. The Father has not left Me alone, for I always do those things that please Him.
John 8:29, NKJV

Everything I did during My life on earth I did with one purpose—to please My Father. If you knew the Father as I know Him, you would make *pleasing Him* the driving purpose of your life. No one knows the Father except Me and the people to whom I reveal Him. Child, I want to reveal Him to *you.* I want you to see Him as He really is—the almighty God. His sovereignty is absolute. His majesty is beyond description. His love can't be contained or measured. The hearts and minds of humans can't conceive of the purity of His holiness and righteousness. His mercies are without number, and His justice is without compromise. I was His mirror image on earth. In My actions you see the Father acting. In My words you hear *Him* speaking. Child, to please Him, all you have to do is to obey My words. Your obedience to My words will please Him beyond measure. As you do this, the Father and I will fulfill Our promise to make Our home with you.

The words I speak are not my own, but my Father who lives in me does his work through me. John 14:10, NLT

→→ *The Greatest Words Ever Spoken,* Loving Christ (p. 280); God's Will (pp. 106–7); Jesus' Relationship with God the Father (pp. 55–60)

I Am Your Only Entrance

I tell you the truth, I am the gate for the sheep. All who ever came before me were thieves and robbers, but the sheep did not listen to them. I am the gate; whoever enters through me will be saved. John 10:7–9

I am the one and only entrance into the safe place for My sheep. Only in Me can they find security, joy, peace, and truth. Only in Me can *all* of their souls' longings be satisfied. Others use charm, false promises, and worldly allurements to entice people to follow them. Their ways seem right, but they end in death. Only in knowing Me can a person gain eternal life. Many would like you to believe that there is no gate and that heaven is open to all. But that is a lie. *I* am the gate for the sheep, and all who enter through Me will be saved. There is no other gate; there is no other way. There is safety and security in no other. When you feel vulnerable or insecure, it is because you have strayed from the safety of the sheepfold. You have lost sight of your Shepherd. Child, I am right here for you and for everyone who will hear My voice and believe Me. Follow Me now, and I will lead you safely through this day and every day to come.

I am the way and the truth and the life. No one comes to the Father except through me. John 14:6

→→ *The Greatest Words Ever Spoken,* The Shepherd and His Sheep (pp. 320–23); Eternal Life (pp. 134–42); The Narrow Way Versus the Broad Way (pp. 170–71)

Many Will Never Believe, Regardless of Proof

I did tell you, but you do not believe. The miracles I do in my Father's name speak for me, but you do not believe because you are not my sheep. John 10:25–26

I know you get discouraged when so many people refuse to listen to your message about Me. No matter what you say or do, they simply won't believe. Child, it has nothing to do with you or the truthfulness of your message. During My ministry on earth, most people would not believe even though I performed miracles. I cast out demons, healed the sick, gave sight to the blind, and even raised people from the dead. Even though the multitudes were amazed, their hearts were not converted. They would not believe because they weren't My sheep. My sheep *will* hear My voice, and they *will* come to Me. Continue to be My witness by doing your works of righteousness and by sowing My words to those around you. Many will debate My words and ignore the light of your life. But My sheep will hear My voice in you, they will see the light of your life, and they will come to Me. Never forget the worth of just *one* soul. After all, I left the ninety-nine to rescue you.

You did not choose Me but I chose you, and appointed you that you would go and bear fruit, and that your fruit would remain. John 15:16, NASB

⊹ *The Greatest Words Ever Spoken,* Unbelief and Motives of Unbelievers (pp. 466–69)

My Father Has a Purpose, Even If You Can't See It

Lazarus's sickness will not end in death. No, it happened for the glory of God so that the Son of God will receive glory from this. John 11:4, NLT

L azarus's sisters sent a messenger to urge Me to come to their home and heal Lazarus. I told My disciples that his sickness would not *end* in death but that it had a different purpose—to glorify the Father and Me. Two days later Lazarus was dead. It was time to go to his home. My disciples thought it was too late. They also were concerned about My safety, thinking that returning to Judea would put My life in danger. But they were wrong. God's complete purposes cannot be determined or explained through human reasoning. They are known only to the Father, the Holy Spirit, and Me. Child, you simply need to know that the Father never does anything without purpose and that His purposes *always* are right and perfect. No matter what you are going through, you never need to ask *why*. You only need to ask *what*—what does the Father want you to do? In My Word I have provided the answer to your every question.

As it is written in the Scriptures, "They will all be taught by God." Everyone who listens to the Father and learns from him comes to me. John 6:45, NLT

→ *The Greatest Words Ever Spoken,* God's Glory (p. 97); Honoring and Glorifying Christ (pp. 267–70)

Don't Try to Redirect God's Will

Lazarus's sickness will not end in death. No, it happened for the glory of God so that the Son of God will receive glory from this. John 11:4, NLT

As I approached Lazarus's home, Martha said, "Lord, if You had been here, my brother would not have died." She assumed that *her* will was My Father's will. She wanted her brother healed, and she assumed if I had gotten there in time, I would have healed him. She was wrong. Our purpose was greater than just restoring Lazarus's health. Martha also assumed that My late arrival had defeated God's will, to save her brother. My late arrival did not defeat God's will; it was the means by which His *perfect* will would be accomplished. His will wasn't about restoring Lazarus's health; it was about glorifying Me. For that glory to be revealed, Lazarus had to die. God's will blessed Mary and Martha in a way far greater than they had conceived. Child, there is nothing wrong with your asking God for your will to be done. But know that the Father and I love you so much that We often have an even better plan. Our will is about more than your temporary circumstances; it's about eternity. Trust Us.

If you then, being evil, know how to give good gifts to your children, how much more will your Father who is in heaven give what is good to those who ask Him! Matthew 7:11, NASB

✦ *The Greatest Words Ever Spoken,* God's Glory (p. 97); Honoring and Glorifying Christ (pp. 267–70)

Will You Love Me Today?

If anyone loves me, he will obey my teaching. My Father will love him, and we will come to him and make our home with him. He who does not love me will not obey my teaching. John 14:23–24

M y followers follow Me by obeying My commands. Obedience is also how My followers become My disciples. Teaching others to obey My commands is how My disciples make disciples of others. Obeying My teachings is how My true followers build their lives on rock instead of sand. Obeying My words is what distinguishes those who truly know Me from those who think they do but don't. And most important, obeying My commands and teachings is how My followers love the Father and Me. People who say they love Me but are apathetic toward My commands only deceive themselves. Child, to obey My commands you must *know* them. They are all contained in My words. Do you meditate on My words daily? Are you discovering My commands and keeping them? My commands not only reveal the Father's will, but they also empower you with the grace you need to *do* His will. Obeying My words is your gateway to intimacy with the Father and Me. Don't let anything keep you from My words.

I have revealed you to those whom you gave me out of the world. They were yours; you gave them to me and they have obeyed your word. John 17:6

✦ *The Greatest Words Ever Spoken,* Loving Christ (p. 280); Commands of Christ (pp. 206–17)

Look at What the Father and I Do for Those Who Love Us

Those who accept my commandments and obey them are the ones who love me. And because they love me, my Father will love them. And I will love them and reveal myself to each of them. . . . All who love me will do what I say. My Father will love them, and we will come and make our home with each of them. John 14:21, 23, NLT

Child, when you obey My commands, you are loving the Father and Me the way *We* want to be loved. When you do this, My Father and I will love you in a very special way. I will reveal Myself to you, and you and I will grow into a greater intimacy. You will see life the way *I* see it. You will see Me as I really am and the Father as He really is. Most important, when you love the Father and Me by obeying My commands, My Father and I will make Our home with you. You will experience Our moment-by-moment presence like never before. I make these promises *only* to those who obey My teachings. I'm not saying that you must obey them perfectly, but your life's direction should be determined by daily discovering and obeying My words.

All things have been handed over to Me by My Father; and no one knows the Son except the Father; nor does anyone know the Father except the Son, and anyone to whom the Son wills to reveal Him. Matthew 11:27, NASB

✈ *The Greatest Words Ever Spoken,* The Promises of Christ (pp. 298–304); Jesus' Love (pp. 44–46)

Do You Really Want to Be Angry?

You have heard that it was said to the people long ago, "Do not murder, and anyone who murders will be subject to judgment." But I tell you that anyone who is angry with his brother will be subject to judgment. Matthew 5:21–22

How merciful is the Father? He has chosen to spare you from the judgment and punishment you deserve. He has chosen to respond to your sin with mercy rather than anger. Instead of executing His judgment and punishment on you, He sent Me to the cross in your place. Knowing that He has shown so much mercy toward you, can you understand why your anger against others is so offensive to Him? The spirit of anger is the spirit of murder. Though it may not seem that serious to you, it *is* that serious to Him. The next time anger wells up inside you, listen to the Holy Spirit. He may whisper, "You are grieving the Father. You're trampling His grace and mercy. You are acting in the spirit of murder." Stop your anger dead in its tracks by meditating on the Word. Listen to the Holy Spirit recount the Father's mercies toward you. At that moment repent, turn around in your heart, and follow Me.

If another believer sins against you, go privately and point out the offense. If the other person listens and confesses it, you have won that person back. Matthew 18:15, NLT

↦ *The Greatest Words Ever Spoken,* Anger (p. 474); Reconciliation Between People (pp. 307–8); The Judgment (pp. 150–60)

You Can Have This Same "Great Faith"

I tell you the truth, I have not found anyone in Israel with such great faith. Matthew 8:10

During My earthly ministry, thousands of people came to be healed. All these people believed that if they could get near Me, they could *see* a miraculous healing. Yet one man, a Roman commander, came with a faith that was the greatest I had ever seen. He pleaded with Me to heal his servant who was at his home, paralyzed and in great pain. But when I offered to go to his home, he told Me that he was unworthy to have Me go there. He said all he needed from Me was a word. He believed that My authority was not bound by time or space. He was right. I spoke the word, and his servant, who was miles away, was instantly healed. Child, like that Roman commander, you do not need Me to be physically present to exercise your faith. You only need a word! Once you have a word from Me, you can rest on it and you can act on it. If you will trust My promises and commands and act on them, you, too, will have great faith. I promise!

All authority has been given to Me in heaven and on earth.
Matthew 28:18, NASB

✦ *The Greatest Words Ever Spoken,* Belief and Faith in Christ (pp. 445–51); The Promises of Christ (pp. 298–304); Commands of Christ (pp. 206–17)

Oh, How the Father Loves You

For the Father himself loves you dearly because you love me and believe that I came from God. John 16:27, NLT

The Father shows His love for humanity in countless ways. He causes the sun to shine and the rain to fall on both the righteous and the unrighteous. He exercises loving-kindness, righteousness, and justice throughout the earth. But He loves one group of people in a special way—a way that brings them into a level of intimacy that is not offered to others. This kind of intimacy-creating love is reserved for those who love Me and believe that I came from Him. I'm not talking about those whose belief is merely an acknowledgment of My divinity. I'm talking about true belief—that which flows from the heart and is expressed by a life of following Me. I'm not talking about a love that is merely expressed by an emotion but a love that is expressed by hearing My words and doing them. Child, this is *not* a love that you can earn. It is a love that comes from the Father. It produces in you a desire to follow Me. You already are the recipient of this special, never-ending love. Oh, what a Father!

For God so loved the world, that He gave His only begotten Son, that whoever believes in Him shall not perish, but have eternal life. John 3:16, NASB

✦ *The Greatest Words Ever Spoken,* God's Love (pp. 99–101)

I Have Demonstrated the Father's Love for You

Greater love has no one than this, than to lay down one's life for his friends. You are My friends if you do whatever I command you. John 15:13–14, NKJV

Child, what would your friends do for you? Would they live their lives for your benefit? Would they give up everything they own to give you what you need? Would they say good-bye to the life they loved and die for you? I have done all this and more for you. I left My throne and became a helpless baby in a manger. Every day I faced the same temptations you have faced, but I never yielded to a single temptation. Had I fallen to even one wrong thought, I could not have been the perfect sacrifice for your sin. I had to perfectly fulfill My Father's will every single moment I was awake. The truth is, I not only laid down My life for you at Calvary, but I laid down My life for you every moment that I walked on earth. And when it came time to present Myself to be a slain sacrifice for you, I didn't hold back. *That* is how much I loved you then; that is how much I love you today. Will *you* be My friend? Will you do what I command?

For I have come down from heaven, not to do My own will, but the will of Him who sent Me. John 6:38, NASB

→→ *The Greatest Words Ever Spoken,* Jesus' Love (pp. 44–46); God's Love (pp. 99–101)

Feast on Me

This is the bread which came down from heaven—not as your fathers ate the manna, and are dead. He who eats this bread will live forever. John 6:58, NKJV

When I came to earth, My Father's Word became flesh. The life I lived and the words I spoke were perfect expressions of the Father's glorious Word. Although many listened, only a few hungered for Me. Unlike the multitudes they wanted to hear My words and intimately know Me. When I was with Mary, her focus was entirely on Me and My words, but her sister, Martha, was focused solely on her tasks. Another time, the woman who washed My feet with her tears was feasting on Me, but My host, a Pharisee, wrongly judged My every action. Child, I am the Bread of Life. There is no true life apart from Me. When you are feasting on My words and experiencing My presence, My life will flow into you. Start your day with Me in My words. Think on Me, My life, and My words throughout your day and into your night. Not only will you live forever, but you will truly live right now on earth. Eternal life doesn't begin when you die; it is experienced every day that you feast on Me.

As the living Father sent Me, and I live because of the Father, so he who feeds on Me will live because of Me. John 6:57, NKJV

⤜ *The Greatest Words Ever Spoken,* The Claims Jesus Made About Himself (pp. 14–22); Heaven (pp. 143–50)

Your Sorrow Will Be Turned to Joy

Most assuredly, I say to you that you will weep and lament, but the world will rejoice; and you will be sorrowful, but your sorrow will be turned into joy. John 16:20, NKJV

On the night of My arrest, I took a few minutes to try to prepare My disciples for what would soon be happening. I knew that My arrest and crucifixion would cause them to experience the most painful sorrow of their lives. I knew that their sorrow would be made worse as they would see people cheering My death. However, I wanted them to know that their terrible sorrow would be turned to joy by My resurrection—a joy that would last for the rest of their lives. Child, I know you, too, experience great sorrows. But I want you to know that if you turn your eyes and heart to all that you have in Me, your sorrow will be replaced with a joy that never can be taken away. When you remain in sorrow, you are choosing to ignore the incomparable, eternal realities that are yours. Turn around and run to Me! Open your eyes to My words, and receive their spirit and life!

Therefore you now have sorrow; but I will see you again and your heart will rejoice, and your joy no one will take from you.
John 16:22, NKJV

✈ *The Greatest Words Ever Spoken,* Joy (pp. 273–75)

Greater Joy Awaits
Than Any You Have Known

It will be like a woman suffering the pains of labor. When her child is born, her anguish gives way to joy because she has brought a new baby into the world. John 16:21, NLT

Some sorrows are so great that even My most committed followers nearly drown in them. This is *not* what My Father desires. Child, your sorrows can divert your path and purpose. When you can't let go of sorrow, you are fixing your gaze on that which is temporary. The pains of childbirth are real, but as soon as a mother holds the newborn baby, the pain is replaced with joy. She would never set the baby aside and spend weeks or months focusing on her former labor pains. My dear one, I want you to know that you have callings and purposes that are eternal. What you have in Me is infinitely greater than any temporary loss you might experience. Don't let sorrow prevent you from laboring in My Father's vineyard. You are so important to Our mission. Fix the gaze of your heart on Me!

So you have sorrow now, but I will see you again; then you will rejoice, and no one can rob you of that joy. John 16:22, NLT

→ *The Greatest Words Ever Spoken,* Spiritual Priorities (pp. 328–37); The Promises of Christ (pp. 298–304); Knowing God and Knowing Christ (pp. 275–77); Gratitude (pp. 262–63)

What Keeps You from Bearing Much Fruit?

I am the true vine, and My Father is the vinedresser. Every branch in Me that does not bear fruit, He takes away; and every branch that bears fruit, He prunes it so that it may bear more fruit. John 15:1–2, NASB

K nowing that the Father wants you to bear much fruit, what prevents you from doing so? Bearing much fruit depends on two things—your abiding in Me and My abiding in you. The fruit of the Spirit is unconditional love, joy, peace, patience, kindness, goodness, faithfulness, gentleness, and self-control. When you abide in Me and I abide in you, you will experience these qualities flowing into you and out of you to others. You abide in Me when *you* obey My commands. Whatever keeps you from abiding in My words and doing them keeps you from bearing much fruit. But when you spend more time in My words and act on them, the Holy Spirit will produce His fruit in abundance. Don't let laziness, pride, or self-centeredness keep you from dwelling in My words and doing them.

I am the vine, you are the branches; he who abides in Me and I in him, he bears much fruit, for apart from Me you can do nothing. John 15:5, NASB

→→ *The Greatest Words Ever Spoken,* Fruitbearing (pp. 257–60); The Holy Spirit and His Ministry (pp. 116–17)

Good Gifts from the Father

You parents—if your children ask for a loaf of bread, do you give them a stone instead? Or if they ask for a fish, do you give them a snake? Of course not! Matthew 7:9–10, NLT

Your heavenly Father wants you to know Him as He really is. He has made His attributes visible in Me and My life, and He has revealed them in His Word. Through the prophet He said, "But let him who glories glory in this, that he understands and knows Me, that I am the LORD, exercising lovingkindness, judgment, and righteousness in the earth. For in these I delight." You know how much you love to give good gifts to those you love. In the same way your heavenly Father loves to give good gifts to His children who ask Him. Does that mean He'll give you whatever you ask for? Of course not. Many of the things you request are not truly good for you. He will withhold them because of His great love for you. But you should know that He is never offended by your requests, no matter how immature or foolish they may be. When you share your heart with Him, He listens, and that is when He can share *His* heart with you.

So if you sinful people know how to give good gifts to your children, how much more will your heavenly Father give good gifts to those who ask him. Matthew 7:11, NLT

✦ *The Greatest Words Ever Spoken,* Prayer (pp. 295–98); God's Goodness (pp. 97–99)

We Are Waiting for You

Ask, and it will be given to you; seek, and you will find; knock, and it will be opened to you. Matthew 7:7, NKJV

As a child, how many times were you afraid to ask your parents for something you really wanted? How many times were you afraid to ask a teacher a question because you didn't want to look foolish? And how many times were you afraid to attempt something new because you didn't want to fail? Child, don't let fears like these creep into your relationship with the Father and Me. We want you to feel safe with Us. How would you feel if *your* children were afraid to ask you for the things they wanted, or didn't ask you questions for fear they might look stupid, or didn't try new things because they didn't want to let you down? The Father and I have proved Our love for you. There are so many things you haven't received because you haven't asked. There are so many things you haven't found because you didn't seek them. And there are so many opportunities you have missed because you wouldn't approach a closed door. Child, go ahead and ask, seek, and knock. We want a loving, intimate relationship with you, just as you want that with your children. Listen to My words and do them.

For everyone who asks receives, and he who seeks finds, and to him who knocks it will be opened. Matthew 7:8, NKJV

→ *The Greatest Words Ever Spoken*, Prayer (pp. 295–98); The Promises of Christ (pp. 298–304)

Following Me
Has No Comfort Zone

Foxes have holes and birds of the air have nests, but the Son of Man has nowhere to lay His head. Matthew 8:20, NKJV

After seeing Me perform a number of miracles, a scribe said, "Teacher, I will follow You wherever You go." I told him I didn't even have a place to sleep. He understood what I was saying— that to follow Me, he would have to be willing to abandon all the comforts and security he was accustomed to. Following Me could cost him everything he valued: his stature, reputation, worldly treasures, and comforts. Sadly, he walked away. He wanted to follow Me but only on *his* terms. Child, if you want to follow Me, it can be done only on My Father's terms. Following Me today offers none of this world's comforts or security. It still requires an *unconditional* surrender of your will to Mine. You must set aside your own rights and desires and take up your cross daily. But in place of earthly comforts and security, you will gain the comfort of the Holy Spirit and the eternal security of knowing Me. In following Me, you trade treasures on earth that you cannot keep for treasures in heaven that you will never lose.

But store up for yourselves treasures in heaven, where neither moth nor rust destroys, and where thieves do not break in or steal. Matthew 6:20, NASB

✦ *The Greatest Words Ever Spoken,* Following Christ (pp. 245–53)

When Storms Overwhelm You, There Are Two Choices

You of little faith, why are you so afraid? Matthew 8:26

During My ministry on earth, My disciples' faith was inconsistent. For example, they left everything they valued to follow Me. They continued to follow Me throughout My ministry. In that, their faith was great. In other areas, however, their faith was small to nonexistent. One night when a violent storm arose on the lake, they were terrified. They shouted, "Lord, save us! We're going to drown!" They were overcome by terror and showed they lacked faith in My sovereignty and power. True faith would have given them all the peace they needed, even when the boat was taking on water. They could have rested, knowing they were safe in My presence. Whenever you are in the midst of a great storm and feel powerless, you have a choice. You can worry and panic or trust in My presence, My words, and My authority to perform My perfect will in your life. You can fear or you can trust. Fear brings loss; trust brings life. If you rely on Me and act on My words, I promise that nothing will remove you from My love and My eternal purposes for your life. I love you and will never leave you or forsake you.

Do not be afraid any longer, only believe. Mark 5:36, NASB

✦ *The Greatest Words Ever Spoken,* Anxiety, Worry, and Fear (pp. 190–93); Belief and Faith in Christ (pp. 445–51)

Do They Really Want the Truth?

I was born and came into the world to testify to the truth.
All who love the truth recognize that what I say is true.
John 18:37, NLT

Nearly everyone says they want to know the truth. Most also say they live according to the truths they know. But most people *don't* want to know the truth or live by it. They simply want to embrace values that justify their sinful behavior. On the other hand, everyone who really *does* love the truth will recognize that what I said is true. Still, many people embrace My words in their minds but not in their hearts. They view My words as ideals to be respected, but they don't commit themselves to following My teachings and commands. Child, that is not you. I know you want to know My truth, not just to consider it but to *do* it! I know you want My truth to dwell in your heart and produce the fruit that your heavenly Father desires—a life that reflects His righteousness, loving-kindness, mercy, forgiveness, and justice. I know you want to follow Me by discovering and doing what I say. And you want to please and glorify the Father with your faith. You know that I am *the* truth, and in knowing Me, the truth will dwell in your heart.

But when He, the Spirit of truth, comes, He will guide you into all the truth. John 16:13, NASB

➤➤ *The Greatest Words Ever Spoken,* Jesus' Missions (pp. 46–51); Jesus' Words, Their Role and Power (pp. 62–64)

Ultimate Authority and Power

You would have no power over me if it were not given to you from above. John 19:11

When Pilate was questioning Me, My silence upset him. He said, "Don't you realize that I have the power to release you or crucify you?" He was wrong! He thought My life was in his hands, but, in truth, his authority was under My Father's authority. My Father had complete control over what was about to happen. When I told this to Pilate, he recognized My innocence and *knew* I was telling the truth. He became desperate to release Me but gave in to the demands of the crowd. He still didn't realize that My sacrifice was not merely a miscarriage of justice but was, in fact, the Father's perfect plan for the atonement of sin. Child, nothing takes the Father by surprise. Though evil may flourish, its seeming victories are only temporary. The Father will overturn all of Satan's work. The Father's eternal victory has already been won. His victory was completed at Calvary. He even uses the seeming victories of Satan to bring about greater victories and His perfect will. Everything in this world will pass away, but the Father's plan for you, My dear child, is eternal. His sovereignty and power reign supreme. Nothing can stay His hand! Your future is secure!

Are not two sparrows sold for a penny? Yet not one of them will fall to the ground apart from the will of your Father. Matthew 10:29

↠ *The Greatest Words Ever Spoken*, God's Sovereignty (pp. 103–5); Security (p. 315)

The Rule for Fasting

And when you fast, don't make it obvious, as the hypocrites do, for they try to look miserable and disheveled so people will admire them for their fasting. I tell you the truth, that is the only reward they will ever get. Matthew 6:16, NLT

The Pharisees were highly religious people and habitual hypocrites. They desperately sought the praise and admiration of other people and had *no* desire for the praise of God. Pride and self-centeredness fed their behavior, which was detestable to the Father. Even their fasting and praying were done to gain the attention of others. But Pharisees aren't the only ones driven by self-centeredness, pride, and a desire to be praised and admired. Such drives are natural to everyone. But My followers are to deny them rather than nurture them. You are a new creation in Me. Let the Holy Spirit replace the fruit of the flesh with the fruit of the Spirit. If you will abide in My words, these drives will lose their grip, and My Father will plant *His* desires and values in your heart. In every area of your life, follow My example and My teaching. Pray and fast in secret, seeking only the presence and praise of the Father.

But when you fast, comb your hair and wash your face. Then no one will notice that you are fasting, except your Father, who knows what you do in private. And your Father, who sees everything, will reward you. Matthew 6:17–18, NLT

✦ *The Greatest Words Ever Spoken,* Fasting (p. 243); Pharisees (pp. 387–89)

Treasure and Protect
That Which Is Holy

Do not give what is holy to dogs, and do not throw your pearls before swine, or they will trample them under their feet, and turn and tear you to pieces. Matthew 7:6, NASB

I have called you to be My witness with your words and your life. I want you to be a beacon of truth so those who desire the truth will be able to find it in you. The more you abide in My words and act on them, the more I will reveal Myself to you. And the more I reveal Myself to you, the greater your intimacy will be with the Father and Me. As our intimacy grows, you will experience the fruits of holiness, which are inherent in Me. Child, the things that are holy are meant to set you apart for the Father's special use. And because they are holy, they are *not* to be carelessly shared with people who do not respect holiness in others and have no interest in hearing about them. God does not reveal His heart or His truths to everyone. He does not delight in those who mock Him and His truths. Child, through your faith in Me, you have been made holy. I took on your sin so you could take on My righteousness and continually cleanse your mind with My Word.

For everyone who does evil hates the Light, and does not come to the Light for fear that his deeds will be exposed. John 3:20, NASB

↠ *The Greatest Words Ever Spoken,* Evangelism (pp. 227–29); The Wicked (pp. 404–6)

How Would You Want to Be Treated?

So in everything, do to others what you would have them do to you, for this sums up the Law and the Prophets.
Matthew 7:12

How do you want others to treat you? Do you want to be criticized and yelled at? Do you want to be gossiped about? Or do you want to be valued and listened to? Do you want others not to judge or condemn you? Do you want them to show you patience? Do you want them to love you unconditionally? Do you want them to be quick to forgive you? Do you want people to honor you rather than belittle you? And finally, who are the people you want to treat you this way? Your parents, brothers and sisters, children, and friends? How about bosses and coworkers? The truth is, you wish that *everyone* would treat you with honor and kindness. Well, child, I want you to treat everyone who enters your life the exact way you want them to treat you. Do this in *everything*. For My followers this is not an option. Doing this will help make you a mirror of My Father's love. You will be loving Me the way I want to be loved, and you will glorify the Father.

And the second is like it: "Love your neighbor as yourself."
Matthew 22:39

→→ *The Greatest Words Ever Spoken,* Desires (pp. 218–19); Conflict (pp. 477–80); Commands of Christ (pp. 206–17)

Power Instead of Deliverance

> My grace is sufficient for you, for my power is made perfect in weakness. 2 Corinthians 12:9

How often have you had a problem so distracting or overwhelming that you prayed the problem would be removed? All My followers have been in that situation many times. Even My apostles pleaded with Me to remove some of their greatest irritations and adversities. There is nothing wrong with making such pleas. My hand is mighty to deliver, and I receive great glory in delivering My followers from adversity. But, child, sometimes deliverance is not what you need. When the Father allows adversity to come into your life, it *always* has a purpose. One purpose is to reveal your weaknesses and to teach you to rely on Me for *My* strength. When you are powerless to overcome an adversity, that is when the power of My love and grace can be perfected in you. What are your weaknesses? Do you lack patience? Strength? Peace? Perseverance? Faith? Love? Mercy? Forgiveness? These heavenly treasures often are *best* developed through adversity. And gaining these eternal treasures is far more important than being delivered from the adversity that helps to perfect you. I have an abundant supply of everything you need. Learn from Me. Lean on Me. Rely on Me. Trust Me. I love you!

Don't let your hearts be troubled. Trust in God, and trust also in me. John 14:1, NLT

→ *The Greatest Words Ever Spoken,* Grace and Mercy (pp. 424–27); God's Sovereignty (pp. 103–5)

How to Stay Centered in My Love

As the Father has loved me, so have I loved you. Now remain in my love. If you obey my commands, you will remain in my love, just as I have obeyed my Father's commands and remain in his love. John 15:9–10

Running a few steps through the rain will not clean dirt from your skin. But remain in the rain for a day, and you will be thoroughly cleansed. Child, I want to shower My love on you, but sometimes you spend so little time in My words that you barely get wet. For Me to truly shower you in My love, you must remain in the place where the water is flowing. That place is found whenever you do with Me what *I* did with My Father. I kept His commands, and *that* kept Me centered in His love. By discovering and keeping My commands, *you* will remain centered in *My* love. My commands will lift you up. They will reveal My Father's will for every situation you encounter, and the Holy Spirit will empower you with the grace and faith you need to *do* His will. But none of this will happen if you don't consistently abide in My words. In My words you will find the answer to every important question, the solution for every problem, and the perfect guidance through every storm.

These things I have spoken to you so that My joy may be in you, and that your joy may be made full. John 15:11, NASB

✦ *The Greatest Words Ever Spoken,* Loving Christ (p. 280); Jesus' Words, Their Role and Power (pp. 62–64)

Some Will Run to You, and Many Will Run Away

For everyone practicing evil hates the light and does not come to the light, lest his deeds should be exposed. But he who does the truth comes to the light, that his deeds may be clearly seen, that they have been done in God.

John 3:20–21, NKJV

The more you become like Me, the more you will experience with other people what I experienced. Some will want to be close to you, and many will run away from you. They may be comfortable when you *don't* talk about Me or the Father. But when you do, they will want to get away from you. Child, it's not *you* they are walking away from. They are running from Me. They love the world, and they love being the god of their own lives. Many practice the deeds of darkness and don't want to be exposed by the light of My truth. But don't be discouraged. Others—those who desire and practice the truth—will be attracted to the light they see in you. As you share My Gospel, the Holy Spirit will open their eyes and give birth to their spirits. Child, they need to see the example of your life—the light of your works of righteousness. They need to hear My words from your lips. Let your light shine! This is one of your glorious callings.

What I tell you in the darkness, speak in the light; and what you hear whispered in your ear, proclaim upon the housetops.

Matthew 10:27, NASB

→→ *The Greatest Words Ever Spoken,* Rejecting Christ (pp. 459–61); Light Versus Darkness (pp. 384–85)

A Glorious Truth to Know and Believe

On that day you will realize that I am in my Father, and you are in me, and I am in you. John 14:20

At our last supper together, I revealed a glorious truth to My disciples. Later, when they finally understood it and believed it, this truth radically changed their lives. Here it is: When people heard Me speak, they *really* were hearing the Father. When they saw My life and works, they *really* were seeing the Father and His works. The Father was in Me, and I was in Him. We were unified in a way that the world could not comprehend. My own disciples had trouble understanding it. But after My resurrection, they realized that I was in the Father, they were in Me, and I was in them. They knew it, believed it, and acted on it. Child, I want you to know that *you* are in Me and *I* am in you. You and I can be as unified and as intimate as I was with My first disciples. I want you to believe this truth and act on it. Let My words and My life dwell in your heart and guide your behavior. If you will do this, *nothing* will be impossible for you.

Truly, truly, I say to you, he who believes in Me, the works that I do, he will do also; and greater works than these he will do; because I go to the Father. John 14:12, NASB

※ *The Greatest Words Ever Spoken,* Christ Living in the Believer (pp. 202–3); The Promises of Christ (pp. 298–304); Abiding in the Words of Christ (pp. 186–88)

The Joy of Seeking the Father's Will

For I have come down from heaven not to do my will but to do the will of him who sent me. John 6:38

How could I have great joy in the midst of great adversity— even when people hated Me and wanted to kill Me? The answer is, My heart and mind were focused on the Father and doing His will instead of Mine. Because My joy was rooted in intimately knowing the Father and doing His will, it was not influenced by circumstances or the actions of other people. Child, you, too, can experience this joy. It is *always* available to you when you set the focus of your mind and heart on doing the Father's will and putting aside *your* will. Because you have My words to reveal the Father's will perfectly, you can know His will and act on it at any time. When you act on My words, the Holy Spirit will give you the grace, power, and faith to do *exactly* what pleases the Father. Doing His will produces a joy that no one can take from you. It's a joy that is centered in His eternal purposes. When you lack joy, realize that it is because your focus has been diverted away from seeking and doing His will.

My food is to do the will of Him who sent Me and to accomplish His work. John 4:34, NASB

↠ *The Greatest Words Ever Spoken,* Jesus' Missions (pp. 46–51); God's Will (pp. 106–7)

Whose Approval Do You Seek?

How can you believe if you accept praise from one another, yet make no effort to obtain the praise that comes from the only God? John 5:44

The Pharisees sought the approval and admiration of others rather than the approval and praise of God. This kept them from believing in Me. Even though human praise is temporary and truly insignificant, it gratifies a person's mind and emotions. God's honor and praise, though eternal, do not produce the same emotional satisfaction. So people naturally seek the praise of others more than the praise of God. But as natural as this is, it belittles the Father and prevents people from truly believing in Me. How about you? In what ways do *you* seek the honor and praise of others? Child, you don't have to be a slave to your old nature. You are a new creature in Me. With your eyes of faith, you can see the Father and Me in ways that people from the world can't. Instead of trying to gain the praise of others, keep your focus continually on Me and on doing the things that please the Father. When you make hearing and doing My words your daily priority, the Father will be glorified, and *you* will receive *His* honor.

For they loved the approval of men rather than the approval of God. John 12:43, NASB

✦ *The Greatest Words Ever Spoken*, Praise (pp. 294–95)

Seeing Is Not Believing

But you haven't believed in me even though you have seen me. John 6:36, NLT

In My day people said they would believe if they could see Me perform more signs and wonders. But for most people, no matter how many miracles they saw, they still would not believe. They kept living the same way they had lived before they saw Me. Today many people say similar things. "If only I could see Jesus, then I would believe." Or "If only He would show me a miracle." Or "If only He would answer my prayer, then I would believe." The truth is, people want to be the rulers of their own lives and continue to do what *they* want to do. Child, don't fall into this trap of unbelief. I have already done *everything* that needs to be done for you to believe. I have already said all I needed to say to give you everything you need to walk in faith. If your faith is weak, it's not because of Me. It's because you are not living in My words. It is *that* simple. I love you!

The words that I say to you I do not speak on My own initiative, but the Father abiding in Me does His works. John 14:10, NASB

→ *The Greatest Words Ever Spoken,* Unbelief and Motives of Unbelievers (pp. 466–69)

The Father Gave You to Me

That is why I said that people can't come to me unless the Father gives them to me. John 6:65, NLT

If My miracles weren't enough, what kind of proof do people need? The truth is, no one can believe unless the Father gives that person to Me. And *everyone* He gives to Me *will* come to Me. Look at the Samaritan woman at the well. She was living in sin and clinging to a false religion with no interest in knowing the truth. She cared only about herself. And yet, the Father drew her to Me. The Holy Spirit opened her heart, and I revealed that I was the Messiah. She repented and believed in Me. Then she became My witness, and many Samaritans believed through her testimony. Child, you, too, were given to Me by the Father. As you witness to others, don't be discouraged if they reject the Gospel. It is *not* your responsibility to prove anything. Spiritual birth is the work of the Holy Spirit. Your calling is to be My witness with your life and your words. Then let the Holy Spirit perform His ministry in the lives of people who see and hear your witness. You are My precious lamb, and I am your Shepherd. Today rejoice that *you* have been given to *Me*.

All that the Father gives Me will come to Me, and the one who comes to Me I will by no means cast out. John 6:37, NKJV

↠ *The Greatest Words Ever Spoken,* God's Sovereignty (pp. 103–5); The Call of Christ (pp. 418–21); Coming to Christ (pp. 452–53)

True Life Is More Than Living

It is the Spirit who gives life; the flesh profits nothing.
John 6:63, NASB

People are more prosperous now than at any time in history. Still, there is a hole in their souls. Many have tasted the life I offer but have been afraid to drink of it. True life does not come from anything this world offers, and it does not come from other people. True life comes only from the Holy Spirit. His fruit of selfless, unconditional love brings true life to all who are born of Him. His fruit of joy overcomes any sorrow. His fruit of peace brings calm in the midst of trials. In My followers His fruit creates an endless patience the world can't explain. His fruit produces self-control and an active outreach of kindness, goodness, and gentleness, even toward people who don't deserve it. Most important, His fruit produces true faithfulness to the Father and to Me. Child, as My follower you have unlimited access to the Holy Spirit and His fruit. Abide in My words, and let Him perform His ministry in *your* life.

If you love Me, keep My commandments. And I will pray the Father, and He will give you another Helper, that He may abide with you forever—the Spirit of truth, whom the world cannot receive, because it neither sees Him nor knows Him; but you know Him, for He dwells with you and will be in you. John 14:15–17, NKJV

→→ *The Greatest Words Ever Spoken,* The Holy Spirit and His Ministry (pp. 116–17); Jesus' Words, Their Role and Power (pp. 62–64); Spiritual Priorities (pp. 328–37)

The Holy Spirit Produces
Rivers of Living Water

If anyone thirsts, let him come to Me and drink. He who believes in Me, as the Scripture has said, out of his heart will flow rivers of living water. John 7:37–38, NKJV

What a glorious day when the Holy Spirit was sent by the Father! Instead of being limited by their nature, which could produce only the fruits of the flesh, My followers could now experience the fruit of the Spirit. Instead of trying to be good on their own, now they could rely on the Spirit to produce His goodness in them. Most important, the Holy Spirit would bring to their memory everything I said so they could abide in My words. For the rest of their lives, He would live in their hearts, guiding them into all truth and teaching them all things. Child, when you were born of the Spirit, He came to live in *your* heart as well. As you abide in My words, He will transform your life, conforming your heart to Mine. And His rivers of living water will fill your heart and flow out of you to bless the lives of others. Listen to His whispers and promptings today and every day!

But the Helper, the Holy Spirit, whom the Father will send in My name, He will teach you all things, and bring to your remembrance all things that I said to you. John 14:26, NKJV

→→ *The Greatest Words Ever Spoken,* Living Water (p. 278); The Holy Spirit and His Ministry (pp. 116–17); Belief and Faith in Christ (pp. 445–51)

Don't Judge by What You See

Do not judge according to appearance, but judge with righteous judgment. John 7:24, NASB

Why are most people's judgments wrong? Because most people judge others only by what they *see*. And what they see is limited by their own faults. Also, people's behavior often is determined by what they *can't* see. So judging someone by what you see will nearly always result in a faulty judgment. And, child, making a faulty judgment can be much worse than making no judgment at all. Also, judging others will nearly always cause you to sin in the area of pride. However, at times it is necessary to make a judgment about someone. Then it is critical to judge with righteous judgment instead of judging according to appearance. The only way to judge righteously is the way I judged. I did not seek My own will but the will of the Father. Child, when you must make a judgment, make it *only* by seeking the will of the Father. Seek answers from My words *before* you make any judgment of another. If you judge according to My words, your judgment will be righteous. Still, almost always it is better not to judge at all.

I can do nothing on My own initiative. As I hear, I judge; and My judgment is just, because I do not seek My own will, but the will of Him who sent Me. John 5:30, NASB. See also Matthew 7:1–3.

✦ *The Greatest Words Ever Spoken,* Judging Others (pp. 483–84)

I Don't Condemn You

Neither do I condemn you; go and sin no more.
John 8:11, NKJV

When the scribes and Pharisees brought an adulterous woman to Me, they wanted to trap Me so I would break either the Law of Moses or the law of Rome. To their dismay I did neither. Instead, I used the occasion to teach an important truth: I did *not* come into the world to destroy lives but to save them. Though this woman's sin was as offensive to the Father as any sin, her heart was broken, and her spirit was repentant. I will not reject a broken heart or a repentant spirit. Everyone who does not believe in Me will be judged for all their sins. But those who have believed will not be judged at all. I have already borne all the judgment for their sins. Child, like all descendants of Adam, your sins are many. In light of God's perfect holiness, they deserve eternal condemnation. But because you have believed in Me, I have already borne *all* the Father's judgment against *all* your sins. I paid your debt in full. You now stand guiltless in My righteousness, free of all condemnation. Today rejoice in the greatness of your salvation, and follow Me!

Whoever believes in him is not condemned, but whoever does not believe stands condemned already because he has not believed in the name of God's one and only Son. John 3:18

→ *The Greatest Words Ever Spoken,* Forgiveness (pp. 253–57)

Everyone Is a Slave, but I Can Set Anyone Free

I tell you the truth, everyone who sins is a slave of sin.
John 8:34, NLT

S in lets people *think* they are free, but in reality they are enslaved. They are bound by invisible chains and are controlled by the world, the flesh, and the devil. They are led into destructive lives with no eternal purpose. Tragically, they will reach the end of their lives having missed the very purpose of their lives. They will die in their sins, forever separated from the Father and His marvelous light. How tragic to be a slave and not even know it. But, child, this is *not* your destiny. At Calvary I cut your chains and set you free—free to be all that the Father created you to be. You are free to know Him and Me intimately, free to experience the purpose for which you were created. And, dear one, you can be used by the Spirit to set others free by the power of My words. My promise is as true for them as it is for you. If they will abide in My words, they will be My true disciples, and they will know the truth, and the truth will set them free. Don't be afraid to share My liberating words. People desperately need your light.

I am the way, and the truth, and the life. John 14:6, NASB

→→ *The Greatest Words Ever Spoken,* Sin (pp. 396–99); Eternal Life (pp. 134–42); Belief and Faith in Christ (pp. 445–51)

Dying to Live

I tell you the truth, unless a kernel of wheat is planted in the soil and dies, it remains alone. But its death will produce many new kernels—a plentiful harvest of new lives. Those who love their life in this world will lose it. Those who care nothing for their life in this world will keep it for eternity.
John 12:24–25, NLT

I came to earth to live the life My Father wanted Me to live. But as important as My life was, had I not been crucified, I would have *missed* the greatest purpose for which I had been sent—and all of humanity would have been forever lost. The only way My Father's great harvest could be accomplished was for Me to die. Child, this same principle applies to you. If you will learn to die to *your* will and *live* for the Father's, you too will reap the abundant harvest of eternal fruit. Denying yourself and living for Him is not a one-time decision. It's a decision you make many times a day. I want you to know that as you die to yourself and live for Him, you will make an *eternal* impact on the lives of others.

And He was saying to them all, "If anyone wishes to come after Me, he must deny himself, and take up his cross daily and follow Me."
Luke 9:23, NASB

✦ *The Greatest Words Ever Spoken,* The Resurrection of the Dead (pp. 171–72); Jesus' Missions (pp. 46–51)

Asking in My Name While Keeping My Commandments

You can ask for anything in my name, and I will do it, so that the Son can bring glory to the Father. Yes, ask me for anything in my name, and I will do it! If you love me, obey my commandments. John 14:13–15, NLT

Asking for something in My name is asking for something you are *confident* I would ask for if I were in your circumstance. But, child, this kind of confidence can be experienced only when you know Me intimately. True intimacy with Me comes only as you obey My commands and teachings. When you obey My words, I will reveal Myself to you. You will begin to know My heart and to see things the way *I* see them. When you are confident that you know My will for a particular circumstance and you are confident that *I* would make the same request that you want to make, *then* you can ask for it in My name. Child, this kind of confidence does not come from taking a few of My statements out of context and trying to use them to supplant the Father's will. Rather, it is the fruit that comes from knowing Me intimately and living in that intimacy day after day.

If you abide in Me, and My words abide in you, ask whatever you wish, and it will be done for you. John 15:7, NASB

⤞ *The Greatest Words Ever Spoken,* Prayer (pp. 295–98); Jesus' Name—Its Power and Meaning (pp. 51–53); Knowing God and Knowing Christ (pp. 275–77)

Don't Let Rejection Get to You

If the world hates you, keep in mind that it hated me first. If you belonged to the world, it would love you as its own. As it is, you do not belong to the world, but I have chosen you out of the world. That is why the world hates you.
John 15:18–19

Those who are of the world love themselves and the things of this world and have no true love for the Father and Me. They want complete independence and security *apart* from God. They have no interest in hearing My words, much less obeying them. Is it any wonder that they have little room in their hearts for My true followers? Child, they may be fine with you as long as you are quiet about Me and silent about the lies of this world. But talk about Me and share the truth about the world and its values, and watch them throw stones. When those of the world distance themselves from you, ridicule you, say terrible things about you, and even do terrible things *to* you, don't fret. Instead, rejoice! Realize that they are treating you the way they treated the prophets and Me. Rejoice, for *great* will be your reward in heaven!

Blessed are you when people insult you and persecute you, and falsely say all kinds of evil against you because of Me. Rejoice and be glad, for your reward in heaven is great; for in the same way they persecuted the prophets who were before you.
Matthew 5:11–12, NASB

↔ *The Greatest Words Ever Spoken,* Rejection and Persecution of Christians (pp. 308–12)

I Don't Want You to Stumble

These things I have spoken to you, that you should not be made to stumble. John 16:1, NKJV

Every fall starts with a stumble. It's never expected. Every fall brings sudden injury. And *nothing* is worse than a spiritual fall that breaks your intimacy with Me. On the night of My arrest, I told My disciples about the trials they were about to experience. I didn't want them to be taken by surprise and made to stumble. Child, you, too, will experience many trials. But every trial you face is only temporary. As the Holy Spirit revealed through Paul, when you are following Me, your afflictions are only temporary, but they produce glorious eternal treasures. So don't fix your gaze on things that are seen, but fix it on Me, My life, and My words. And know that being weighed down by sin can cause you to stumble and fall. If you will continually dwell in My words, the truth will set you free from your bondage to sin. Today cast off all distractions that take your eyes off Me and cause you to stumble. Keep My yoke upon you, and let Me carry your load. You will not stumble when you are harnessed to Me.

Take My yoke upon you and learn from Me, for I am gentle and humble in heart, and you will find rest for your souls. For My yoke is easy and My burden is light. Matthew 11:29–30, NASB

++ *The Greatest Words Ever Spoken,* Rejection and Persecution of Christians (pp. 308–12); Stumbling Blocks (pp. 488–89)

The Glory of the Thief's Salvation Is Yours as Well

Assuredly, I say to you, today you will be with Me in Paradise. Luke 23:43, NKJV

In My darkest hour the Father performed an amazing work of grace with a person who least expected it. Included in the crowd that cheered My crucifixion were the nation's most respected religious leaders. There also were others who were deeply religious. But the Father's work of grace was not performed in their hearts. Instead, He chose one of the two hardened criminals hanging on crosses by each side of Me. Though his sins were great, one of the men was transformed before My eyes. Even though he knew we both would soon be dead, he asked Me to remember him when I came into My kingdom. What was the source of his great faith? The answer is, he had been born again. The work of God had been performed in his heart, and he believed. Child, the glory of his salvation is also the glory of yours. In spite of the greatness of your sins, the Father has performed His same work of grace in *your* heart. His mercy is no less to you than it was to the thief. Can you see why you should praise Him day and night? Oh, how great is your salvation!

Nevertheless do not rejoice in this, that the spirits are subject to you, but rejoice that your names are recorded in heaven. Luke 10:20, NASB

↠ *The Greatest Words Ever Spoken*, Eternal Life (pp. 134–42)

The Thief's Timing Is *Not* Yours

Assuredly, I say to you, today you will be with Me in Paradise. Luke 23:43, NKJV

How many people have foolishly thought, *I'll be like the thief on the cross. I'll live my life my way, and when I'm at the end of my life, I'll believe*? It doesn't work that way. When someone rejects the Father's offer of mercy, nothing requires the Father to repeat the offer. Although God performed His work of grace in one thief's heart, He did not perform it in the other thief's heart. Child, realize there is a tragic side to the timing of the thief's spiritual birth. He missed the very purpose of his life. Instead of glorifying the Father and bearing fruit, he defied the Father. He wasted his life pursuing things of no eternal worth. Even worse, he never came to know the Father and Me intimately on earth. He never experienced Our love until his final moments. Unlike this man, you were born of the Spirit *before* your final day. You have been given the time, the grace, and the faith to know the Father and Me intimately. You have time to fulfill your calling and store up treasures in heaven.

Do not store up for yourselves treasures on earth, where moth and rust destroy, and where thieves break in and steal. But store up for yourselves treasures in heaven, where neither moth nor rust destroys, and where thieves do not break in or steal.
Matthew 6:19–20, NASB

→→ *The Greatest Words Ever Spoken,* Eternal Life (pp. 134–42); The Mission of a Christian (pp. 281–89); Fruitbearing (pp. 257–60)

Your Power to Forgive

Father, forgive them, for they do not know what they are doing. Luke 23:34

How badly have you been hurt? Does your mind keep reflecting on the hurt a person inflicted on you? I know your pain exactly as you know it. I feel it exactly as you feel it. The Father and I want to give you the power to forgive the one who caused your pain. That power can be gained only when you set the eyes of your heart on Me on the cross, where the Father and I *chose* to forgive you. Forgiveness is not a feeling; it's a choice to set a person free from your condemnation. You don't forgive people because they deserve it or because you feel like it. You forgive them because I suffered and died to forgive *your* sins. While I was hanging from the cross in agony, instead of cursing you I chose to forgive you. Child, when you refuse to forgive someone, you heap more sin on Me. You belittle and reject My love and forgiveness of you. Repent, forgive, and follow Me. Pray with Me, "Father, forgive them, for they know not what they are doing." By obeying My command to forgive, you will be loving Me.

But if you do not forgive men their sins, your Father will not forgive your sins. Matthew 6:15

Forgive, and you will be forgiven. Luke 6:37

✦ *The Greatest Words Ever Spoken,* Jesus' Words from the Cross (pp. 64–65); Forgiveness (pp. 142–43; 253–57; 481–83)

Paid in Full

It is finished. John 19:30

How many sins have you committed? How many more will you commit before your life ends? I'm talking about all the times you acted or will act contrary to My Father's commands. I'm also talking about all the times you *didn't* act when you should have. How many times have you failed to love the Father with *all* your heart, mind, soul, and strength? How many times have you failed to love others as you love yourself? The psalmist wrote, "If you, O LORD, kept a record of sins, O Lord, who could stand?" The truth is, a record has been kept, and the number of your sins is incomprehensible. Your offense against the Father is beyond measure. That is why you desperately needed a Savior. And *that* is why I sacrificed My life on the cross. When I said, "It is finished," that is exactly what I meant. Child, I didn't pay for some of your sins or even most of your sins. I paid for *all* your sins. All your earthly circumstances are truly insignificant when compared to this one fact.

Thus it is written, that the Christ would suffer and rise again from the dead the third day, and that repentance for forgiveness of sins would be proclaimed in His name to all the nations, beginning from Jerusalem. Luke 24:46–47, NASB

→→ *The Greatest Words Ever Spoken,* Jesus' Words from the Cross (pp. 64–65); Forgiveness (pp. 142–43; 253–57; 481–83)

Where I Came from
and Where I'm Going

Even if I bear witness of Myself, My witness is true, for I
know where I came from and where I am going; but you do
not know where I come from and where I am going.
John 8:14, NKJV

People know a lot less than they think. Everyone is limited by
their earthly perspective. They are unsure of the past and have
no knowledge of the future. But you are *not* limited by the perspective and values of this world. You are My lamb. Unlike everyone else,
I did not come from this world. I came from the Father, and He has
shown Me all things. Even when I walked the earth, I knew *exactly*
where I was going, even through death. And I want you to know that
I, as your Shepherd, will lead you according to My knowledge. This
knowledge is not limited by human understanding. As you abide in
My words, I will fill your heart and mind with all that you need. And
My Spirit will fill your spirit. As long as you follow Me, you will
never have to worry about getting lost in this world's darkness. Your
life will be filled with purpose and will not end at death. Follow Me
closely. I know exactly where we are going!

My sheep hear My voice, and I know them, and they follow Me.
John 10:27, NKJV

The Difference Between Me and All Others

You are from below; I am from above. You belong to this world; I do not. That is why I said that you will die in your sins; for unless you believe that I AM who I claim to be, you will die in your sins. John 8:23–24, NLT

Most religious leaders of My day belonged to the world and lived by its values. Without believing in Me, they continued to live in hypocrisy and ultimately died in their sins. No one can believe in Me unless he is set free from his blinding bias to see that I was sent to earth by My Father. Child, My Father chose to reveal the truth about Me to *you*! He removed the blindfold from your eyes and the bias from your heart. More and more you are seeing Me as I really am. Your belief in Me is a gift from the Father, delivered to you by the Holy Spirit. You heard the Gospel, and you repented and believed. You have been saved from this world and its destiny. You have passed from death to life! Praise the Father for His grace toward you.

For I have come down from heaven, not to do My own will, but the will of Him who sent Me. This is the will of Him who sent Me, that of all that He has given Me I lose nothing, but raise it up on the last day. John 6:38–39, NASB

↠ *The Greatest Words Ever Spoken,* The Claims Jesus Made About Himself (pp. 14–22); Belief and Faith in Christ (pp. 445–51); Coming to Christ (pp. 452–53)

Your Time Is Limited—
Stop Wasting It

Are there not twelve hours in the day? If anyone walks in the day, he does not stumble, because he sees the light of this world. But if one walks in the night, he stumbles, because the light is not in him. John 11:9–10, NKJV

As I entered the final days of My ministry on earth, My disciples didn't realize that our time together was coming to an end. But I knew My hour was near, and there was still much to be done. I knew something they had not yet learned—that *time* was their most limited resource. Your time on earth is also extremely limited. One of Satan's great deceptions is that you can do the most important things later. Don't believe it! You are a light in a dark world. If that light flickers for only a few moments each day, how will others find the truth? Let your light shine every moment you are awake. Make the most of your time by letting Me live My life through you. Your life truly is like a mist that appears in the morning and vanishes by noon. Commune with Me, and be My witness with your life and words.

Behold, I say to you, lift up your eyes and look on the fields, that they are white for harvest. Already he who reaps is receiving wages and is gathering fruit for life eternal; so that he who sows and he who reaps may rejoice together. John 4:35–36, NASB

✢ *The Greatest Words Ever Spoken,* Stewardship, Generosity (pp. 338–41); Spiritual Priorities (pp. 328–37); Light Versus Darkness (pp. 457–58)

Avoid Darkness
and Remain in the Light

If anyone walks in the day, he does not stumble, because he sees the light of this world. But if one walks in the night, he stumbles, because the light is not in him. John 11:9–10, NKJV

A s My hour drew near, My disciples had no idea what they would soon be facing. For more than three years, I had been their light—their source for truth and power. I had been their full-time provider and counselor. They had come to rely on Me for everything, and yet My light and I would soon be gone. Thankfully, the Holy Spirit would later bring My light back into their lives. Their souls would be safe, and they would bear much fruit. Child, even though you can't see Me, I *am* with you. My words and their light are available to you as they were to My disciples. If you let them guide your choices, you *will not* stumble. You will see everything from My perspective. You will see the Father as I see Him. Sadly, when you ignore My words or set aside My teachings, you stray into darkness. In darkness you *will* stumble and fall. You *will* get hurt, and you *will* hurt others. Store My words in your heart and walk in their light. Instead of stumbling, you will be safe.

I am the light of the world. He who follows Me shall not walk in darkness, but have the light of life. John 8:12, NKJV

→→ *The Greatest Words Ever Spoken,* Light Versus Darkness (pp. 457–58)

How to See God's Glory in Your Life and Your World

Did I not say to you that if you would believe you would see the glory of God? John 11:40, NKJV

Lazarus's sisters had the faith to believe that if I had arrived before he died, I could have saved him. But when I told them to remove the stone from the tomb entrance, they had no faith. Instead of obeying My command, Martha pointed out the circumstance that seemed impossible to overcome. Lazarus already smelled of decay, she said, because he had been dead four days. Child, I understand when your heart is like Martha's. You can't see that I can make a difference that defies human experience. But realize that I see what you can't see. When Martha finally chose to believe Me and obey My words, she saw God's glory. Her dead brother came back to life. Child, there is a special blessing for those who believe *before* they see, and that applies to *you*. Every time you take a step of faith based on My words, you please the Father, and your faith grows. However, to take a step of faith, you must first hear My words, just as Martha did. Believing Me is simply acting in response to My commands, teachings, and promises. Every time you do, you will glorify the Father and Me, and you will see His glory in your life.

With people this is impossible, but with God all things are possible. Matthew 19:26, NASB

→ *The Greatest Words Ever Spoken,* Belief and Faith in Christ (pp. 445–51); The Promises of Christ (pp. 298–304); Commands of Christ (pp. 206–17)

How to Gain the Father's Honor

Anyone who wants to serve me must follow me, because my servants must be where I am. And the Father will honor anyone who serves me. John 12:26, NLT

People are foolish to seek one another's honor. Honor from other people is as fleeting as a passing cloud, and it delivers even less benefit. But My Father is the almighty God, whose glory is greater than that of all creation. There is no greater honor than His. And unlike the honor of people, the *Father's* honor is life-giving and eternal. His honor is not awarded for educational or social achievements. It's not based on gender or age. Any of My followers can receive His honor, and that includes *you.* Everyone who serves Me will receive His honor, and those who follow Me are those who serve Me. When you honor My words by abiding in them and doing them, you are following Me. You also serve Me when you serve My sheep. And, child, when you follow Me, you are believing, honoring, and loving the One who sent Me. The Father will honor you with *His* treasures stored up for you in heaven. They are yours for all eternity.

Then the King will say to those on his right, "Come, you who are blessed by my Father; take your inheritance, the kingdom prepared for you since the creation of the world." Matthew 25:34

✦ *The Greatest Words Ever Spoken,* Following Christ (pp. 245–53); Servants (pp. 316–19)

The Trouble with Walking in Darkness

A little while longer the light is with you. Walk while you have the light, lest darkness overtake you; he who walks in darkness does not know where he is going. John 12:35, NKJV

It's not that bad. Everybody does it! This may be your last thought before you step away from the light to dabble in darkness. You think you'll return to God's light later, but at the moment, you just want to do what *you* want to do. My child, don't be so naive. Even taking one step into darkness can put you in a place where the darkness may suddenly overwhelm you. You may quickly lose your way. You may go where you never intended, and you may get lost, never to return. In the darkness you will stumble and fall. You might suffer great injury to your soul. I did not give you My words so you could merely *consider* them, accepting some and ignoring others. I gave them to you so you could walk in the light and remain in the light. In the light you will bear much fruit, and your life will bring great glory to Me and the Father. You will be *safe,* and your life will fulfill its eternal purpose. And, child, only in the light will you have continuous intimacy with the Father and Me. We will not walk with you in darkness.

But he who practices the truth comes to the Light, so that his deeds may be manifested as having been wrought in God. John 3:21, NASB

✦ *The Greatest Words Ever Spoken,* Light Versus Darkness (pp. 384–85)

How to Become a Child of Light

While you have the light, believe in the light, that you may become sons of light. John 12:36, NKJV

Many who say they believe in Me agree that I am the Light of the World—the Light of Life. They *think* they believe this truth, but they don't really. True beliefs are shown not through words or feelings but by what a person does. Those who truly believe I am the Light of Life will *walk* in My light. They desire and even crave My truth and righteousness. They want to know the Father's will, not so they can think about it, but so they can *do* it. Those who continually ignore My commands do not believe in My light, no matter what they say. They do what *they* want to do, not what the Father wants them to do. Child, I am your light, and My light is available to you every moment. But the only way to believe in the light is to walk in it. Meditate on My teachings and walk in them. Then you will be a child of light. Follow Me. I will never lead you into the peril of darkness but will keep you safe in My light.

When he puts forth all his own, he goes ahead of them, and the sheep follow him because they know his voice. John 10:4, NASB

✈ *The Greatest Words Ever Spoken,* Light Versus Darkness (pp. 384–85)

Don't Trust in
Your Own Strength

Will you lay down your life for My sake? Most assuredly, I say to you, the rooster shall not crow till you have denied Me three times. John 13:38, NKJV

Shortly before My arrest, I told My disciples that the night's events would cause them to fall away. Peter insisted that even if everyone else left Me, he would not. When I told him he would deny Me three times before the rooster crowed, he replied, "Even if I have to die with you, I will never disown you." Peter made the same mistake that many of My followers make. He thought he was able, in his *own* strength, to follow Me. Following Me is *not* a matter of your will. As Peter and My other disciples learned, though they were willing in their spirit, their flesh was weak. All My followers must learn that same lesson. By yourself, you do not have the power to overcome your own will and, instead, do Mine. Child, you need to rely wholly upon Me for My strength. I will provide the grace you need for any situation at the moment you need it. But you must receive it and act on it. As you obey My words, the Holy Spirit will give you all the power you need to take each step. Remember, you only need to follow Me one step at a time.

My grace is sufficient for you, for my power is perfected in weakness. 2 Corinthians 12:9, NASB

✦ *The Greatest Words Ever Spoken,* Pride (pp. 391–93); Self-Deception and Self-Justification (pp. 394–95)

I Didn't Come to Judge but to Save

If anyone hears My words and does not believe, I do not judge him; for I did not come to judge the world but to save the world. John 12:47, NKJV

Today many people think I am like a judge on a throne, ready to execute immediate judgment and condemnation. But I did not come to earth and lay down My life to judge the world. I came to *save* it. I sacrificed My life so that those who would believe in Me would gain eternal life. Child, you have believed. Every time you obey My words, you are believing Me. I am not sitting by the Father waiting to condemn your every mistake and failure. I am *not* your judge; I am your Advocate. I am your faithful Friend who sticks closer than a brother. No one has a greater love for you than the Father and I have. I laid down My life for you. I promised that I will never leave you. I am the Good Shepherd, and you are My dear lamb. I am the One who left the ninety-nine to seek and save you. And I will do it again if I need to. Even the Father doesn't judge you. All of His judgment for your sin was executed against Me on Calvary.

The thief comes only to steal and kill and destroy; I came that they may have life, and have it abundantly. I am the good shepherd; the good shepherd lays down His life for the sheep. John 10:10–11, NASB

→ *The Greatest Words Ever Spoken*, Jesus' Missions (pp. 46–51); The Shepherd and His Sheep (pp. 320–23)

Rejecting My Words
Is Rejecting Me

He who rejects Me, and does not receive My words, has that which judges him—the word that I have spoken will judge him in the last day. John 12:48, NKJV

There are many who think they believe in Me because they acknowledge Me as the Son of God. But merely agreeing that I am the Son of God is not the same as *believing* in Me. Though they may have good beliefs *about* Me, if they don't hear and do what I say, they do not believe *in* Me. They will be judged by the words I have spoken. Whenever anyone rejects My words, they are rejecting Me. Those who truly believe in Me hear My words and obey them. They do not do this perfectly, but obedience is the desire of their hearts and the direction of their lives. I know your hunger for My words is ever growing! I know your life is guided by My words. But I also know there are times when you reject My words, choosing your will instead. As you grow in your relationship with Me, you'll find yourself rejecting My words less and obeying them more. Keep building your life on the rock and not on sand. Keep abiding in My words.

Therefore everyone who hears these words of Mine and acts on them, may be compared to a wise man who built his house on the rock. Matthew 7:24, NASB

→ *The Greatest Words Ever Spoken,* Abiding in the Words of Christ (pp. 186–88); Loving Christ (p. 280)

Have You Discovered the Glory of Serving Others?

If I then, your Lord and Teacher, have washed your feet, you also ought to wash one another's feet. For I have given you an example, that you should do as I have done to you. Most assuredly, I say to you, a servant is not greater than his master; nor is he who is sent greater than he who sent him. If you know these things, blessed are you if you do them. John 13:14–17, NKJV

Most people would rather be served than serve. My disciples were no exception. On the night of My arrest, they were shocked when I washed their feet. But I wanted them to see that even in My hour of greatest need, I could still focus on serving *their* needs. Child, if I were with you, I would not hesitate to wash *your* feet. In My kingdom those who will be the greatest will be those who have focused their lives on serving. I want you to serve with a joyful heart instead of a complaining one. I want you to serve humbly, often in ways that others don't see. But the Father and I see what you do in secret. Serve, not because others deserve it, but as one more way you can love the Father and Me. Whenever you serve My followers with a joyful heart, you are really serving Me.

But the greatest among you shall be your servant. Whoever exalts himself shall be humbled; and whoever humbles himself shall be exalted. Matthew 23:11–12, NASB

⤙ *The Greatest Words Ever Spoken,* Serving Others and Serving God (pp. 319–20); Servants (pp. 316–19)

The Identifying Mark of a Disciple

A new commandment I give to you, that you love one another; as I have loved you, that you also love one another. By this all will know that you are My disciples, if you have love for one another. John 13:34–35, NKJV

My disciples, like most people, were competitive and contentious. They were quick to criticize and judge one another. When offended, they found it hard to forgive. If they continued in this behavior after My ascension, their hearts would become hardened toward one another. Their intimacy with Me would be broken, and their ministry to the world would be weakened. So I gave them a new, compulsory commandment: to love one another in the same way I had loved them. If they would love one another that way, *nothing* could defeat them. Child, I give this same command to *you*. I want *you* to love My other followers in the same ways that I have loved you: unselfishly and without demands, expectations, judgment, or destructive criticism. This is the type of love that people of the world cannot duplicate or counterfeit. If you will love My other followers in this way, you will become known as My disciple. You can love this way because My unconditional love is the fruit of the Holy Spirit. He lives within you. Let Him love others through you.

If you love Me, you will keep My commandments. John 14:15, NASB

⤞ *The Greatest Words Ever Spoken,* Love (pp. 278–80); Following Christ (pp. 245–53)

Another Vital Ministry of the Holy Spirit

> However, when He, the Spirit of truth, has come, He will guide you into all truth; for He will not speak on His own authority, but whatever He hears He will speak; and He will tell you things to come. He will glorify Me, for He will take of what is Mine and declare it to you. John 16:13–14, NKJV

Truth is critical, even a matter of life and death. You live in a dark world, and its ruler is a liar. His greatest weapon is deception, and he uses it skillfully to keep people from knowing and following Me. Without the truth *no one* could escape his domain. Child, you desperately need the truth—not just to *know* it, but also to *do* it. The Father sent the Holy Spirit initially to guide My apostles into all truth. But this ministry of the Spirit didn't end with My apostles. Today His ministry is to take the perfect truths of My words and write them on *your* heart. This, too, is critically important, because all of your behavior flows out of your heart. When My words bear their fruit in your heart, your behavior will flow from the truth of My words. And out of your heart will flow rivers of living water that will glorify the Father and bless those He brings into your path.

For this I have been born, and for this I have come into the world, to testify to the truth. Everyone who is of the truth hears My voice. John 18:37, NASB

↣ *The Greatest Words Ever Spoken,* The Holy Spirit and His Ministry (pp. 116–17)

Praying Honestly,
Seeking Peace and Power

O My Father, if it is possible, let this cup pass from Me; nevertheless, not as I will, but as You will. Matthew 26:39, NKJV

I n Gethsemane I knew I was about to be arrested, tried, and unjustly sentenced. I knew I would be beaten mercilessly and nailed to a cross. But My greatest burden was that I would soon experience sin for the first time. As always, My prayers were completely honest and transparent. Three times I shared My desire first, asking the Father to spare Me this terrible ordeal if possible. Each time I asked Him, His peace flowed into My heart. Then I could honestly ask that His will be done. After My third prayer, His peace flooded My heart, and I was ready to fulfill the Father's calling. This is how I want you to pray. Be transparent and honest. First, share how you truly feel and what you really want. Then My peace will flow into your mind and heart. In the time that follows, whether seconds or days, your desire will change from wanting your will to truly wanting the Father's. Then you'll be able to honestly ask for His will to be done. You will receive your request for His will, by His power!

But when you pray, go away by yourself, shut the door behind you, and pray to your Father in private. Then your Father, who sees everything, will reward you. Matthew 6:6, NLT

✦ *The Greatest Words Ever Spoken,* Prayer (pp. 295–98); Jesus' Prayers (pp. 53–55)

Accepting Adversity and Overcoming It

Put your sword back into its sheath. Shall I not drink from the cup of suffering the Father has given me? John 18:11, NLT

As I was being arrested, Peter pulled out his sword. He wanted to end My adversity *his* way, as quickly as possible. He didn't realize that the Father intended this adversity. It would be the means through which Peter's redemption and that of all My sheep would be provided. I needed to endure it to the end. But the good news is, the so-called end was *not* the end. My victory didn't come by avoiding the trial; it came by enduring it. Child, I know that when you experience devastating trials, like Peter, you try to work your way out of them. And yet sometimes the Father has a greater purpose than merely eliminating or solving a problem. When you follow Me, the ultimate victory will *always* be yours, even in death. So when trials come, don't despair. Run to Me. Cast your cares upon Me. Fast, pray, and abide in My words. Listen to the whispers of the Holy Spirit. Know that even your worst trials are only temporary and that they are producing for you treasures in heaven that are eternal. Trust Me!

My grace is sufficient for you, for power is perfected in weakness. 2 Corinthians 12:9, NASB

✤ *The Greatest Words Ever Spoken,* Adversaries and Human Enemies (pp. 188–90); Rejection and Persecution of Christians (pp. 308–12)

Why Are You Crying?
Whom Do You Seek?

Woman, . . . why are you crying? Who is it you are looking for? John 20:15

On the morning of My resurrection while it was still dark, I first appeared to Mary Magdalene, who was weeping. She thought someone had taken My body. In the darkness she didn't recognize Me through her tears. But when I spoke her name, she realized who I was. I was *alive!* I told her to let My disciples know, but they didn't believe her. They missed an opportunity to glorify the Father with faith. Instead, they remained grieving in their unbelief. Child, how often do you remain in unbelief, grieving in the midst of trials? How often do you act as if I'm still dead? *Seek* Me. I am alive and I am with you. Unbelief renders you fruitless, and My Father and I want you to bear much fruit. From the moment Mary believed I was alive, she listened to My words and obeyed them. I want *you* to do the same. Hear My words and obey them. In them your unbelief will be replaced by faith, and your fears and sorrows will be replaced by courage and joy! Hear My voice now, and follow Me.

The work of God is this: to believe in the one he has sent. John 6:29

↣ *The Greatest Words Ever Spoken,* Faith (pp. 231–40; 445–51)

A Greater Blessing for You

You believe because you have seen me. Blessed are those who believe without seeing me. John 20:29, NLT

In the evening of My resurrection day, I appeared to My disciples, and they *finally* believed that I had risen from the dead. Their hearts were filled with inexpressible joy. They told Thomas they had seen Me, but he refused to believe. He said he would have to see Me and place his hands in My wounds. How sad. For the next eight days, his heart remained in unbelief. Then he saw Me and truly believed. He served Me faithfully for the rest of his life. But because he insisted on seeing Me, he did not receive the same blessing that I offer to you and to all My followers who haven't seen Me. The blessing is yours because you walk by faith even though you have *not* seen Me. For you to follow Me requires a greater faith than was required of My disciples, because they would not believe until they saw. My Father and I love you for that. As you keep My words, My Father and I will continually make Our home with you.

All who love me will do what I say. My Father will love them, and we will come and make our home with each of them. John 14:23, NLT

✈ *The Greatest Words Ever Spoken,* Faith (pp. 231–40; 445–51)

I Can See What You Cannot—
Trust Me

Cast the net on the right side of the boat, and you will find some. John 21:6, NKJV

One night following My resurrection, Peter and several other disciples fished all night but caught nothing. When morning came, I was standing on the shore and called to them, "Children, you do not have any fish, do you?" Not knowing it was Me, they answered, "No." When I told them to cast their net on the other side of the boat, they must have thought I was crazy. But they obeyed My words and immediately caught so many fish that John said to Peter, "It is the Lord." Peter got so excited he threw on his shirt and jumped into the water and came to Me. Child, there are so many times when even your best efforts fail to accomplish what you want to achieve. Next time don't wait until you fail before you decide to come to Me. Look to *Me* for direction. Jump out of your boat and into My words. Listen to My instructions and follow them. Then *I* will fill your nets. Your joy will overflow, you will bear much fruit, and your Father will be glorified.

Take My yoke upon you and learn from Me, for I am gentle and humble in heart. Matthew 11:29, NASB

✢ *The Greatest Words Ever Spoken,* Faith (pp. 231–40; 445–51)

Don't Compare My Dealings with Others to My Dealings with You

---

If I want him to remain alive until I return, what is that to you? As for you, follow me. John 21:22, NLT

How often have you compared your circumstances to those of others and thought, *That's not fair*? My disciples did the same thing. When I warned Peter that in the future he would be killed, he looked at John and asked, "What about him?" Instead of being thankful for the knowledge I had given him, he wanted to compare his future with what lay in store for John. Peter was more concerned about My being fair than he was about doing My will. I replied, "What is that to you?" Child, I know there are so many times when you compare your circumstances to those of others. You wonder why you don't have what they have or why you have to go through hard trials and they do not. My answer to you is the same: "What does *that* have to do with *you*?" The Father and I deal with you according to Our eternal purposes for you. Comparing yourself to others blinds you to Our love for you. Don't worry about fairness. Stop the comparisons. My call to you is the same as it is to *all* My sheep: follow Me!

For everyone who exalts himself will be humbled, and he who humbles himself will be exalted. Luke 14:11, NASB

✤ *The Greatest Words Ever Spoken,* Commands of Christ (pp. 206–17); Pride (pp. 391–93); Jealousy (pp. 383–84)

My Call Is the Same for All My Sheep

Follow me! John 21:19

Though My Father's will is different for each of My sheep, My *call* is the same to everyone: follow Me. When My first disciples heard that call, they gave up everything—their livelihoods, time with their families, even their futures. After My ascension they could no longer follow Me physically. But they continued to follow Me in the most important ways: with their hearts, minds, attitudes, and actions. I am calling you to follow Me in those same ways. Following Me begins with hearing My words. My disciples heard My words as I spoke them. Later the Holy Spirit reminded them of My words. You have My words recorded in the Gospels. As you read them, they will seep into your mind and heart. Then the Holy Spirit will bring them to your memory whenever you need them. But *hearing* My words is just the beginning. Following Me requires faith that I am who I claim to be and that I will do everything I have promised to do. Most important, it takes faith to do daily what I say. Child, follow Me, and I will lead you where *I* want you to go.

Greater love has no one than this, that one lay down his life for his friends. You are My friends if you do what I command you.
John 15:13–14, NASB

✦ *The Greatest Words Ever Spoken,* Following Christ (pp. 245–53); The Call of Christ (pp. 418–21)

Knowing Me and
Seeing the Father

Have I been so long with you, and yet you have not come to know Me, Philip? He who has seen Me has seen the Father; how can you say, "Show us the Father"? John 14:9, NASB

Have you ever felt as though even the people closest to you don't *really* know you? I had been with My disciples for more than three years. And yet, at our last supper, they showed that they still didn't *know* Me. I told Thomas, "If you had known Me, you would have known My Father also; from now on you know Him, and have seen Him." Philip then said, "Lord, show us the Father and that will be enough for us." They still did not understand that when they looked at Me, they were seeing the *Father* in Me. It was the Father doing His marvelous works *through* Me. Child, I want you to know the Father and Me intimately. As you abide in My words and obey My commands, I will fulfill My promise to reveal Myself and the Father to you, and you will come to know the Father and Me as never before. *Knowing* Me begins the moment you abide in My words! And as you continue in My words, our intimacy will continue to grow! I promise!

My teaching is not Mine, but His who sent Me. John 7:16, NASB

✦ *The Greatest Words Ever Spoken,* Jesus' Relationship with God the Father (pp. 55–60); The Claims Jesus Made About Himself (pp. 14–22)

Believe Me

Believe Me that I am in the Father and the Father in Me, or else believe Me for the sake of the works themselves.
John 14:11, NKJV

I t's one thing to hear My words; it's a very different thing to believe them. It was important for My first disciples to understand My relationship with the Father, but mere understanding was not enough. I wanted them to *believe* Me. Although you may never fully understand My relationship with the Father, I want you to believe what I tell you about it. Believing Me does not mean you merely embrace an opinion about what I say. Rather, believing leads to *acting* on My words. On the same night that My disciples *said* they believed I had come from God, they ran away and hid in fear. Though they held an opinion about Me, they didn't really *believe* Me. The evidence of true belief is demonstrated by one's behavior. Child, you believe Me, not when you say you do, but when you *do* what I say. When you *believe* that the Father is in Me and that I am in Him, your whole life—who you are and everything you do—will flow out of that belief. Believe Me!

And He who sent Me is with Me; He has not left Me alone, for I always do the things that are pleasing to Him. John 8:29, NASB

⤜ *The Greatest Words Ever Spoken,* Jesus' Relationship with God the Father (pp. 55–60); The Claims Jesus Made About Himself (pp. 14–22)

When Traditions Replace the Father's Will

And why do you break the command of God for the sake of your tradition? Matthew 15:3

The Pharisees were deeply offended when My disciples failed to follow their traditions. The Pharisees were more concerned about keeping their traditions than they were about obeying God's commands. They didn't realize that their traditions were *worthless* in God's eyes. Their practice of elevating traditions above My Father's Word and commands was vile and detestable to Him. Today many who claim to be My followers elevate their religious traditions and teachings above knowing and obeying My words. They follow their own teachings but remain unaware of or indifferent to Mine. They will be judged by My Word. Child, examine yourself. Your beliefs that are based wholly on My words will stand. They will empower you to obey My words and to *do* the will of the Father. But any beliefs based on mere traditions or on human teachings will bear no eternal fruit. Set them aside! Everything you need, in spirit and in truth, is available to you in Me and My words.

These people honor me with their lips, but their hearts are far from me. They worship me in vain; their teachings are but rules taught by men. Matthew 15:8–9

✧ *The Greatest Words Ever Spoken,* The Traditions of Men (p. 404); Hypocrites, Hypocrisy, and Self-Righteousness (pp. 378–83)

Can You Love Me the Way I Told Peter to Love Me?

Simon son of John, do you love me more than these? . . . Then feed my lambs. John 21:15, NLT

Three times I asked Simon Peter if he loved Me. The first two times I asked if he loved Me with *agape* love (the unconditional, selfless love of God). Each time he answered that his love for Me was *phileo* love (brotherly affection). Because he had denied and abandoned Me, he knew he couldn't honestly claim anything more than phileo love for Me. The third time I asked, "Do you *phileo* Me?" He was deeply grieved that I questioned even his claim of phileo love. I wanted him to recognize his spiritual poverty so that when the Holy Spirit came, Peter would rely wholly on Him. I also knew that after the Holy Spirit came upon him, Peter would finally possess agape love for Me and so many others. Agape is a fruit of the Spirit. Child, those who are poor in spirit are the ones who run to *Me* to be forgiven and made whole. That's what I wanted for Peter, and it is what I want for you. The more you realize the bankruptcy of your own nature, the more you will hunger for Me and rely on the Holy Spirit. And, dear one, in Him you, too, can *agape* Me.

Blessed are the poor in spirit, for theirs is the kingdom of heaven. Matthew 5:3, NASB

✦ *The Greatest Words Ever Spoken,* Loving Christ (p. 280); The Mission of a Christian (pp. 281–89)

Many *Say* They Know Me, but They Don't

If I want glory for myself, it doesn't count. But it is my Father who will glorify me. You say, "He is our God," but you don't even know him. I know him. If I said otherwise, I would be as great a liar as you! But I do know him and obey him. John 8:54–55, NLT

During My time on earth, nearly everyone *said* they knew God, but most did not. Today people may hold the opinion that God exists, but that is *not* the same as believing in Him. Knowing *about* Him is not the same as *knowing* Him. To believe in God is to surrender your will to His will and daily to allow Him to rule your life. Those who truly believe in Him obey His Word and enjoy an intimate relationship with Him. The fact that the Pharisees did *not* obey God proved that they did not know Him. Child, I know *you* have surrendered your life to My lordship. That shows you truly believe Me. And because you believe in Me, you have an ever-increasing desire to obey My words. Your faith to obey My teachings will create a growing intimacy with the Father and Me. I will continue to manifest Myself to you, and the Father and I will continually abide with you.

If you keep My commandments, you will abide in My love; just as I have kept My Father's commandments and abide in His love. John 15:10, NASB

→→ *The Greatest Words Ever Spoken,* Knowing God and Knowing Christ (pp. 275–77); The Claims Jesus Made About Himself (pp. 14–22)

How to Get Out of the Darkness

I have come as a light into the world, that whoever believes in Me should not abide in darkness. John 12:46, NKJV

Before people believe in Me, they live and walk in darkness. They do not know the Father or Me or the Father's truth, so they accept the world's deceptive values. Satan is the Father of Lies and the master of deception. In the darkness he makes everything he offers seem acceptable and good and everything the Father offers seem unimportant and without value. Those who remain in darkness will end their lives in despair. But, child, *you* believe in Me. You are the Father's dear child, and He does not want you to remain in darkness. My words are light, and as long as your heart remains in them, you need not fear being drawn into darkness. When your behavior steps out of My light into darkness, realize that you have forsaken My words. But you don't have to remain there. Get back to My words. Hear them and obey them. There is no other way to escape the darkness and no other way to remain in the light. Remain in My words—to love Me, to grow your faith, to become My true disciple, to know the truth, and to remain free.

If you continue in My word, then you are truly disciples of Mine; and you will know the truth, and the truth will make you free. John 8:31–32, NASB

→→ *The Greatest Words Ever Spoken,* Light Versus Darkness (pp. 384–85); The Promises of Christ (pp. 298–304)

When You Feel Deeply Troubled

Now my soul is deeply troubled. Should I pray, "Father, save me from this hour"? But this is the very reason I came! Father, bring glory to your name. John 12:27–28, NLT

I know there may be times when you are hurting beyond description. Your pain is so deep you can't understand it. It is rooted in your soul. I experienced anguish such as this as the hour of My sacrifice drew near. The realization of becoming the sins of humanity was excruciating. But instead of letting My focus remain on the agony that lay ahead, I turned My focus to the Father and His purpose for Me. He purposed to use My sacrifice to redeem all who would believe in Me. Child, when your soul is deeply troubled, your only path to victory is to turn your focus to the Father and His purposes for you! He wants an intimate relationship with you, and He wants you to bear much fruit. You can accomplish this only as you abide in Me and My words abide in you. Then your prayers will be answered, you will bear much fruit, and the Father will be glorified!

If you remain in me and my words remain in you, ask whatever you wish, and it will be given you. This is to my Father's glory, that you bear much fruit, showing yourselves to be my disciples.
John 15:7–8

✈ *The Greatest Words Ever Spoken,* Anxiety, Worry, and Fear (pp. 190–93); Jesus' Missions (pp. 46–51); The Mission of a Christian (pp. 281–89); Spiritual Priorities (pp. 328–37)

You Don't Have to Understand Right Now

You don't understand now what I am doing, but someday you will. John 13:7, NLT

M y disciples were stunned when I began to wash their feet. That's something only the lowliest of servants would do! How could the One who had calmed the sea, healed the sick, and raised the dead descend to the level of the lowliest servants? When Peter resisted, I gave him the promise that he would understand all this in the future. I know there are many times when you ask, "How could God let this happen?" Dear one, realize that your vision is limited. You can't see even a minute into the future, but the Father's vision has no limits. It is still true that not even a single sparrow falls to the ground apart from His loving will—and even your greatest trials can't remove you from His care. You don't understand now, but someday you will. Your only question should be "Lord, what do You want me to do?" That question will *always* be answered in My words recorded in the Gospels. Let Me carry your burden. Let Me serve you so you can serve others in My name.

My sheep hear My voice, and I know them, and they follow Me; and I give eternal life to them, and they will never perish; and no one will snatch them out of My hand. John 10:27–28, NASB

➤ *The Greatest Words Ever Spoken*, The Shepherd and His Sheep (pp. 320–23); Serving Others and Serving God (pp. 319–20)

That My Joy Will Overflow in You

Now I am coming to you. I told them many things while I was with them in this world so they would be filled with my joy. I have given them your word. John 17:13–14, NLT

Dear one, what is the difference between My *joy* and your *happiness*? Your happiness depends on circumstances. When something happens that you like, you are happy. But when things turn out otherwise, you lose your happiness. If something bad happens, happiness is replaced with sadness or discouragement. On the other hand, My joy never varies with changing circumstances. My joy resides in Me and My words—the words the Father gave Me to speak. On the night of My arrest, I can't say that I was happy. But as My heart focused on My Father and His glory, He delivered peace to My soul and His sustaining joy to My Spirit. *That* is the joy I want to pour into your soul. When you abide in My words, My joy will abide in you! And you will receive even more joy when you spend more time abiding in My words. My joy will fill you up and overflow to those around you.

If you keep My commandments, you will abide in My love, just as I have kept My Father's commandments and abide in His love. These things I have spoken to you, that My joy may remain in you, and that your joy may be full. John 15:10–11, NKJV

→ *The Greatest Words Ever Spoken,* Joy (pp. 273–75); The Promises of Christ (pp. 298–304)

Glorifying God

Now is the Son of Man glorified and God is glorified in him. If God is glorified in him, God will glorify the Son in himself, and will glorify him at once. John 13:31–32

My driving purpose has always been to glorify the Father. On earth I said everything He wanted Me to say, exactly the way He wanted it said. In every situation I performed His will perfectly. I never fell to temptation in thought, word, or deed. But the Father's greatest glory was accomplished at Calvary, where I completed His work of redemption. Child, you, too, can bring glory to the Father. In fact, that should be the focus and purpose of your life. My bond servant James wrote, "What is your life? You are a mist that appears for a little while and then vanishes." My Father has given you a way to make your brief life on earth count for eternity. That happens when you glorify Him. So the question is, how can you glorify Him? You glorify the Father by honoring Me. And you honor Me by building your life on the rock of hearing My words and doing them. When you do these things, you will bear much fruit. And in bearing much fruit, you glorify My Father.

This is to my Father's glory, that you bear much fruit, showing yourselves to be my disciples. John 15:8

⤞ *The Greatest Words Ever Spoken,* Honoring and Glorifying God (pp. 270–71); Fruitbearing (pp. 257–60); Fruit, Both Good and Bad (pp. 454–55)

Do You Desire the Gift
More Than the Giver?

You unbelieving and perverted generation, how long shall I
be with you and put up with you? Bring your son here.
Luke 9:41, NASB

A desperate father begged Me to deliver his son from a spirit that
tormented him. My response stunned My disciples. I called
the crowd an "unbelieving and perverted generation." I didn't come
to earth merely to be known as a healer or a miracle worker. I am the
Anointed One of God and the Redeemer of humanity. I came to
reveal the truth about My Father and Me and to fulfill His promise
of the atonement. But the multitudes only wanted My healing and
miracles. They knew My works, but they didn't know Me. They felt
the same way about My Father. They wanted His help but had no
desire for *Him*. My dear child, He is *so* much greater than His works!
As you come to know Him, you will stand in awe and amazement.
Your heart will be filled with joy and love. That's why He said, "Let
him who glories glory in *this,* that he understands and knows Me."
In Me you can know the Father like never before. Look at My life
and listen to My words. We love you.

This is eternal life, that they may know You, the only true God,
and Jesus Christ whom You have sent. John 17:3, NASB

✦ *The Greatest Words Ever Spoken,* Unbelief and Motives of Unbelievers
(pp. 466–69)

Making Your Old Self Better Does Not Work

And no one puts new wine into old wineskins. For the new wine would burst the wineskins, spilling the wine and ruining the skins. New wine must be stored in new wineskins.
Luke 5:37–38, NLT

The Pharisees focused on outward performance. They demanded strict adherence to every aspect of their traditions, but they did *not* know the Father. They knew nothing of His love, grace, mercy, or Spirit. I came to proclaim a *new* covenant between the Father and humanity, one that required more than mere compliance with laws and traditions. My new covenant requires a whole new person, a person created by a new birth, a birth of the Spirit. And, child, that is you. Now that you have a new nature, I don't want you to try to make your old nature and old values fit into your new nature and your new life in Me. Instead, I want you to abandon your old way of life. Concentrate on nourishing your spirit with My words. That's why Peter wrote, "As newborn babes, desire the pure milk of the word, that you may grow thereby." Don't waste your time trying to make your old way of life fit into the new. Cut your ties to your former ways and follow Me.

That which is born of the flesh is flesh, and that which is born of the Spirit is spirit. Do not be amazed that I said to you, "You must be born again." John 3:6–7, NASB

→→ *The Greatest Words Ever Spoken,* Spiritual Birth (pp. 178–81)

Be Careful Whom You Follow

Can one blind person lead another? Won't they both fall into a ditch? Luke 6:39, NLT

In My day a multitude of voices competed for the adoration and allegiance of the people. The scribes, Pharisees, and Sadducees wanted everyone to believe what they were pretending to believe and do what they themselves would *not* do. They said God was their Father, and yet they didn't know Him. They were blind to His heart and His will. They studied the Scriptures, which testified of Me, but they refused to come to *Me* for life. They were the blind leading the blind. Today things are even worse. More people than ever know the Scriptures but do *not* know *Me*. They tickle the ears of the multitudes, making them feel comfortable in the world and good about themselves. My dear one, don't be fooled. Abide in Me, and let My words become the standard by which you measure the teachings of all who claim to know Me. My true disciples will lead *you* as they follow *Me*. They will not ignore or contradict My words. I glorify the Father, and the Father glorifies Me. The true shepherds of My flock glorify the Father and Me and not themselves. Look for shepherds after My heart. They abide in My words and obey them.

Beware of the false prophets, who come to you in sheep's clothing, but inwardly are ravenous wolves. You will know them by their fruits. Matthew 7:15–16, NASB

→→ *The Greatest Words Ever Spoken,* False Prophets (pp. 368–69)

Your Reality May Not Be My Reality

Stop the weeping! She isn't dead; she's only asleep.
Luke 8:52, NLT

As Peter, James, John, and I entered the home of Jairus, we were surrounded by his family members and friends who were mourning his young daughter's death. When I told them to stop weeping, that she wasn't dead but only sleeping, they laughed and ridiculed Me. They were limited by *their* reality. The girl was dead in their view but merely asleep in Mine. Their reality had no hope, but *My* reality had no limits. A word from Me was all it took to wake up Jairus's little girl and bring her back to life. I told Jairus to stop being afraid and instead to believe. He obeyed My word, and I fulfilled My promise and awakened his daughter. Child, it is no different today. You are limited by your reality, but I am not! In My words I have given you many promises, and they are never limited by your circumstances. When you act on My words, I will fulfill My promises to you. Let Me cut the chains of your reality and lift you into Mine.

Truly, truly, I say to you, he who believes in Me, the works that I do, he will do also; and greater works than these he will do; because I go to the Father. John 14:12, NASB

✦ *The Greatest Words Ever Spoken,* The Promises of Christ (pp. 298–304); Following Christ (pp. 245–53); Belief and Faith in Christ (pp. 445–51)

Whom Do You Want to Be Like?

Students are not greater than their teacher. But the student who is fully trained will become like the teacher.
Luke 6:40, NLT

Many shepherds have been called to feed My sheep the truths that I revealed. They are also called to lead My sheep by the example of their lives. But, child, I never intended for you to rely entirely on the words or examples of your teachers. All teachers are human, and it's only natural for them to add their own opinions and even personal biases to their teachings. And no matter how much they love Me, they are *not* Me! So let *Me* be your *ultimate* Teacher. Let My words be the standard by which the teachings and lives of all others are viewed. My words came directly from the Father. Everything I said is *exactly* what the Father commanded Me to say. So when you hear My words, you are hearing *directly and perfectly* from the Father. And My life is the only perfect life to follow. Child, fully trained students will become like their teachers. If you are going to become like anyone, the Father wants you to become like *Me. I* must be your Teacher so *you* can become more like *Me.*

But do not be called Rabbi; for One is your Teacher, and you are all brothers. . . . Nor are you to be called "teacher," for you have one Teacher, the Christ. Matthew 23:8, NASB; 23:10, NIV

↬ *The Greatest Words Ever Spoken,* Following Christ (pp. 245–53)

How to Love Me More

A man loaned money to two people—500 pieces of silver to one and 50 pieces to the other. But neither of them could repay him, so he kindly forgave them both, canceling their debts. Who do you suppose loved him more after that?
Luke 7:41–42, NLT

I was invited to have dinner at the home of a Pharisee. He was disgusted to see a sinful woman there with Me, weeping as she washed My feet with her tears and an expensive perfume. He concluded that I could not be a prophet because it was obvious that I didn't know what kind of woman she was. He was wrong. I knew her heart. She was overwhelmed by hopelessness because her sins were so great in number. She believed she could *never* be forgiven. Now, in My presence, she couldn't believe I was *not* condemning her. Astonished by My unconditional love, she was filled with gratefulness. Because I forgave her, this woman's love for the Father and for Me was greater than that of anyone else in the house. Child, have *you* realized the great number of your sins? Have you realized the hopelessness of the debt your sins created? If you have, don't despair. For the more you understand how much you've been forgiven, the more you will be able to love the Father and Me.

For this reason I say to you, her sins, which are many, have been forgiven, for she loved much; but he who is forgiven little, loves little. Luke 7:47, NASB

✦ *The Greatest Words Ever Spoken,* Forgiveness (pp. 142–43; 253–57)

Another Way You Can Glorify the Father

I have brought you glory on earth by completing the work you gave me to do. John 17:4

I had only a few disciples to send into the world to proclaim the Gospel. The harvest was great, but there were not enough laborers to complete the work. That's why I told them to ask the Lord to send more workers into His harvest. They prayed, and the Father answered. Child, today the harvest is greater than ever. I want you to pray that the Father will send forth laborers to reap His harvest. And realize that today there are many who *begin* to accept their calling and labor in His fields, but they cease their labors before they complete the work. Believe Me, it would have been easy for Me to cease My labors before Calvary. But I didn't! I knew that completing the work would bring great glory to the Father. Child, you can glorify the Father more than you have thought possible. If you will heed His calling and persevere in your labors in the power of the Holy Spirit, you will bring Him glory. No matter how unimportant you think your work might be, your work and calling are very important to Us.

Teach these new disciples to obey all the commands I have given you. And be sure of this: I am with you always, even to the end of the age. Matthew 28:20, NLT

✦ *The Greatest Words Ever Spoken,* Honoring and Glorifying God (pp. 270–71); Honoring and Glorifying Christ (pp. 267–70)

Understand *This* Promise, and Gratitude and Joy Will Fill Your Heart

---

Most assuredly, I say to you, he who hears My word and believes in Him who sent Me has everlasting life, and shall not come into judgment, but has passed from death into life. John 5:24, NKJV

Have you wondered why so many who say they believe in Me are unhappy? Why are they overcome by stress, worry, and even despair? Their faith in the Father has grown cold, they are not abiding in My words, or they have forgotten the *miracle* of their salvation. Child, don't be like them. Always remember that you were *dead* in sin, having *no* hope. You were headed toward the full wrath of God and eternal separation from the Father. But I bore all your sin, received all your judgment, and endured all of God's wrath in *your* place. I want you to believe in Him who sent Me and believe My words. Your destiny has been forever changed. You have passed from death into life; you will be spared *all* judgment. When you *don't* rejoice in this, you are letting your circumstances blind you to the greatness of My Father's love, My sacrifice on the cross, and the miracle of your salvation. Open your eyes and rejoice! I love you!

Nevertheless do not rejoice in this, that the spirits are subject to you, but rejoice that your names are recorded in heaven. Luke 10:20, NASB

✦ *The Greatest Words Ever Spoken,* The Promises of Christ (pp. 298–304); Abiding in the Words of Christ (pp. 186–88); Eternal Life (pp. 134–42)

The Father's Commission,
Fulfilled in Me

The Spirit of the Lord is upon Me, because He anointed Me to preach the gospel to the poor. He has sent Me to proclaim release to the captives, and recovery of sight to the blind, to set free those who are oppressed, to proclaim the favorable year of the Lord. Luke 4:18–19, NASB

A s I proclaimed this passage from Isaiah, a hush fell over those who were in the synagogue. When I announced that this passage about the Messiah was *fulfilled* in *Me,* the listeners were stunned. They had no idea how to handle such a bold proclamation made by the son of a carpenter. But I fulfilled this proclamation every day of My earthly life. I preached the Gospel to those who were spiritually destitute, and they received its riches. I set free those who were enslaved to the taskmaster of sin. I gave sight to those who were physically blind and opened the spiritual eyes of those who could not see. I set free those who were oppressed by spirits, despair, and darkness. I proclaimed the time of God's favor and forgiveness and delivered it all at Calvary! Now I am calling *you* to follow Me. Follow Me by continuing My ministry. My dear child, as the Father sent Me, now *I* am sending *you.*

Peace be with you; as the Father has sent Me, I also send you. John 20:21, NASB

→→ *The Greatest Words Ever Spoken,* Jesus' Missions (pp. 46–51); The Claims Jesus Made About Himself (pp. 14–22)

As the Father Sent Me,
So Send I You

The Spirit of the Lord is upon Me, because He anointed Me to preach the gospel to the poor. He has sent Me to proclaim release to the captives, and recovery of sight to the blind, to set free those who are oppressed, to proclaim the favorable year of the Lord. Luke 4:18–19, NASB

The Gospel is good news for the poor and *great* news for the poor in spirit. Apart from Me, the poor have no joy in the moment and little hope for the future. But in Me they *can* have joy in the moment, eternal purpose in their lives, and hope for the future. Even though they have few *earthly* treasures, they can lay up eternal treasures in heaven. The news is even better for the poor in spirit. They believe they could *never* be cleansed or forgiven. But when they hear that *I* bore all their sins, paid all their debt, and offer cleansing and forgiveness from the cross, they run to Me. Child, you are now My mouthpiece to the poor and the poor in spirit. You are My hands, arms, and legs. Give them the Good News that no one else can give. Tell them about Me and the redemption I offer. You are My light in their dark world. Let your light shine brightly.

Let your light shine before men in such a way that they may see your good works, and glorify your Father who is in heaven. Matthew 5:16, NASB

⤝ *The Greatest Words Ever Spoken,* Jesus' Missions (pp. 46–51); The Claims Jesus Made About Himself (pp. 14–22); Commands of Christ (pp. 206–17)

As the Father Sent Me,
So Send I You

The Spirit of the Lord is upon Me, because He anointed Me to preach the gospel to the poor. **He has sent Me to proclaim release to the captives,** and recovery of sight to the blind, to set free those who are oppressed, to proclaim the favorable year of the Lord. Luke 4:18–19, NASB

If you have ever been held against your will, you know the terrible feeling of being imprisoned. Think how terrible being enslaved your entire life with no means of escape would be. Those who sin are *slaves* to sin. Sin has bound them in chains that cannot be broken, apart from Me. Gloriously, the Father sent Me to proclaim *release* to the captives. I broke their chains through My work on the cross and through the truth of My word. Mary Magdalene, Zacchaeus, the Samaritan woman, My disciples, the thief on the cross, and countless others discovered the joy of being set free from the merciless task-master of sin. Child, I want you, too, to proclaim release to those who are captive. Let them know they *can* be set free from the sin that entices and entraps them. Let them know I have promised that if they will *abide* in My words, they will come to know Me, and I *will* set them free. Join Me in My mission to set captives free.

And you will know the truth, and the truth will set you free. John 8:32, NLT

➻ *The Greatest Words Ever Spoken,* Deliverance (pp. 125–29); Evangelism (pp. 227–29); Jesus' Missions (pp. 46–51); The Claims Jesus Made About Himself (pp. 14–22)

As the Father Sent Me, So Send I You

The Spirit of the Lord is upon Me, because He anointed Me to preach the gospel to the poor. He has sent Me to proclaim release to the captives, **and recovery of sight to the blind,** to set free those who are oppressed, to proclaim the favorable year of the Lord. Luke 4:18–19, NASB

During My earthly ministry I restored sight to many who were blind. There is another type of blindness that is even more terrible. It is blindness of the heart. Without a new birth those blinded by pride, self-centeredness, greed, envy, bitterness, anger, and lust will never come to know Me. But the Father gave Me the authority and power to open the eyes of their hearts. Through My atonement and the new birth given by the Spirit, they can see My light. Child, I want you to proclaim recovery of sight to the blind of heart. Let them see My life and My love in all you do. Let them see the power of My words at work in your life. Let them hear My words from your lips. Let them experience My mercy, grace, and forgiveness through you. You may be the only light that will ever come their way.

You are the light of the world. A city on a hill cannot be hidden. Neither do people light a lamp and put it under a bowl. Instead they put it on its stand, and it gives light to everyone in the house. Matthew 5:14–15

→→ *The Greatest Words Ever Spoken,* Jesus' Missions (pp. 46–51); The Claims Jesus Made About Himself (pp. 14–22)

As the Father Sent Me, So Send I You

The Spirit of the Lord is upon Me, because He anointed Me to preach the gospel to the poor. He has sent Me to proclaim release to the captives, and recovery of sight to the blind, **to set free those who are oppressed,** to proclaim the favorable year of the Lord. Luke 4:18–19, NASB

What makes it hard to get through your day or causes you to lose sleep? What brings you to the point of despair? Are you weighed down by grief, anger, bitterness, or envy? Are you enslaved by pride, greed, or lust? How often are you burdened with stress or fear? It doesn't have to be that way. My Father sent Me to *set free* those who are oppressed, and that includes you. The Father does not want you to continue under the weight of your oppression. I have the authority, the power, and the means to set you free and keep you free from all that oppresses you. First, come to Me with all your burdens. Let *Me* carry your load. Learn from Me by abiding in My words. Let My words form your attitudes and determine your behavior, moment by moment. As you follow Me, I will free you from oppression. And, child, I want *you* to use My words to set *others* free!

It is the Spirit who gives life; the flesh profits nothing; the words that I have spoken to you are spirit and are life. John 6:63, NASB

⊁⊁ *The Greatest Words Ever Spoken,* Deliverance (pp. 125–29); Jesus' Missions (pp. 46–51); The Claims Jesus Made About Himself (pp. 14–22)

As the Father Sent Me, So Send I You

The Spirit of the Lord is upon Me, because He anointed Me to preach the gospel to the poor. He has sent Me to proclaim release to the captives, and recovery of sight to the blind, to set free those who are oppressed, **to proclaim the favorable year of the Lord.** Luke 4:18–19, NASB

During My time on earth, Israel was oppressed by Roman conquerors. People had no hope of being delivered. They lived in fear and sought just to survive. Yet the Father commanded Me to proclaim that I had brought forth the time of His abundant favor. How could *this* be the time of His favor? The answer was simple. The Father's favor was shown by His sending *Me.* I was the ultimate expression of His favor to humanity. In Me, people would have the truth about the Father. They would have the only acceptable payment for all their sins. They could receive God's forgiveness, redemption, and eternal life. They could see the Father perfectly in My life and hear His words without distortion from My lips. Today people are more oppressed than ever. Child, I want *you* to proclaim that *this* is the favorable time of the Lord. I want you to tell others of all that the Father has provided in Me.

What I tell you now in the darkness, shout abroad when daybreak comes. What I whisper in your ear, shout from the housetops for all to hear! Matthew 10:27, NLT

→← *The Greatest Words Ever Spoken,* Jesus' Missions (pp. 46–51); The Claims Jesus Made About Himself (pp. 14–22); God's Goodness (pp. 97–99); God's Mercy (pp. 101–2)

If You Don't Believe It in Your Heart, You Don't Believe It

O foolish ones, and slow of heart to believe in all that the prophets have spoken! Luke 24:25, NKJV

Two of My disciples were deeply grieved as they walked toward Emmaus. I joined them on their journey, but they didn't recognize Me. When I asked about their sadness, they explained that a prophet they had hoped would redeem Israel had been crucified, and His body had been taken from His tomb. Before I was crucified they had been excited about My teachings. But they had never believed in their *hearts* that I was the Christ. I had been sent by the Father to lay down My life as a ransom for all who would believe in Me. I was to be raised on the third day. In My final minutes with these men, their eyes were opened, and they believed in their hearts. That belief came as they listened to My words and received them. Child, simply agreeing with My words in your mind is *not* the same as belief in your heart. Belief is born in your heart as you hear My words and act on them. When you *obey* My words, the faith of your heart is expressed and rapidly grows. There is no other way to grow faith in your heart. That's why Paul proclaimed that "faith comes from hearing, and hearing by the word of Christ."

He who believes in Me, as the Scripture has said, out of his heart will flow rivers of living water. John 7:38, NKJV

++ *The Greatest Words Ever Spoken,* Unbelief and Motives of Unbelievers (pp. 466–69); Foolishness (pp. 369–71); The Heart (pp. 374–78)

The World's Values Are Built on the Lies of Its Ruler, Satan

He has always hated the truth, because there is no truth in him. When he lies, it is consistent with his character; for he is a liar and the father of lies. So when I tell the truth, you just naturally don't believe me! John 8:44–45, NLT

The devil is a liar, and those of the world believe his lies. It is only natural for them *not* to believe *Me*. Child, Satan will do all he can to keep you from bearing fruit and building the kingdom of God. He will use every scheme he can to deceive and defeat you. He wants you to love the world rather than the Father. He reminds you of the offenses of others to prevent *you* from forgiving them. He magnifies their weaknesses, hoping you will judge them. And He accuses *you* to yourself, reminding you of all your faults. He wants to steal your attention away from the Father and Me and Our love and mercy. But, child, remember that My love for you is not based on your goodness. Don't listen to his whispers. Let the light of My words expose his lies, false values, and destructive schemes.

I am the light of the world. Whoever follows me will never walk in darkness, but will have the light of life. John 8:12

→→ *The Greatest Words Ever Spoken,* Satan (pp. 175–78); Unbelief and Motives of Unbelievers (pp. 466–69)

Hypocrisy and Self-Righteousness Are Poisonous

You hypocrites! Each of you works on the Sabbath day! Don't you untie your ox or your donkey from its stall on the Sabbath and lead it out for water? This dear woman, a daughter of Abraham, has been held in bondage by Satan for eighteen years. Isn't it right that she be released, even on the Sabbath? Luke 13:15–16, NLT

Hypocrisy filled the Pharisees' hearts and corrupted everything they said and did. And yet they were blind to it. They felt no guilt for taking care of their animals on the Sabbath, but they condemned and hated Me for healing *people* on the Sabbath. The people I healed and those who witnessed their healings glorified God. But not these hypocrites. They were filled with rage and hatred and even conspired to kill Me. Child, hypocrisy is ingrained in human nature. I know there are times you too struggle with hypocrisy. But the difference between you and the Pharisees is that they did not feel guilty about hypocrisy. You repent; they did not. Child, the more you abide in My words and do them, the faster your struggle with hypocrisy will fade. All hypocrisy flows from pride and self-righteousness. In My words you see Me as I really am and yourself as you really are. Your gratefulness for the Father's grace and mercy will soar, and your pride, self-righteousness, and hypocrisy will decline. You will truly become more and more like Me.

Beware of the yeast of the Pharisees—their hypocrisy. Luke 12:1, NLT

→→ *The Greatest Words Ever Spoken,* Hypocrites, Hypocrisy, and Self-Righteousness (pp. 378–83); Pride (pp. 391–93)

It's Not What You *Say*— It's What You *Do*

Not everyone who says to Me, "Lord, Lord," will enter the kingdom of heaven, but he who does the will of My Father who is in heaven will enter. Matthew 7:21, NASB

Many people wanted to be near Me to see My miracles and to hear what I would say. But most never came to know Me. Today many think that because they call Me "Lord" they will be granted entrance into the kingdom. Though they may know *about* Me, they haven't come to *know* Me. When people know Me, the direction of their lives changes from doing their own will to doing My Father's will. I know that *you* are often unsure of what His will is. You ask yourself, *Does He want me to do this or that or something else?* You have wondered how you can know the Father's will. The answer is to abide in My words *daily.* They reveal the Father's will for every situation. Let the Holy Spirit teach you from My words, which not only reveal My Father's will but empower you to *do* His will.

But when He, the Spirit of truth, comes, He will guide you into all the truth; for He will not speak on His own initiative, but whatever He hears, He will speak; and He will disclose to you what is to come. He will glorify Me, for He will take of Mine and will disclose it to you. John 16:13–14, NASB

↠ *The Greatest Words Ever Spoken,* Eternal Life (pp. 134–42); Knowing God and Knowing Christ (pp. 275–77); Abiding in the Words of Christ (pp. 186–88)

The World Does Not Know the Father

O righteous Father, the world doesn't know you, but I do; and these disciples know you sent me. John 17:25, NLT

This world does not know the Father. Those who are of the world fully embrace its values. In contrast, the Father has revealed all that is good and all that is evil. What He has revealed as evil, the world accepts and promotes. And what the Father calls good, the world scoffs at. Child, knowing that those who are of the world do not know the Father, why would you use their standards to guide your decisions? Why would you tempt your Father by playing in their arena or engaging in their activities? The Father and I do not want to take you *out* of the world, but We want you to be Our light *in* the world. The Father sent Me not just to save you but also to lead you through this dark world. As you follow Me, others will see your works of righteousness, and they will hear My voice and follow Me. But your light must remain visible. If you become like them, then your light will go out, and they will remain in darkness. Let your light shine brightly.

All things have been handed over to Me by My Father; and no one knows the Son except the Father; nor does anyone know the Father except the Son, and anyone to whom the Son wills to reveal Him. Matthew 11:27, NASB

↦ *The Greatest Words Ever Spoken,* The World (pp. 408–9); Following Christ (pp. 245–53); Light Versus Darkness (pp. 384–85)

Don't React Against Those Who Act Against You or Me

You do not know what manner of spirit you are of. For the Son of Man did not come to destroy men's lives but to save them. Luke 9:55–56, NKJV

While we were traveling to Jerusalem, My disciples went ahead and entered a Samaritan village. But the village would not receive Me because we were headed to Jerusalem. When James and John, two of My most trusted disciples, saw this, they reacted without love or mercy. They asked if I wanted them to call fire down from heaven to destroy the village. Not only would such an action violate My teachings, but it would also be contrary to My heart and Spirit. My disciples had heard Me teach that they should turn the other cheek, love their enemies, and pray for those who persecute them. But they often acted as if they had not heard Me at all. Child, I don't want you ever to react with a spirit of vengeance or condemnation when people reject Me. I also don't want you to react that way when they reject you. Don't act like them—as if you are of this world. You are not. You know My heart. Follow Me!

But I say to you who hear: Love your enemies, do good to those who hate you, bless those who curse you, and pray for those who spitefully use you. Luke 6:27–28, NKJV

→→ *The Greatest Words Ever Spoken,* Following Christ (pp. 245–53); Adversaries and Human Enemies (pp. 188–90)

When I Tell You to Do the Impossible, I'll Give You the Way to Do It

---

You give them something to eat! . . . Have them sit down to eat in groups of about fifty each. Luke 9:13–14, NASB

My disciples urged Me to send the multitudes away to nearby towns so they could find food and lodging. They were stunned when I told them to go ahead and feed the people. They looked to their limited resources. "We have no more than five loaves and two fish," they said. They acted as if *their* limitations were *My* limitations. They still looked at situations through the eyes of unbelief. Then I told them to have the crowd sit in groups of fifty. Finally they trusted Me and obeyed, and I was able to perform the miracle that followed. Child, in every situation you encounter, you will be tempted to look at your own resources and let them limit your belief and actions. That's only natural. But I don't want you to do what's natural—I want you to walk by faith. Apply My words to each situation, and by faith obey them. Then watch what I will do through you and around you. Your limitations are *not* My limitations. Trust Me!

Do not work for food that spoils, but for food that endures to eternal life, which the Son of Man will give you. On him God the Father has placed his seal of approval. John 6:27

✤ *The Greatest Words Ever Spoken,* The Promises of Christ (pp. 298–304); Faith (pp. 231–37; 445–51)

Be Careful Not to Be Self-Righteous

You are the ones who justify yourselves in the eyes of men, but God knows your hearts. What is highly valued among men is detestable in God's sight. Luke 16:15

The Pharisees were constantly criticizing and condemning others while excusing their own sins. They always tried to appear righteous even though they were far from it. Not only did they think of themselves as more righteous than others, but they believed they were more acceptable to God. But God knew their hearts, which were filled with evil. They craved the praise of people but cared nothing about the praise of God. They adorned themselves with material treasures that made them appear more worthy to others, not knowing that what people consider valuable has *no* value to God. The sinner who admitted his sinfulness and pleaded for God's mercy was forgiven and justified. The self-righteous Pharisees were not. Child, God resists the proud, but gives grace to the humble. Today acknowledge your own unrighteousness and unworthiness. Then look to My atonement at Calvary. Accept that I took upon Myself all your sin, and *believe* that I have clothed you in *My* righteousness. You are cleansed and forgiven! The Father will flood your heart with grace and gratefulness, and the kingdom of heaven will be yours.

Go home to your family and tell them how much the Lord has done for you, and how he has had mercy on you. Mark 5:19

✦ *The Greatest Words Ever Spoken,* Hypocrites, Hypocrisy, and Self-Righteousness (pp. 378–83); Self-Deception and Self-Justification (pp. 394–95)

My Daily Call

I have come to call not those who think they are righteous, but those who know they are sinners and need to repent. Luke 5:32, NLT

The Pharisees couldn't understand how I could attend a feast filled with tax collectors and sinners. They didn't know the Father's heart. He sent Me to earth to seek and to save those who were lost. People who are self-righteous and excuse their sin don't see their need for a Savior. But those who see themselves as sinners with no hope of their own see their desperate need. My call to repent is *not* a once-in-a-lifetime call. I call upon My sheep to follow Me every time they make a moral choice. I call them to repent every time they make a wrong choice. When the Holy Spirit reminds you of a prideful thought or action, an attitude of envy or greed, a moment of anger or a lustful thought, don't try to justify your behavior. Instead, acknowledge your sin to Me. Then turn away from your self-centeredness and turn back toward Me to hear and obey My words. Remember, in your weakness My strength is made perfect, and My Father gives grace to the humble. Stay close and let *Me* carry your load.

I tell you that in the same way, there will be more joy in heaven over one sinner who repents than over ninety-nine righteous persons who need no repentance. Luke 15:7, NASB

✦ *The Greatest Words Ever Spoken,* Repentance (pp. 462–66); The Call of Christ (pp. 418–21)

Faith in God, Not in Yourself

Have faith in God. I tell you the truth, you can say to this mountain, "May you be lifted up and thrown into the sea," and it will happen. But you must really believe it will happen and have no doubt in your heart. Mark 11:22–23, NLT

E verything you do is an example of expressing faith in something. When you get out of bed, you express faith in your legs to hold your weight. When you cross a bridge, you express faith in the strength of the bridge. When a physician gives you medicine, you express faith in his diagnosis and in the effectiveness of the medicine. But faith in itself is not a virtue. The faith that pleases the Father and Me is the faith you place in Us. That is the only faith that glorifies the Father and Me. It is the faith that creates an open channel through which We can provide the miraculous power for you to do the impossible. This kind of faith flows from your heart, and its source is the Holy Spirit. Faith in God is the foundation on which miracle-producing faith must be built. But, child, there is only one way to grow it, and that is to continually live in My words.

Truly I say to you, if you have faith and do not doubt, you will not only do what was done to the fig tree, but even if you say to this mountain, "Be taken up and cast into the sea," it will happen. Matthew 21:21, NASB

✦ *The Greatest Words Ever Spoken,* The Promises of Christ (pp. 298–304); Faith (pp. 231–37; 445–51)

Adding Belief to Your Prayers

Therefore I tell you, whatever you ask for in prayer, believe that you have received it, and it will be yours. Mark 11:24

My earliest disciples asked Me to teach them to pray. I taught them the most important aspects of prayer—glorifying the Father with praise, seeking His will, petitioning for daily needs, asking for forgiveness of sins, and, finally, asking for daily protection from temptations and the schemes of the Evil One. Child, you need to pray in this same manner. Prayer is also a time when you should tell the Father your desires and hold nothing back. It's a time when you should listen for the whisperings of the Holy Spirit. But there's one more crucial facet, and that is faith. Faith opens a channel through which God's blessings and miraculous answers can flow. My words will create and grow your faith as you hear and obey them. Because your heart will be conformed to My heart by your hearing and doing, your desire for the Father's desires will increase. When you add heart-based faith to your prayers, *nothing* will be impossible.

Again I say to you, that if two of you agree on earth about anything that they may ask, it shall be done for them by My Father who is in heaven. For where two or three have gathered together in My name, I am there in their midst. Matthew 18:19–20, NASB

✈ *The Greatest Words Ever Spoken,* Prayer (pp. 295–98); The Promises of Christ (pp. 298–304); Faith (pp. 231–37; 445–51)

Removing the Roadblock to Intimacy with the Father

And whenever you stand praying, if you have anything against anyone, forgive him, that your Father in heaven may also forgive you your trespasses. Mark 11:25, NKJV

Have you noticed that sometimes when you pray, someone who offended you comes to mind? It is the Holy Spirit reminding you of a person you haven't wholly forgiven. He wants you to know the fullness of the Father's forgiveness: total forgiveness of *all* your sin. But as long as you withhold forgiveness, your intimacy with the Father will be diminished. I have called you into the Father's kingdom of light. But when you withhold forgiveness, you are rejecting His light and choosing to remain in darkness. You are belittling the magnitude of your sin and the terrible price I paid to atone for your sin. Repent and forgive! Release that person from all your judgment, and pray for his or her redemption. Then you will experience the fullness of the Father's forgiveness. Intimacy will be restored. He will listen to your heart and share His heart with you. Child, this is My call. Will you answer?

For if you forgive men when they sin against you, your heavenly Father will also forgive you. But if you do not forgive men their sins, your Father will not forgive your sins. Matthew 6:14–15

→→ *The Greatest Words Ever Spoken,* Forgiveness (pp. 253–57); Knowing God and Knowing Christ (pp. 275–77); Loving Christ (p. 280)

The Cornerstone of Your Faith

Do you believe that I am able to do this? Matthew 9:28, NASB

Two blind men, hoping I would give them their sight, cried out to Me, pleading for mercy. I asked them, "Do you believe that I am able to do this?" They replied, "Yes, Lord." Of course, anyone can *say* they believe. But that doesn't mean they truly believe in their hearts. I then touched their eyes and said, "According to your faith let it be to you." If they *didn't* believe in their hearts that I could do this, their blindness would remain. But they *did* believe, and their eyes were opened. Child, so often you ask Me to do things for you and for others, and I love that. But My question is, do you believe in your heart that I am able to do what you are asking? Sometimes you do, and sometimes you don't. Sometimes your nagging doubts remain. It doesn't have to be that way. If you have even the slightest doubt, run to My words and pour them into your mind. The Holy Spirit will reveal My will, and your doubts will be washed away. Then you will be able to answer from your heart, "Yes, Lord, I believe!"

This is the work of God, that you believe in Him whom He sent. John 6:29, NKJV

↠ *The Greatest Words Ever Spoken*, Faith (pp. 231–37; 445–51)

Keeping Your Mind and Heart Set on God's Interests

Get behind Me, Satan! You are a stumbling block to Me; for you are not setting your mind on God's interests, but man's. Matthew 16:23, NASB

When Peter said, "You are the Christ, the Son of the living God," I told him I would build My church on the rock of that revelation. But a short time later I gave him the strongest rebuke I had ever given one of My disciples. I told him, "Get behind Me, Satan!" How could Peter go so quickly from being an instrument of the Holy Spirit to being an unknowing tool of Satan? The answer is, his mind had changed its focus from the interests of God to earthly interests, including his own self-interest. Peter thought he would be doing the right thing to prevent My capture and death, but that would have defied the Father's plan. Child, today Satan uses this same tactic. He will try to shift your attention from the purposes of God to your own self-interests. How can you discern the difference between God's true callings and purposes and those that aren't His? You need to let My teachings be the standard by which your purposes and activities are measured. When they guide your decisions, you will *always* know the Father's will!

I don't speak on my own authority. The Father who sent me has commanded me what to say and how to say it. John 12:49, NLT

→→ *The Greatest Words Ever Spoken,* Spiritual Priorities (pp. 328–37); Satan (pp. 175–78); The Spirit Versus the Flesh (pp. 337–38)

If You Follow Me with Conditions, You Don't Understand Me

Foxes have dens to live in, and birds have nests, but the Son of Man has no place even to lay his head. Luke 9:58, NLT

As I walked along a road, a scribe called out, saying that he would follow Me wherever I would go. But his commitment changed when I told him I didn't even have a place to sleep. He wanted to follow Me but not if he had to leave his comfortable life. He would follow Me only on *his* terms. Why would anyone base their decision to follow Me on their conditions being met? Either they don't understand who I am or they don't believe My message. Child, do you set conditions that determine to what extent *you* will follow Me? Do you say, "I'll follow You if . . ."? Or "I'll follow You when . . ."? Or "I'll follow You, but don't ask me to do this or that"? If you have been a conditional follower, it might indicate that you don't yet fully know Me. Or perhaps you have not yet learned My priority of seeking eternal things over temporal things. Both of these shortcomings can be changed. Just get to know Me better and *grow* your faith. The more you get to know Me and do what I say, the faster you will grow into an unconditional follower.

You are my friends if you do what I command. John 15:14, NLT

↠ *The Greatest Words Ever Spoken,* Following Christ (pp. 245–53)

If the Father and I Don't Judge Anyone, Why Do You?

For the Father judges no one, but has committed all judgment to the Son. John 5:22, NKJV

You judge according to the flesh; I judge no one. John 8:15, NKJV

The Father, who is perfect in knowledge and holiness, could perfectly judge all humanity. But He has chosen not to judge anyone. Instead, He committed all judgment to Me. And even though I received the Father's authority to judge, I, too, have chosen not to judge. Those who reject Me and My words *will* be judged, but My words will judge them. So, child, if the Father and I are the only Ones with the knowledge and authority to judge perfectly and We choose not to judge, what gives *you* the right to judge? I know that judging others is part of your natural reaction. But you don't have to be a slave to your old nature. You are a new creature in Me; you have a new nature. The Holy Spirit can produce His fruit in you—love, joy, peace, patience, kindness, goodness, faithfulness, gentleness, and self-control. Let Him replace your judgmental spirit with His fruit. *This* is the will of the Father. Will you ignore it, resist it, or obey it?

For I did not come to judge the world, but to save it. John 12:47

→ *The Greatest Words Ever Spoken,* Judging Others (pp. 483–84); The Spirit Versus the Flesh (pp. 337–38)

Don't Stop Anyone from Acting in My Name

Don't stop him! . . . No one who performs a miracle in my name will soon be able to speak evil of me. Anyone who is not against us is for us. Mark 9:39–40, NLT

My first disciples came upon someone who was casting out demons in My name. They told Me, "We told him to stop, because he was not one of us." But I told them not to stop him. Who were they to judge anyone who was doing good in My name? They didn't know the details of the Father's plan. They certainly couldn't discern the hearts and motives of others. I'm sure they were afraid this man might not adhere to My teachings or might misrepresent Me. But even if that were true, *they* were not the ones to judge him. Child, that same spirit of judgment is rampant today among those who want to follow Me. I know that you, just like My first disciples, don't want anyone to misrepresent Me. I appreciate that, but I don't want you to sit in judgment of anyone! You do not know people's hearts or their relationship with the Father. I have not called you to be a judge. Set your eyes and heart on following Me.

A new command I give you: Love one another. As I have loved you, so you must love one another. John 13:34

✦✦ *The Greatest Words Ever Spoken,* Judging Others (pp. 483–84); Commands of Christ (pp. 206–17)

What's the Proof That God
Is Your Father?

If God were your Father, you would love me, because I have come to you from God. I am not here on my own, but he sent me. John 8:42, NLT

The Pharisees claimed God as their Father. They studied the Scriptures diligently, yet they would not come to Me. So they had no right to claim God as their Father. The truth is, they never knew the Father or Me. When they rejected Me, they were rejecting the Father. So how can people *know* if they are truly children of God? It's very simple. If God is their Father, they will love Me. And the only way to love Me is to obey My commands and teachings. As I told My first disciples, those who *don't* love Me *don't* obey My teachings. So obedience to My words is the proof that a person loves Me. And this love for Me is the proof that they are indeed children of God. Child, I know of your growing desire to abide in My words and do what they say. By keeping My words you are loving Me, and this love for Me is *proof* that you are a blessed child of God!

Those who accept my commandments and obey them are the ones who love me. And because they love me, my Father will love them. And I will love them and reveal myself to each of them. John 14:21, NLT

↣ *The Greatest Words Ever Spoken,* Loving Christ (p. 280); Obedience and Good Works (pp. 289–94); Knowing God and Knowing Christ (pp. 275–77)

In Me You Have the Power to Do Mighty Works

Yes, I am sending you to the Gentiles to open their eyes, so they may turn from darkness to light and from the power of Satan to God. Then they will receive forgiveness for their sins and be given a place among God's people, who are set apart by faith in me. Acts 26:17–18, NLT

I called the apostle Paul to take the Gospel to the Gentiles so they could turn from darkness and the power of Satan to Me, My light, and My power. My dear child, you, too, can open the eyes of those I bring into your path. Through the power of the Holy Spirit, you can turn people from the darkness of this world to My light. Because you know Me, you can proclaim that I am alive. You can *reveal* Me with your words and *prove* Me with your life. Share My life and My words with others, and love them with My love. Let them know that no matter how lost they may feel, they can be delivered by My atonement and its cleansing power. Though their sins be as scarlet, they can be as white as snow. So don't be afraid. Lift Me up each day, and the Holy Spirit will draw people to Me. Child, you can make an eternal difference in the lives of your family, your friends, and even people you haven't yet encountered.

Behold, I say to you, lift up your eyes and look on the fields, that they are white for harvest. John 4:35, NASB

→→ *The Greatest Words Ever Spoken,* Evangelism (pp. 227–29); The Call of Christ (pp. 418–21)

If You Don't Let Down Your Net, You Can't Catch Fish

Now go out where it is deeper, and let down your nets to catch some fish. Luke 5:4, NLT

When I told Simon to go to deeper water and let down his nets, he couldn't understand *why* I would give such a command. But what he did next can teach you a valuable lesson. First, he *honestly* shared his feelings with Me. He said that they had worked all night without catching anything and that fishing any longer would be futile. He went on to say, "Nevertheless *at Your word* I *will* let down the net." Though My command defied his logic, he still obeyed it. This was his first lesson in placing his faith in My words. Because he acted on it, the catch was so large it nearly sank his boat and the boat of his partners. How about you? If My command doesn't fit within your understanding or is contrary to your desires, do you reject it or obey it? Child, to act in faith you must first have a word from Me that applies to your situation and reveals My will. That's why it's critical that you fill your heart with My words. As you obey My words, I will reveal Myself to you. You will know My presence and see the mighty works that accompany faith in Me.

It is written: "Man does not live on bread alone, but on every word that comes from the mouth of God." Matthew 4:4

✦ *The Greatest Words Ever Spoken,* Faith (pp. 231–37); Obedience and Good Works (pp. 289–94)

The Power of Having Faith in Me

Daughter, your faith has healed you. Go in peace. Luke 8:48

A woman had suffered from a bleeding problem for twelve years. Though no physician had been able to heal her, the woman believed that if she could receive a touch from Me, or even a word, she would be healed. But she soon realized the crowd was pressed so tightly against Me that she could not get close enough to receive either a touch or a word. And yet she didn't give up. She believed if she could get close enough to touch the edge of My robe, she would be healed. That is childlike faith, pure and simple. When she reached out and touched My robe, she was instantly healed. Child, you can have this pure and simple faith. Although you can't physically touch Me, you have an even *greater* opportunity. You have My words to provide a sure foundation upon which your faith can securely stand. And as you act in faith on My words, I will channel My power into you. And like this woman, you can have faith in Me, and I will make you whole.

Heaven and earth will pass away, but my words will never pass away. Luke 21:33

✦ *The Greatest Words Ever Spoken,* Faith (pp. 231–37); Jesus' Words, Their Role and Power (pp. 62–64)

I Want You to Know the Father as He Really Is

No one knows the Son except the Father, and no one knows the Father except the Son and those to whom the Son chooses to reveal him. Matthew 11:27

Though many may know *about* the Father, most do not truly know Him. In fact, the only people who truly know Him are those to whom I personally reveal Him. Child, I want to reveal the Father to *you*. I want you to see Him and His works in My life. I want you to hear His voice and know His will in My words. This can take place only as you abide in My words. When you obey My teachings, you are loving the Father and Me the way We want to be loved. When you do this, the Father and I will take up residence with you. Look intently at My life—the ways I interacted with people. Watch Me with My disciples, with My followers, and with strangers. I dealt with men, women, children, the rich, the poor, the educated and the uneducated, the healthy and the sick, the righteous and the unrighteous. Look at Me closely and hear My words and act on them. Then you will not only come to know Me, but you will also come to know the Father.

The words that I say to you I do not speak on My own initiative, but the Father abiding in Me does His works. John 14:10, NASB

✦ *The Greatest Words Ever Spoken,* Jesus' Relationship with God the Father (pp. 55–60); The Claims Jesus Made About Himself (pp. 14–22); Jesus' Missions (pp. 46–51)

Who Will You Be More Like Today?

The Pharisee stood and prayed thus with himself, "God, I thank You that I am not like other men—extortioners, unjust, adulterers, or even as this tax collector. I fast twice a week; I give tithes of all that I possess." And the tax collector, standing afar off, would not so much as raise his eyes to heaven, but beat his breast, saying, "God, be merciful to me a sinner!" Luke 18:11–13, NKJV

I t is so easy to be like the Pharisee who, blinded by his own pride, could see only what he thought he had done right. He justified himself by recounting what he *thought* pleased God and by comparing himself to others. He left the altar with no forgiveness from God. Meanwhile, the tax collector was under the full weight of his sin and knew he had *no* hope in himself or his works. His *only* hope was God's mercy—and that's exactly what he received. His sins were forgiven, and he left justified. Child, see yourself as you really are. See the Father and Me as We really are. Rely *entirely* on the Father's mercies, for they are greater than all your sins. Today instead of walking in pride, comparing yourself to others, walk around in humility and extreme gratitude. Rejoice that, like that tax collector, you have been forgiven, cleansed, and justified.

For God so loved the world, that He gave His only begotten Son, that whoever believes in Him shall not perish, but have eternal life. John 3:16, NASB

⤞ *The Greatest Words Ever Spoken,* Repentance (pp. 462–66); Hypocrites, Hypocrisy, and Self-Righteousness (pp. 378–83); Justification (pp. 160–61)

The Holy Spirit Empowers You to Follow Me

But you shall receive power when the Holy Spirit has come upon you; and you shall be witnesses to Me in Jerusalem, and in all Judea and Samaria, and to the end of the earth. Acts 1:8, NKJV

Watching My disciples on the night of My arrest could have been so discouraging. On the hardest night of My life, they were more concerned about themselves than they were about Me. They were still arguing about which of them would be the greatest in My kingdom. They acted as if I had taught them nothing. And when I asked them to watch and pray, they fell asleep. But I wasn't discouraged, because I knew everything would change when the Holy Spirit was sent—and it did! Child, just as the ministry of the Holy Spirit changed their lives, His ministry should change yours as well. One of His ministries is to bring to your memory everything I have said. But He can't bring My words to your memory if you haven't been abiding in them. Abiding in My words every day is as important to your spiritual life as food and water are to your physical life. How long can you live without food or water? Don't limit the ministry of the Holy Spirit for even a day.

But the Helper, the Holy Spirit, whom the Father will send in My name, He will teach you all things, and bring to your remembrance all that I said to you. John 14:26, NASB

✦ *The Greatest Words Ever Spoken,* The Holy Spirit and His Ministry (pp. 116–17); The Great Commission (p. 263)

You Have Been Given So Much

For everyone to whom much is given, from him much will be required; and to whom much has been committed, of him they will ask the more. Luke 12:48, NKJV

Consider how much *you* have received. You were blessed to hear the Gospel. You have been given the greatest gift ever given, the gift of eternal life. You have abundant access to My words. You have been delivered from the kingdom of darkness into My glorious kingdom of light. You have been born again. You can hear My words and understand them. But, child, you were not given all of this *just* for your own blessing. My Father wants you to share these blessings with others. The Father never intended that you be a *storage container* for His blessings, but rather that you would be an open pipeline through which His blessings could flow freely to others. Imagine the joy of being an open channel of the Father's love, mercy, forgiveness, and grace. Imagine being a channel of His wealth to meet the needs of others. My promise is that, as you share His blessings with others, what you share will be multiplied. Your well will never run dry.

But the seed in the good soil, these are the ones who have heard the word in an honest and good heart, and hold it fast, and bear fruit with perseverance. Luke 8:15, NASB

✦ *The Greatest Words Ever Spoken*, Stewardship, Generosity (pp. 338–41); Commands of Christ (pp. 206–17)

Do You Realize What You Have?

Again, the kingdom of heaven is like treasure hidden in a field, which a man found and hid; and for joy over it he goes and sells all that he has and buys that field.

Matthew 13:44, NKJV

As a chief tax collector, Zacchaeus was rich and dishonest. And yet he saw that the kingdom of God was near. He didn't just see it; he *believed* it. He believed My words, and He believed in Me. He was born again! He was convicted of sin, and he repented. He freely gave up most of his wealth to repay those he had cheated. Most of the rest of his money he gave to the poor. Child, do *you* see Me as I really am? Do you see the priceless worth of the kingdom of God and the incomparable gift of eternal life? It cost Me everything, and yet the Father has freely given it to you. The more you understand and believe these truths, the faster the enticements of this world will lose their attraction. If you continue to struggle with the allure of the things of this world, you haven't seen the true worth of everything you have in Me. Spend more time feasting on My words, and the Holy Spirit will do the rest.

Again, the kingdom of heaven is like a merchant seeking beautiful pearls, who, when he had found one pearl of great price, went and sold all that he had and bought it. Matthew 13:45–46, NKJV

→→ *The Greatest Words Ever Spoken,* The Kingdom of God and the Kingdom of Heaven (pp. 161–70); Spiritual Priorities (pp. 328–37)

When Your Love for Me Fades

Yet I hold this against you: You have forsaken your first love. Remember the height from which you have fallen! Repent and do the things you did at first. If you do not repent, I will come to you and remove your lampstand from its place. Revelation 2:4–5

When men and women are born again, the eyes of their hearts are opened. They long to get to know Me. They hunger to hear My words and know My will. They express their love for Me by obeying My commands. My followers in Ephesus endured hardships and didn't grow weary. But, sadly, they lost their heart for Me and their desire to live according to My words. Child, don't let that be true of you. I am the Light of the World, but the only way you can remain in My light is to continually expose your heart to My words and do what they say. If this kind of love has faded, then My call to you is the same as My call to those at Ephesus. Repent and do the things you did when your eyes were first opened. Then I will fulfill My promise of intimacy with you.

O righteous Father! The world has not known You, but I have known You; and these have known that You sent Me. And I have declared to them Your name, and will declare it, that the love with which You loved Me may be in them, and I in them. John 17:25–26, NKJV

※ *The Greatest Words Ever Spoken,* Loving Christ (p. 280); Repentance (pp. 462–66)

The Father's Love Story for You

But when he was still a great way off, his father saw him and had compassion, and ran and fell on his neck and kissed him. . . . But the father said to his servants, "Bring out the best robe and put it on him, and put a ring on his hand and sandals on his feet. And bring the fatted calf here and kill it, and let us eat and be merry; for this my son was dead and is alive again; he was lost and is found." Luke 15:20, 22–24, NKJV

When people heard Me tell the parable of the lost son, they thought *I* was telling them of the Father's love even for those who turn their back on Him. But everything I said on earth was what the Father had commanded Me to say. Child, this parable is from the *Father.* It is *Him* telling *you,* "Even when you were lost in sin, I loved you and ran to you, forgave you, and joyfully received you!" Can you see His amazing love and compassion for you? You were dead in sin. But the Father's love sent Me to sacrifice My life to ransom you. Before you could even repent, the Father had compassion on you and extended His love and mercy. As My Father loves you, so do I. You are My lamb, and I am your Shepherd.

For God did not send his Son into the world to condemn the world, but to save the world through him. John 3:17

✦ *The Greatest Words Ever Spoken,* Grace and Mercy (pp. 424–27); God's Love (pp. 99–101); Jesus' Words in Parables (pp. 65–84); The Worth of an Individual (pp. 410–14)

When You Give,
Remember the Poor Widow

I tell you the truth, . . . this poor widow has given more than all the rest of them. For they have given a tiny part of their surplus, but she, poor as she is, has given everything she has. Luke 21:3–4, NLT

There are so many things that people value but *God* does not. There also are many things that God values but people do not. People value wealth and status; God does not. God values humility, love, and mercy, but people don't. In the temple I noticed a number of rich people depositing gifts into the treasury. They took pride in the size of their gifts. Then came a poor widow whose gift of two coins was minuscule. She loved God greatly and wanted to express her love with that offering. Although people look at the outside, God looks at the heart. Though her gift was ever so small, it was *everything* she had. When measured by God's values, its worth was far greater than all the other gifts combined. The Father has provided for you so you can be a wise and righteous steward of His gifts. But more than that, He wants your heart, like the heart of the poor widow, to overflow with gratefulness to Him and love and mercy to others.

Give, and it will be given to you. A good measure, pressed down, shaken together and running over, will be poured into your lap. For with the measure you use, it will be measured to you. Luke 6:38

→→ *The Greatest Words Ever Spoken,* Stewardship, Generosity (pp. 338–41)

When You're Serving Me, Don't Miss Small Opportunities

The kingdom of heaven is like a mustard seed, which a man took and sowed in his field, which indeed is the least of all the seeds; but when it is grown it is greater than the herbs and becomes a tree, so that the birds of the air come and nest in its branches. Matthew 13:31–32, NKJV

How often do you miss opportunities to do My will in small things because they don't seem important? Maybe you don't take an opportunity to show My love to someone because you have only a few minutes, so you do nothing. You may let a hundred opportunities pass by while you wait for a bigger one to come along. But if you don't minister in the little opportunities, you may not minister at all. Child, in a brief *moment* you can give a smile or a hug. You can give an encouraging word or a listening ear. The smallest seed of My love can change people's day or even their eternity. Don't judge anything's worth by its size. At the time of My crucifixion, the kingdom was like a tiny mustard seed. But today it covers the earth. Even the *tiniest* thing you do in My name brings glory and delight to your heavenly Father. Your small seeds of ministry will grow into trees that produce life-giving fruit.

And if you give even a cup of cold water to one of the least of my followers, you will surely be rewarded. Matthew 10:42, NLT

→→ *The Greatest Words Ever Spoken,* Small Beginnings, Big Outcomes (p. 327); The Mission of a Christian (pp. 281–89); The Kingdom of God and the Kingdom of Heaven (pp. 161–70)

Be Diligent in Your Love for Me

But if that servant says in his heart, "My master is delaying his coming," and begins to beat the male and female servants, and to eat and drink and be drunk, the master of that servant will come on a day when he is not looking for him, and at an hour when he is not aware, and will cut him in two and appoint him his portion with the unbelievers.
Luke 12:45–46, NKJV

You are a child of the Most High God and a servant in the kingdom. If you knew I was coming in two days, how much more diligent would you be in serving the Father? You would immerse yourself in My words and listen carefully for every prompting of the Holy Spirit. You would marshal all your resources, time, talents, and money to make the greatest possible kingdom impact. You would cast off every sin that has distracted you. You would plead with the Holy Spirit to produce His fruit in your life. Child, you cannot know the day or the hour of My return. But I want you to live every day in a way that expresses your love for Me by obeying My words. If that becomes the central focus of your life, you will be ready for Me, no matter when I return! I love you!

Blessed is that servant whom his master will find so doing when he comes. Truly, I say to you that he will make him ruler over all that he has. Luke 12:43–44, NKJV

→→ *The Greatest Words Ever Spoken,* Faithfulness (pp. 237–40); Attitudes (pp. 196–98); Spiritual Priorities (pp. 328–37)

Are You Looking at Logs or Specks?

And why worry about a speck in your friend's eye when you have a log in your own? How can you think of saying, "Friend, let me help you get rid of that speck in your eye," when you can't see past the log in your own eye? Hypocrite! First get rid of the log in your own eye; then you will see well enough to deal with the speck in your friend's eye.
Luke 6:41–42, NLT

Why is it so easy to notice even the smallest faults of others? Why is it so easy to add your voice to someone else's criticism of another person? The answer lies within your heart. Pride can blind you to your own faults while magnifying the faults of another person. Pride creates a fertile soil in which all sin is spawned. Nothing breaks your intimacy with Me faster than pride. It is the log that blocks your vision and makes it impossible for you to see clearly enough to remove a small splinter from another person's eye. Each time you find yourself criticizing or judging someone, ask the Father to expose your pride, and then repent. Stop judging, criticizing, and gossiping. Ask for the grace He promises to the humble. Then if you're prompted by the Spirit, gently and lovingly offer your help to the person with the splinter.

For those who exalt themselves will be humbled, and those who humble themselves will be exalted. Luke 14:11, NLT

✦ *The Greatest Words Ever Spoken,* Judging Others (pp. 483–84); Pride (pp. 391–93)

It's the Doing That Counts

But what do you think? A man had two sons, and he came to the first and said, "Son, go, work today in my vineyard." He answered and said, "I will not," but afterward he regretted it and went. Then he came to the second and said likewise. And he answered and said, "I go, sir," but he did not go. Which of the two did the will of his father?
Matthew 21:28–31, NKJV

The Pharisees and other religious leaders made covenants to do the Father's will. But instead they did their own. They were all about themselves. They didn't know the Father and desired people's praise more than His. When they were convicted by the preaching of John the Baptist, instead of repenting, they became even more set in their ways. On the other hand, many sinners who had previously rejected God heard the same preaching and repented. They became *doers* of God's will. Intentions and commitments do not transform a heart. Expressing faith in Me by acting on My words *does* transform a heart. Intentions and commitments without actions are fruitless. Hearing My words and doing them bears much fruit. Child, today and every day when the Holy Spirit brings My words to your mind, do them! I don't want your promises; I want your obedience. That is how you follow Me.

Not everyone who calls out to me, "Lord! Lord!" will enter the Kingdom of Heaven. Only those who actually do the will of my Father in heaven will enter. Matthew 7:21, NLT

↠ *The Greatest Words Ever Spoken,* Obedience and Good Works (pp. 289–94); Faithfulness (pp. 237–40); Attitudes (pp. 196–98)

I Want You to Be Unified with Others Who Follow Me

I do not pray for these alone, but also for those who will believe in Me through their word; that they all may be one, as You, Father, are in Me, and I in You; that they also may be one in Us, that the world may believe that You sent Me. John 17:20–21, NKJV

D o you wonder why there is so much division among My followers? It's because so many no longer make *following Me* the focus of their lives or their teaching. Instead, they concentrate on doctrinal issues that were never meant to be the focus of My shepherds or My sheep. I have called *all* My sheep and their shepherds to focus their hearts on My teachings and commands and to follow Me. My call is clear. "If anyone wishes to come after Me, he must deny himself, and take up his cross daily and follow Me." Although it's impossible to unite around doctrines, *anyone* whose heart is centered on following Me *can* unite with anyone else whose heart has that same focus. Following Me by faith must become the driving focus of My sheep. Child, take up your cross daily, follow Me, and unite with *all* My followers who do likewise.

Any kingdom divided against itself will be ruined, and a house divided against itself will fall. Luke 11:17

→→ *The Greatest Words Ever Spoken,* Unity Versus Division (p. 342)

My Presence and Power
Demonstrated in Your Oneness

Again I say to you that if two of you agree on earth concerning anything that they ask, it will be done for them by My Father in heaven. For where two or three are gathered together in My name, I am there in the midst of them.

Matthew 18:19–20, NKJV

When My disciples asked Me to teach them how to pray, I taught them to ask that the Father's will would be done. I also taught them to ask the Father to *reveal* His will concerning the issues and requests they were praying for. Seeking the Father's will in everything was to be the foundation upon which their prayer life and prayer requests would stand. Later I promised that even if only two of My followers were in agreement about what they should ask for, the Father would grant their request. Whenever two or more of you come together in My name, ask the Father to *reveal* His will. When you reach agreement concerning *His* will, ask for it, and He will do it. If you are not in agreement, simply agree to ask that His will be done. He is not obligated to give you an answer that lies outside His will. And, child, I want you to *know* that whenever two or more of you come together in My name, I will be in your midst in a very special way.

Your kingdom come, your will be done on earth as it is in heaven.

Matthew 6:10

→→ *The Greatest Words Ever Spoken,* Prayer (pp. 295–98); The Promises of Christ (pp. 298–304); Following Christ (pp. 245–53); Jesus' Name—Its Power and Meaning (pp. 51–53)

This Is Why So Many Lives Are Empty

It is the Spirit who gives life; the flesh profits nothing. The words that I speak to you are spirit, and they are life. But there are some of you who do not believe. John 6:63–64, NKJV

How many people do you know whose lives seem empty? No matter what they pursue or acquire, they never seem to be fulfilled. They are trying to fill their emptiness with the very things that create and amplify it—things of the flesh that merely gratify their desires. They chase after money, power, immorality, and the approval and praise of others. But the fact is, the flesh profits *nothing*. Child, have you felt an emptiness that you couldn't understand or explain? If you try to fill the emptiness with things of the world, they will only enlarge the void. But I can fill your void. Unlike the flesh, which profits nothing, the *Spirit* gives *life*. My words are spirit and life. Anytime you feel empty, don't turn to the things of the flesh or to the empty words of others. Run to *My* words, and pour them into your mind and heart. They will replace the emptiness of your soul with My Spirit and My life!

He who believes in Me, as the Scripture said, "From his innermost being will flow rivers of living water." John 7:38, NASB

→ *The Greatest Words Ever Spoken,* Spiritual Priorities (pp. 328–37); Abiding in the Words of Christ (pp. 186–88); Jesus' Words, Their Role and Power (pp. 62–64)

You Can't Honor the Father
If You Don't Honor Me

For the Father judges no one, but has committed all judgment to the Son, that all should honor the Son just as they honor the Father. He who does not honor the Son does not honor the Father who sent Him. John 5:22–23, NKJV

All who enter a courtroom yield to the judge's authority. If this is true of an earthly judge, whose judgment is only temporal, what degree of honor is due the One to whom the Father has committed the eternal judgment of all humanity? If the Father has so honored His Son, know that He is greatly offended by those who do not honor His Son. When people minimize or ignore My words, they are rejecting them. And when people reject My words, they are rejecting Me. Child, don't listen to My words with the intention of merely *considering* them. And don't try to bend them to *your* will. Instead of trying to make My words fit into your plans, change your plans to conform to *My* words. When you do what I say, you are honoring Me. And when you honor Me, you honor the Father.

Why do you call Me, "Lord, Lord," and do not do what I say?
Luke 6:46, NASB

✦ *The Greatest Words Ever Spoken,* Honoring and Glorifying Christ (pp. 267–70); Loving Christ (p. 280); The Claims Jesus Made About Himself (pp. 14–22)

When You Receive More Than You Give Up, Is It a Sacrifice?

Assuredly, I say to you, there is no one who has left house or parents or brothers or wife or children, for the sake of the kingdom of God, who shall not receive many times more in this present time, and in the age to come eternal life.
Luke 18:29–30, NKJV

My call has always been the same. Some ignore it, many rationalize it, and most reject it. But My call remains the same. "If anyone desires to come after Me, let him deny himself, and take up his cross daily, and follow Me." Setting aside your desires sounds bad enough. But picking up your cross and carrying it sounds like a sacrifice that is too hard to accept. You are giving up all your perceived "rights"—the right to happiness, love, health, possessions, respect, time, and even relationships. A person carrying a cross has only the right to suffer and die. How could I ask *anyone* to make such a sacrifice? It's because I know that your life on earth is merely a moment when compared to eternity. Any sacrifice made in the moment, though painful at the time, is no great sacrifice when it produces an infinitely greater gain that lasts forever. When you take up your cross and follow Me, lives will be impacted for eternity. The heavenly treasures you gain will never be lost!

But store up for yourselves treasures in heaven, where moth and rust do not destroy, and where thieves do not break in and steal.
Matthew 6:20

✦ *The Greatest Words Ever Spoken,* Sacrifice and Self-Denial (pp. 313–14); Rewards (pp. 172–75)

Hidden from the Wise,
Revealed to Babes

I thank You, Father, Lord of heaven and earth, that You have hidden these things from the wise and prudent and have revealed them to babes. Matthew 11:25, NKJV

In a number of cities, I performed miracles that amazed the multitudes, and yet most would not believe and repent. How could *anyone* not believe and repent when people had just witnessed such signs and wonders? They saw the blind receive their sight and the deaf receive their hearing. Paralyzed people were made to walk, and the demon possessed were set free. Everyone who received a word or a touch from Me was healed. The truth is, the multitudes were excited by the miracles, but they missed the meaning. However, the humble of heart, the uneducated, and the children *did* see the meaning of the miracles and understood My message. The Father chose to reveal the truth to the humble and hide it from those who were arrogant. No one can know Me unless the Father reveals Me to them. Look around you. Most people will never know Me. But, child, you have believed in Me, and you are believing My words. Rejoice and praise the Father's grace to you!

No one knows the Son except the Father, and no one knows the Father except the Son and those to whom the Son chooses to reveal him. Matthew 11:27

✦ *The Greatest Words Ever Spoken*, Revelation of God's Truth (pp. 312–13); Humility (pp. 271–73); Pride (pp. 391–93); Hypocrites, Hypocrisy, and Self-Righteousness (pp. 378–83)

When You Are Troubled
or Struggle with Doubts

Why are you troubled? And why do doubts arise in your hearts? Luke 24:38, NKJV

You have experienced My love and forgiveness, and you have felt My presence and peace. And yet at times you are troubled by anxiety and doubts. Why? Because either you don't *know* My words that apply to your circumstances *or* you choose *not* to believe and act on them. My earliest disciples had the same problem. Even when I appeared to them after My resurrection, they were *still* troubled with fear and doubts. But when the Holy Spirit came, everything changed! He reminded them of the words I had spoken. Then they were able to abide in My words and obey them. Child, the Holy Spirit wants to perform that same ministry for *you*. But for Him to *remind* you of My words, you must *abide* in them. The more you abide in My words and do them, the greater your faith will grow. When faith floods your heart, your anxiety and doubts will be washed away. Anytime you find yourself struggling with doubts or fears, let that be an alert that you have *not* been abiding in My words. The more you abide in My words and do them, the *less* you will struggle with fears and doubts.

Everyone who comes to Me and hears My words and acts on them, I will show you whom he is like: he is like a man building a house, who dug deep and laid a foundation on the rock. Luke 6:47–48, NASB

➤➤ *The Greatest Words Ever Spoken*, Anxiety, Worry, and Fear (pp. 190–93); Abiding in the Words of Christ (pp. 186–88)

Your Ministry May Start with Friends and Family, but It Doesn't End There

---

Do not be afraid. From now on you will catch men.

Luke 5:10, NKJV

When Peter obeyed My words, rowed out to deeper water, and let down his nets, the catch was so great his boat and that of his partners began to sink. He fell down at My knees, crying out, "Go away from me Lord, for I am a sinful man!" But instead of leaving him, I simply replied, "Do not be afraid. From now on you will catch men." When we returned to shore, Peter and his partners left their boats and their business behind and followed Me. You might wonder why I would answer his fear by giving him a vision of "catching men." Child, when you focus on serving yourself, anything that threatens *you* creates fear. But when your heart is turned away from yourself and focused on reaching, loving, and serving others, your fears will be replaced with My love. My beloved John said it perfectly when he wrote, "There is no fear in love. But perfect love drives out fear." Child, this is My desire for you too—that you continually reset your focus from yourself to loving others. I want you to become an active "fisher of men."

Whoever acknowledges me before men, I will also acknowledge him before my Father in heaven. Matthew 10:32

→ *The Greatest Words Ever Spoken,* The Mission of a Christian (pp. 281–89); Following Christ (pp. 245–53); Evangelism (pp. 227–29); Anxiety, Worry, and Fear (pp. 190–93)

Giving Without the Desire to Receive Back

And if you lend to those from whom you hope to receive back, what credit is that to you? For even sinners lend to sinners to receive as much back. Luke 6:34, NKJV

C hild, I want you to be a wise manager of everything the Father has entrusted to you. The Father does not delight in the naiveté of the simple or the foolishness of the proud. But I also want you to know that everything the Father has given you is not intended to merely gratify your own desires. He wants you to *use* your money to meet your family's needs and the needs of others. Remember, where your treasure is, there will your heart be also. Child, treasure the Father and Me. Instead of viewing your money as your possession, see it as a tool that We placed in your hand—a tool for ministering to others and building up the kingdom of God. Give without any expectation of being repaid. When you give to others in response to the prompting of the Holy Spirit, you are really giving back to Us what We entrusted to you. Child, I gave *you* that which is far more precious than gold or silver. I gave you My life—*My life!*—as a ransom for *you*. Follow Me!

The Son of Man did not come to be served, but to serve, and to give His life a ransom for many. Matthew 20:28, NASB

✦ *The Greatest Words Ever Spoken,* Stewardship, Generosity (pp. 338–41); Commands of Christ (pp. 206–17); Sons of God (pp. 327–28)

Who Are My Friends, Who Are My Disciples, Who Loves Me, and Who Will Enter the Kingdom of Heaven?

You are My friends if you do whatever I command you.
John 15:14, NKJV

If you abide in My word, you are My disciples indeed.
John 8:31, NKJV

If anyone loves me, he will obey my teaching. John 14:23

He who does not love me will not obey my teaching.
John 14:24

Not everyone who says to Me, "Lord, Lord," shall enter the kingdom of heaven, but he who does the will of My Father in heaven. Matthew 7:21, NKJV

Therefore whoever hears these sayings of Mine, and does them, I will liken him to a wise man who built his house on the rock. Matthew 7:24, NKJV

But everyone who hears these sayings of Mine, and does not do them, will be like a foolish man who built his house on the sand. Matthew 7:26, NKJV

My sheep hear My voice, and I know them, and they follow Me. John 10:27, NKJV

✦ *The Greatest Words Ever Spoken,* Obedience and Good Works (pp. 289–94); God's Will (pp. 106–7); Loving Christ (p. 280)

I Want You to Make Disciples *My* Way

Therefore go and make disciples of all nations, baptizing them in the name of the Father and of the Son and of the Holy Spirit, and teaching them to obey everything I have commanded you. Matthew 28:19–20

I have said much about the necessity of obeying My words and doing My Father's will. So why do so many who profess to know Me still act as if My call is about something else? Truly, it is far easier to *talk* about religion and doctrine than it is to obey what I have commanded. Many teachers have made the church about so many other things, and their followers may hear Me say those terrible words "I never knew you; depart from Me, you who practice lawlessness." Child, don't be deceived. I have called you to follow Me, and the only way to follow Me is to act on My words. When you obey My words, you will be doing My Father's will. Don't be distracted by man-made teachings and doctrines. Be My disciple and lead others into discipleship. The *only* way to make disciples is to do it *My* way—to teach them to obey everything I have commanded you. Follow Me, and I will lead you and those you disciple safely home. I love you so much!

If you continue in My word, then you are truly disciples of Mine. John 8:31, NASB

→→ *The Greatest Words Ever Spoken,* The Great Commission (p. 263); Following Christ (pp. 245–53); The Mission of a Christian (pp. 281–89); Evangelism (pp. 227–29)

How to Save Your Life
Instead of Losing It

For whoever desires to save his life will lose it, but whoever loses his life for My sake will save it. Luke 9:24, NKJV

It's only natural to want to stay alive as long as possible. The Father created every creature with that instinct. But people who make preserving their lives and lifestyles their priority no longer hold Me as their Lord. Instead, they want to *use* Me to fulfill their desires. Child, I will not take on that role, nor will I have an intimate relationship with anyone under those conditions. Anyone who thinks I will is trading My offer of eternal life for a momentary gain in a momentary life. On the other hand, people whose eyes have been opened to who I am are seeing the incredible offer of God's mercy and eternal salvation. They will joyfully trade a self-focused life on earth for a life of eternal purpose with Me! When I talk about *losing* your life for *My* sake, I'm not talking about dying physically. I'm talking about dying to your own desires and then *living* for My desires. Child, when I talk about saving your life, I'm not talking about saving it physically but taking on an eternal purpose and significance that can be found only in following Me. When you give up your life each day to follow Me, you will be saving your life.

Put your trust in the light while you have it, so that you may become sons of light. John 12:36

→→ *The Greatest Words Ever Spoken,* Sacrifice and Self-Denial (pp. 313–14); Rewards (pp. 172–75)

Even the Smallest Deed Will Not Go Unrewarded

And if anyone gives even a cup of cold water to one of these little ones because he is my disciple, I tell you the truth, he will certainly not lose his reward. Matthew 10:42

Your Father in heaven is amazing in so many ways! He can speak galaxies into existence. In a single moment He can create life. And though His power is unlimited and His majesty is beyond description, no sparrow falls to the ground apart from His loving will. Child, your *smallest* effort to serve even the youngest of My followers will be generously rewarded with treasures in heaven. When you feed others, you will be rewarded as if you were feeding Me. When you give a drink to them, you will be rewarded as if you were giving it to Me. When you clothe them, you will be rewarded as if you had clothed Me. When you minister to anyone of the household of faith, you will be rewarded as if you had ministered to Me. So don't belittle even your smallest efforts to minister in My name. When we meet face to face, I will say to *you,* "Come, you blessed of My Father, inherit the kingdom prepared for you from the foundation of the world."

The King will answer and say to them, "Truly I say to you, to the extent that you did it to one of these brothers of Mine, even the least of them, you did it to Me." Matthew 25:40, NASB

✦ *The Greatest Words Ever Spoken,* Small Beginnings, Big Outcomes (p. 327); The Promises of Christ (pp. 298–304); Rewards (pp. 172–75)

Those Who Diligently Serve Me Until I Come Will Be Greatly Blessed

---

Who then is that faithful and wise steward, whom his master will make ruler over his household, to give them their portion of food in due season? Blessed is that servant whom his master will find so doing when he comes. Truly, I say to you that he will make him ruler over all that he has.
Luke 12:42–44, NKJV

When the master left his estate for a season, some of his servants became lazy, doing only the absolute minimum. Others became abusive to their fellow servants. But some acted no differently. They were as diligent, as honest, and as loving as they were when the master was home. When he returned, those who were lazy or abusive were severely punished, but those who remained diligent were greatly rewarded. Child, I know that many who profess to be My followers act as if I will never return. Their zeal for Me and the kingdom has faded. But I *will* return at the exact hour the Father has appointed. Those who have been faithful in My absence will be honored above all. Continue to follow Me moment by moment. Don't set your mind on the future, but live in the present. Though you can't see Me yet, I am with you. The night is coming soon, so labor in My fields while there is still light. Your faithfulness glorifies Me and delights the Father.

So you, too, must keep watch! For you don't know what day your Lord is coming. Matthew 24:42, NLT

→ *The Greatest Words Ever Spoken,* Faithfulness (pp. 237–40); Attitudes (pp. 196–98)

Discipleship Is for All My Followers, Including You

And whoever does not bear his cross and come after Me cannot be My disciple. For which of you, intending to build a tower, does not sit down first and count the cost, whether he has enough to finish it. Luke 14:27–28, NKJV

Dear one, I am calling *you* to take up your cross and be My disciple. But don't be afraid of My call. I am *not* asking you to bear your cross alone. I have given you the Holy Spirit to guide you and empower you. Take My yoke upon you, and let *Me* bear your burden. The *cost* of being My disciple is dying to your will and living to Mine. The cost is hearing My commands and stepping out in faith to obey them. You can do that because you have *Me.* I am the vine, and you are the branch. Without Me you can do nothing. But *with* Me there is nothing I ask that you can't do. I know your weaknesses and infirmities. They make no difference to Me. I have disciples who are paralyzed, yet they pray without ceasing. I have disciples who are blind, yet they see My glory and tell of it. I have disciples who cannot speak, yet they extend their arms in love to those who need them. I have chosen you and appointed you to bear much fruit. Let's gather the harvest together!

Behold, I say to you, lift up your eyes and look on the fields, that they are white for harvest. John 4:35, NASB

→ *The Greatest Words Ever Spoken,* Following Christ (pp. 245–53)

I Am with You, and I Will Never Leave You

And lo, I am with you always, even to the end of the age.
Matthew 28:20, NKJV

Child, although you cannot see Me, I am with you. Even when you feel most alone, I am beside you. Because you have believed in Me, I see you covered in My righteousness, cleansed from all your sin. I have paid off your entire debt to God. Child, even though you still struggle to yield some areas of your heart to Me, I know that you will! Yielding each area of your life is not a one-time decision; it's something you do each day as the Holy Spirit reveals your weaknesses. Know that in your weaknesses My strength is made perfect. I will supply all that you lack so that I might receive the glory and pass that glory on to the Father. In your struggles to forgive, look to My cross and release the ones who offend you. In the midst of your fears, look to My words and act on them. When you lack love, let My love flow through you. Obey My commands as the Holy Spirit brings them to your mind. Child, I love you infinitely more than you love yourself. I will remain with you always—always! And soon we will be together.

My sheep hear My voice, and I know them, and they follow Me. And I give them eternal life, and they shall never perish; neither shall anyone snatch them out of My hand. John 10:27–28, NKJV

→→ *The Greatest Words Ever Spoken,* The Promises of Christ (pp. 298–304); The Great Commission (p. 263)

January 9—*Increase our faith!* Luke 17:5.

January 10—*Lord, even the demons are subject to us in Your name.* Luke 10:17, NKJV.

January 13—*Let not the wise man glory in his wisdom, let not the mighty man glory in his might, nor let the rich man glory in his riches; but let him who glories glory in this, that he understands and knows Me.* Jeremiah 9:23–24, NKJV.

January 18—*Well done, my good servant!* Luke 19:17.

January 24—*Fear not, be of good courage!* See Mark 6:50.

February 1—*God, have mercy on me, a sinner.* Luke 18:13.

February 3—*You shall worship the LORD your God, and Him only you shall serve.* Matthew 4:10, NKJV.

February 22—*Teacher, don't you care if we drown?* Mark 4:38.

March 3—*Teaching them to obey everything I have commanded you.* Matthew 28:20.

March 14—*Lord, Lord, have we not prophesied in Your name, cast out demons in Your name, and done many wonders in Your name?* Matthew 7:22, NKJV.

March 14—*I never knew you; depart from Me, you who practice lawlessness!* Matthew 7:23, NKJV.

March 21—*In this world you will have trouble.* John 16:33.

March 23—*No servant can serve two masters; for either he will hate the one and love the other, or else he will be devoted to one and despise the other. You cannot serve God and wealth.* Luke 16:13, NASB.

March 23—*But seek first the kingdom of God and his righteousness, and all these things will be added to you.* Matthew 6:33, ESV.

March 28—*Guard your heart above all else, for it determines the course of your life.* Proverbs 4:23, NLT.

March 29—*Even if I have to die with you, I will never deny you!* Matthew 26:35, NLT.

March 30—*Who is My mother, or My brothers? . . . Here are My mother and My brothers!* Mark 3:33–34, NKJV.

April 4—*God is opposed to the proud, but gives grace to the humble.* 1 Peter 5:5, NASB.

April 4—*Therefore humble yourselves under the mighty hand of God, that He may exalt you at the proper time.* 1 Peter 5:6, NASB.

April 5—*Come, you who are blessed of My Father, inherit the kingdom prepared for you from the foundation of the world.* Matthew 25:34, NASB.

April 7—*You will know them by their fruits.* Matthew 7:16, NASB.

April 9—*For as the heavens are higher than the earth, so are My ways higher than your ways, and My thoughts than your thoughts.* Isaiah 55:9, NKJV.

April 16—*I never knew you; depart from Me, you who practice lawlessness!* Matthew 7:23, NKJV.

April 21—*Deny yourself, take up your cross daily, and follow Me.* See Luke 9:23.

April 28—*There is a way that seems right to a man, but in the end it leads to death.* Proverbs 14:12.

May 7—*How much better it is to get wisdom than gold! And to get understanding is to be chosen above silver.* Proverbs 16:16, NASB.

May 12–*Love the Lord your God with all your heart.* Matthew 22:37.

May 22–*I am the way, the truth, and the life. No one comes to the Father except through Me.* John 14:6. NKJV.

May 27–*"Come now, and let us reason together," says the* LORD, *"though your sins are as scarlet, they will be as white as snow; though they are red like crimson, they will be like wool."* Isaiah 1:18, NASB.

May 28–*I have hidden your word in my heart, that I might not sin against you.* Psalm 119:11, NLT.

May 29–*Heaven and earth will pass away, but My words will never fail.* See Matthew 24:35.

June 10–*Increase our faith!* Luke 17:5.

June 14–*Above all else, guard your heart, for it is the wellspring of life.* Proverbs 4:23.

June 18–*He who believes in Me will live even if he dies.* John 11:25, NASB.

June 21–*To those who call evil good, and good evil; who substitute darkness for light and light for darkness.* Isaiah 5:20, NASB.

June 30–*You shall call His name Jesus, for He will save His people from their sins.* Matthew 1:21, NKJV.

July 2–*I am the way, the truth, and the life.* John 14:6, NKJV.

July 9–*I never knew you; depart from Me, you who practice lawlessness.* Matthew 7:23, NASB.

July 9–*No eye has seen, no ear has heard, and no mind has imagined what God has prepared for those who love him.* 1 Corinthians 2:9, NLT.

July 11–*Love your enemies and pray for those who curse and abuse you.* See Matthew 5:44.

July 16–*I am the way, the truth, and the life.* John 14:6, NKJV.

July 19–*To whom much is given, much is required.* See Luke 12:48.

August 5–*Therefore I tell you, do not worry about your life, what you will eat or drink; or about your body, what you will wear.* Matthew 6:25.

August 7–*Who sinned, this man or his parents, that he was born blind?* John 9:2.

August 8–*If you abide in My word, you are My disciples indeed. And you shall know the truth, and the truth shall make you free.* John 8:31–32, NKJV.

August 9–*"Do you believe in the Son of Man?" . . . "Who is He, Lord, that I may believe in Him?"* John 9:35–36, NASB.

August 12–*Father, forgive them, for they do not know what they are doing.* Luke 23:34.

August 13–*My God, My God, why have You forsaken Me?* Matthew 27:46, NKJV.

August 19–*Lord, if You had been here, my brother would not have died.* John 11:21, NKJV.

August 30–*But let him who glories glory in this, that he understands and knows Me, that I am the* LORD, *exercising lovingkindness, judgment, and righteousness in the earth. For in these I delight.* Jeremiah 9:24, NKJV.

September 1–*Teacher, I will follow You wherever You go.* Matthew 8:19, NASB

September 2–*Lord, save us! We're going to drown!* Matthew 8:25.

September 4–*Don't you realize that I have the power to release you or crucify you?* John 19:10, NLT.

September 24–*Your afflictions are only temporary, but they produce glorious eternal treasures. So don't fix your gaze on things that are seen, but fix it on Me, My life, and My words.* See 2 Corinthians 4:17–18.

September 28–*If you, O LORD, kept a record of sins, O Lord, who could stand?* Psalm 130:3.

October 7–*Even if I have to die with you, I will never disown you.* Matthew 26:35.

October 17–*Children, you do not have any fish, do you?* John 21:5, NASB.

October 17–*It is the Lord.* John 21:7.

October 18–*What about him?* John 21:21.

October 18–*What does that have to do with you?* See John 21:22.

October 20–*If you had known Me, you would have known My Father also; from now on you know Him, and have seen Him.* John 14:7, NASB.

October 20–*Lord, show us the Father and that will be enough for us.* John 14:8.

October 29–*What is your life? You are a mist that appears for a little while and then vanishes.* James 4:14.

October 30–*Let him who glories glory in this, that he understands and knows Me.* Jeremiah 9:24, NKJV.

October 31–*As newborn babes, desire the pure milk of the word, that you may grow thereby.* 1 Peter 2:2, NKJV.

November 13–*Faith comes from hearing, and hearing by the word of Christ.* Romans 10:17, NASB.

November 19–*We have no more than five loaves and two fish.* Luke 9:13, NASB.

November 20–*God resists the proud, but gives grace to the humble.* James 4:6, NKJV.

November 25–*"Yes, Lord."* Matthew 9:28, NASB.

November 25–*According to your faith let it be to you.* Matthew 9:29, NKJV.

November 26–*You are the Christ, the Son of the living God.* Matthew 16:16, NASB.

November 29–*We told him to stop, because he was not one of us.* Mark 9:38.

December 1–*Though their sins be as scarlet, they can be as white as snow.* See Isaiah 1:18.

December 2–*Nevertheless at Your word I will let down the net.* Luke 5:5, NKJV.

December 16–*If anyone wishes to come after Me, he must deny himself, and take up his cross daily and follow Me.* Luke 9:23, NASB.

December 20–*If anyone desires to come after Me, let him deny himself, and take up his cross daily, and follow Me.* Luke 9:23, NKJV.

December 23–*Go away from me Lord, for I am a sinful man!* Luke 5:8, NASB.

December 23–*There is no fear in love. But perfect love drives out fear.* 1 John 4:18.

December 24–*Where your treasure is, there will your heart be also.* Matthew 6:21, KJV.

December 26–*I never knew you; depart from Me, you who practice lawlessness.* Matthew 7:23, NASB.

December 28–*Come, you blessed of My Father, inherit the kingdom prepared for you from the foundation of the world.* Matthew 25:34, NKJV.

December 30–*Without Me you can do nothing.* John 15:5, NKJV.

"*...experience His power like never before!*"

—**JOSH D. MCDOWELL**, author and speaker

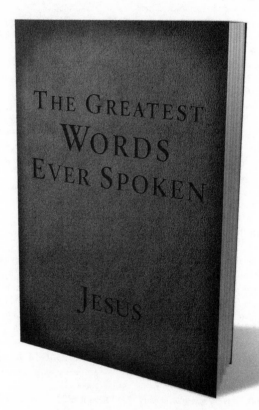

The Greatest Words Ever Spoken—an ideal companion to *Jesus Speaks*—offers you a fast, easy way to find everything Jesus said about hundreds of issues that are crucial to your life, relationships, faith, and spiritual growth.

"Packed with every word Jesus spoke and grouped by topic, this book should be a constant companion to your Bible."

—**DR. DAVID JEREMIAH,** founder of Turning Point Ministries, best-selling author of *Captured by Grace*

Read an excerpt from this book and more at WaterBrookMultnomah.com!